THE REBEL ACCOUNTANT is a chartered tax advisor who has worked widely behind the scenes in London and Australia, everywhere from major accountancy firms to tiny start-ups.

He chose his career because he loves to be creative.

TAXTOPIA

TAXTOPIA

HOW I DISCOVERED THE INJUSTICES, SCAMS AND GUILTY SECRETS OF THE TAX-EVASION GAME

THE REBEL ACCOUNTANT

monoray

First published in Great Britain in 2023 by Monoray, an imprint of
Octopus Publishing Group Ltd
Carmelite House
50 Victoria Embankment
London EC4Y 0DZ
www.octopusbooks.co.uk

An Hachette UK Company
www.hachette.co.uk

ISBN (Hardback) 978 1 800 96088 6
ISBN (Trade paperback) 978 1 800 960893

A CIP catalogue record for this book is available from the British Library.

Printed and bound in UK.

1 3 5 7 9 10 8 6 4 2

Typeset in 11.75/18pt Heldane Text by Jouve (UK), Milton Keynes.

This FSC® label means that materials used for
the product have been responsibly sourced.

This **monoray** book was crafted and published by
Jake Lingwood, Sybella Stephens, Caroline Taggart,
Mel Four, David Eldridge and Peter Hunt.

Disclaimer

I'd love it if this was entirely a work of fiction, but it isn't. This book is an accurate depiction of a certain kind of career in accountancy. Where I have used real names it is in instances where there is a clear factual basis for doing so. Other places and names have been changed to protect the innocent (or guilty) and have been blended, merged and obscured in order to prevent individuals or institutions being recognised, when they are not my target. I hope that does not obscure the insights I want to share with you about a culture that exists within the global tax industry, and a horrifying truth about the world's tax systems themselves.

CONTENTS

INTRODUCTION

There's a sketch I like by a cartoonist called Shannon Burns of a balding man sitting at a desk in front of a computer in what could be an office anywhere in the world. The man has a little smile on his face as he thinks to himself, *I'll round this column off to the nearest nickel.*

The cartoon is captioned "REBEL ACCOUNTANT".

When I first saw this picture, it made me smile (though as a Brit I had to check which coin a nickel was). But there was something unsettling about it, too. I realised that I'd heard the phrase *rebel accountant* before.

Some years ago I was in an old Victorian pub in the Square Mile – the financial district of London – sharing a beer with a partner at a major accountancy firm. Actually it was more than one beer. He loosened up enough to tell me about a tax scheme he was working on in which he had simply *invented* a £10-million expense for one of his clients, which was going to save the client a few million pounds of tax.

I've spent a career around such people, but even so this admission seemed a little bold, and not least because I barely knew the man. Inventing expenses on this scale is not just illegal, it's spending-a-long-time-in-jail illegal.

I asked him if he was afraid of getting caught.

"Nah," he said. "It's not like the tax office want to mess with us. And besides, I see myself as a Rebel Accountant."

This is what unsettled me when I saw the light-hearted sketch of the accountant who rebels with a bit of clandestine rounding – out there in the real world, accountants are cheating the system to ensure that their clients, people with serious money, are paying a lot less tax than they should be. And as a consequence of these rebel accountants, not only are schools and hospitals and roads and the rest receiving a lot less money, but you are paying a lot more tax than you need to be. That's not quite as funny.

Except the maddening thing is that most accountants don't even need to be rebels. Most of the time the rules don't need circumventing or manipulating, because the rules have been written under the guidance of those people with very serious money.

Perhaps you knew that already. But do you know exactly *how* the rich avoid their taxes and, by extension, whether you could, too?

About half your wealth will disappear as tax over the course of your life – a little less if you're Australian or American, a little more if you're European. You'll probably spend more on tax than you will on all the homes you'll live in, the cars you'll drive and the food you'll eat *combined*, but I'll bet you find it easier to read a nutrition label than the deductions coming out of your payslip. I bet you know more about whether a neighbourhood is a nice one to live in than you are able to figure out how much tax you'll pay to live there.

You're not meant to know about tax. It's kept complex for a reason. If you knew what was *really* going on, you'd be the one who would want to rebel. If you understood that you were paying perhaps four times the tax rate of multi-millionaires, and more in absolute terms than some billionaires, would you stand for it?

Something's gone wrong here. We're being mocked. *Hand over your cash, but don't ask how we calculated how much you have to pay, because we're not going to tell you.*

It's like we're being forced to play a game but we don't know the rules – yet the rules were written by the person insisting we play.

So how do you fix this situation? Learn the rules? Are you kidding? It takes months of hard study and years of experience to become a professional tax advisor (I know, because that's what I did).

There are some books on this subject, guides for laypeople about their taxes, but mostly they are, well – how do I put this? – *boring*.

So here's my solution. I've written a book about tax that explains how it works and how you're being screwed over by it and what you can do about that screwing, written in a way that hopefully disguises the fact that you're reading a book about tax at all.

This is a book about cheats and scandals, sex and violence, conflict and lies, smuggling cash in suitcases and awkward situations in toilet cubicles. There's death and war and gore and a fish called Starbuck.

This was the challenge I set myself – to overcome the problem that everyone *needs* to read a book about tax, but no one *wants* to. I hope that changes, now.

I've decided to remain anonymous, and use the name "The Rebel Accountant", not least because it lets me tell this story in a way that I otherwise wouldn't be able to. In short, in a much more *fun* way. That does mean that a few names are made up, and a few places and events merged together. One or two people who have read early drafts of this book have already said, "Hey, this is a description of *me*", and of course they're wrong, but I can't help but smile, just a little, at their mistake.

In reading this book, I want you to feel like you're playing a game – because that's how the tax professionals see it. You don't know the rules? Don't worry too much about that – I'll explain them as we go along. The good news is that if you win this game, you can double your wealth, as you will no longer be paying tax (someone else will be paying it instead of you, but we'll deal with that a little later on).

And if you lose this game? Well, here's the secret. Don't tell anyone. Once you know the rules you can't lose – it's a rigged game.

The place you get to when you reach the end of this game is called Taxtopia. You'll find out why.

PROLOGUE

Driving into the town of Kersey, Pennsylvania, I saw a teenager holding up a homemade sign. He had used a spray can to spell out three words on a large piece of cardboard. I was on a small rural road and there can't have been more than one car every five minutes passing along it, so it was clear that he was waving the sign just for me. Before I could make out the words I assumed that if it wasn't an advert it would be something religious, political or obscene. I rather hoped it would be obscene. As I drew closer I saw that he had a smile on his face, and he gave me a wide-grinned wink.

The sign said:

Was he warning me of an accident up ahead? Was he giving me his opinion on local law enforcement? Either way, should I slow down? I eased off what the lady at the rental company called the *gas* and over-analysed the situation.

What if it was a trick? Would a 14-year-old in rural Pennsylvania go to all that trouble just to laugh at making cars slow down for no reason? Was it some incomprehensible TikTok challenge? For that matter, had the lady at the rental company been flirting with me? She probably wasn't. Though she had said my accent was "cute".

I was going about 40mph. I had no idea what the speed limit was. I had very little experience of driving on American roads. I knew I was approaching a small town, so it seemed reasonable to assume that I was going too fast. I started to brake.

I always over-analyse the situation. In my career you can charge by the hour, so it becomes a habit to consider every last detail. But in this case the analysis didn't last long.

The *cop* was well concealed. He had parked his car a dozen or so yards up a dirt drive to hide it from traffic like me and was crouched down holding a radar gun, and clocked my speed at about 22mph. It was slow enough not to get a ticket.

The cop flapped his hand a little as I drove by, as if asking me to slow down further, and I gave him a little wave in response. I meant it to be friendly, but he didn't look in the mood for niceties. Not long after, I found out why.

A minute or two down the road, approaching the crossroads where most of the small town's white wooden houses are situated, I saw another teenager. He, too, held up a sign as I approached. This one had only one word sprayed onto it, and the kid had an even broader grin than his friend. The sign read:

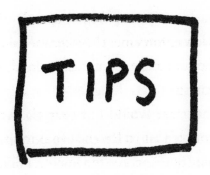

He'd chosen his spot well. There was a stop sign at the crossroads, so I was slowing to a standstill anyway. I didn't immediately realise what had just happened. It was the friends I was visiting in the town who had to explain it to me.

"Kids are doing it all over the place," they said. "It started with some photos and bragging on the internet and now it's really caught on. They make good money."

"What do the police think about it?" I asked.

"Well, yeah, they're kinda pissed, but the kids aren't breaking any laws. If anything, they're helping people obey the law. And I think most people would rather pay the kids a few bucks than a hundred-dollar fine."

I mulled this over. I would like you to mull it over too.

Be honest with yourself, would you have tipped the kids?

I mean, sure, it's a little cheeky. And sure, that speeding fine would have paid for things we all need. But you didn't know what that speed limit was and there was no easy way to find out. Be really, really honest with yourself. No one's looking.

There's another version of this story. In this other version, the cop isn't a cop.

The cop is the taxman. The cop is His Majesty's Revenue & Customs, the Internal Revenue Service, the Australian Taxation Office, le Ministère de l'Action et des Comptes Publics. The cop is working within a system that really is designed to catch you out. He knows you don't know how fast you're allowed to go. He's waiting behind a bush, at the bottom of a hill, at the end of a long open road.

And the speeding fine's not really a fine – it's tax. It's cash you have to pay because you don't know how to work the system.

You might think this isn't a fair comparison. Perhaps you think a fine is for when you do something wrong, whereas tax is just something we all pay, regardless of the choices we make. That may be how tax works for you, but it is not how it works for people richer than you. In this version of the story, the cop puts his radar gun away when a Lamborghini drives by at 90mph. Would it still be fair that you paid the fine, but the Lambo guy didn't?

Because that's what's happening. Across the world, tax systems are designed to let the richest people off. I don't mean "designed" in some abstract sense, like something that economists debate at dinner parties, tipsily drawing diagrams on their host's napkins. I mean the system of taxes we have is *actually designed* to reward the very wealthy. As in, someone sat down and said, "Let's write a tax code where the poorest in society pay at least quadruple the tax rates of the richest" and then, worried that wasn't fair, added, "Though if that puts too much burden on the *really* wealthy we'll let the rich buggers pay nothing at all."

Now, where were we? The cop is the taxman and the fine is a tax, and the billionaires are speeding through in their sports cars without so much as a frown from the cop (who is actually the taxman). Still with me?

You've probably gathered that you're the guy in the regular car. You're the guy who doesn't know what the speed limit is – which if I've got this metaphor right means I'm saying you don't know what the tax rules are, which maybe sounds like I'm insulting you, though who gets offended for being told they don't know much about tax?

You might think you do know the rules, or at least how they apply to you, but I can assure you that you don't. No matter how simple your financial affairs are, you are paying *way* more in tax than you think you are. Governments have become experts at plucking your wealth from you without you noticing.

But what's more, most of the tax you're paying isn't even going towards schools or hospitals or nukes or a slightly quicker train to somewhere you'll never visit. Most of the time it's being used to subsidise the wealthy.

You might think you're being an ethical citizen by paying your taxes, but our system is so warped that more often than not you're not helping the state *at all*. Indeed most of the time you'd help the economy more if you asked your boss for a pay *cut*. We'll find out exactly why a bit later on, because right now we're dealing with you speeding into Kersey, Pennsylvania.

The speeding ticket you'd get if the kids weren't there to warn you isn't fair. You're the only one who has to pay it – none of the rich people do. And the cop is more likely to use the cash to go for beers with his mate in the Lamborghini than to spend it on "things we all need".

Remember that if you're the guy in the regular car, this makes you the guy who has the chance to pay a few dollars to the kids with the signs instead of a hundred dollars to the taxman.

And this is where I come in. You may have worked out who I am by now. I'm those kids with the signs. I'm waving the signs at you. I'm the person you pay to "rearrange your financial affairs". That's my industry's preferred term for "make your tax bill disappear".

Of course, my signs have more than three words on them (though I'll happily accept tips). You might think at this point I'm about to tell you how to not pay any tax (and you're not necessarily wrong), and you may or may not have a moral issue with that, but I'm afraid it's not that simple.

For a start, you're already a fraudster and a money-launderer. You may not realise it, but you've committed theft and fraud and tax evasion and yes, money-laundering, on more than one occasion. I don't want to repeat myself too much, but the system really is designed to catch you out.

In my country, England, if you've ever so much as paid for a sandwich "to take away", then changed your mind and sat down in the café, you've defrauded the government – you've committed a crime with a maximum prison sentence more severe than if you'd prepared to commit an act of terrorism, all because of a quirk of the tax rules and a table that became available. The examples are pretty similar in other countries, too, so no matter where you are in the world *something* like this will have caught you out.

You may have even taken advantage of a tax-avoidance scheme of sorts, too. I have a friend who prides herself on her good ethical behaviour, including the fact that she is helping to save the planet by scrapping her old car and leasing an electric one. She's doing so by using a salary sacrifice scheme that saved her almost half the cost of leasing her Nissan Leaf. Saved *her*, but someone has to pick up the tab. That someone is you.

Or a simpler example: you might not be happy to read that Amazon pays very little tax, but do you wish this book cost more?

To make it all worse, you're also really not paying for all the good stuff. If you're a doctor or a nurse, a teacher, a lecturer, a civil servant, a policeman, a fireman, a judge, a soldier, a prison warden or a politician, then your wages are probably being paid by the government – your tax contributions are akin to a child handing back their pocket money as rent. The family is no richer for it. Though like any proud parent we're all glad you're doing what you're doing (except you politicians: I've got a whole chapter on what you get up to).

But that doesn't mean that the rest of us are pulling more than our weight. Perhaps the most shocking thing I've learned about tax is that most of us aren't paying for the doctors and teachers and civil servants and firemen and judges and soldiers. Most of us aren't making the government richer *at all*, yet you'll almost never hear the reason why.

Here's the crux of the issue – most of us are paying far more in tax than we realise, yet contributing far less to the government's coffers than we think we are.

Most of our tax is being used to subsidise the rich, yet the rich are routinely avoiding paying their taxes.

We abhor the tax cheats we read about, but often, unwittingly, we are tax cheats ourselves.

And sometimes it's not *unwittingly*. Sometimes we know exactly what we're doing – a cash payment to the plumber here, a pocketed tip there, an illicit download off the internet perhaps, or using a side business to deduct a few bogus expenses. But when *we* do it it's harmless, right? After all, we're just the little guy up against an inflexible system, and who doesn't root for the little guy? But then again, don't we just hate to see that system beaten by anyone else, especially anyone richer than us?

And the people who really are richer than us can beat the system more easily because they can afford to pay for advice from someone like me.

Let me tell you what I do for a living.

1

DON'T BECOME A TAX ADVISOR

It did not begin well.

Three months in I realised I'd been tricked. I remember the exact moment it dawned on me, a weighted shadow of regret and dismay, made worse by the empty seat next to me where my party guest had failed to show.

In front of me was a curtain that hung heavy from the ornate ceiling of this Knightsbridge hotel. Behind me was the rest of the party. A thousand other guests, any of them more amiable than the two to the right of me.

They were a couple, old and tired. Tired of each other as much as this party. The theme changed every year, the format didn't. I tried hard with them, I really did.

He was a partner at a small firm near Heathrow that had just been purchased by my firm. His name was Norman. He worked in Value Added Tax. In a profession known for its Aspergic members, VAT is at the far end of the spectrum. You charge VAT on what you sell, you recover it on what you buy. Norman had advised on this for our clients day in, day out, for 40 years.

So I asked his wife what she did.

"I work in VAT," she said.

I thought hard. *Where do I go with this?*

"So was it your love of VAT that brought the two of you together?" I asked. I thought this was a nice thing to say – light-hearted, friendly, a hint of sauciness perhaps. A conversational hook, if nothing else.

They looked at each other, turning their heads slowly, as their osteopath had advised. Then she turned slowly back to me.

"No," she said. There was no smile.

Then she took her turn to look at the curtain.

—

In the September of that year I had decided to rebel against my parents.

It was astonishingly difficult to do.

We lived in a posh but trendy part of London, my parents were both relaxed and liberal, had enjoyed the Sixties appropriately then sobered up in the Seventies, squeezed out kids in the Eighties and sent us to undemanding private schools in the Nineties. I didn't have the emotional trauma to become a drug addict or the musical ability to justify tattooing or piercing myself. If I'd announced at dinner that I was going to join an ashram in Peshawar, my old man would have recommended a restaurant he knew on the Khyber Road while my mother would have told me politely that I had my religions confused.

My father had got me a job making music videos and commercials – the kind of thing that some people dream of doing. Without any effort or inclination on my part I had found myself in what was supposed to be a creative maelstrom, working as part of a team that was filming the comeback of an Eighties pop icon.

So how to rebel? How do you do something that no one expects you to? How do you raise eyebrows and start conversations?

Yup, I became an accountant.[†]

There were aptitude tests and interviews and all that, but frankly so few people want to be accountants and so many accountants are needed that as long as you can tell which of two numbers is bigger you're pretty much guaranteed to get a training contract.

Most people are recruited by one of the "Big 4" firms. Between them, they're responsible for around 96 per cent of the significant business of accounting. You might know that there used to be a "Big 5", until something really bad happened to one of them.

But I made a mistake. This is where the trick came in.

I interviewed at the Big 4, but I also went along to an assessment day at a smaller firm. For legal reasons I can't tell you which one. This is a shame, as there's a good joke about this firm's name.

The assessment day was amazing. There were six of us attending – I fell instantly in love with three of the other assessees; we were taken out for lunch in the City; given a speech about how this firm was different, how they wanted fresh ideas, a youthful perspective, how we could be part of a dynamic, evolving team from Day 1. We would be trained by the best in the world and become leaders in our chosen field. We took part in an inspired business exercise to test our commercial acumen. "The decisions you make in this exercise will reflect the decisions that you are making in your jobs."

To help you understand how this affected me, compare it to the interview I had at one of the Big 4 firms:

"Tell me something about your CV."

[†]   Actually, now I come to think of it, I may also have been influenced by a family friend recounting a conversation he overheard in a lift at a big accountancy firm in the city. There were two partners discussing their careers, and one turned to the other and said, in all earnestness, "I can't decide whether to earn £400,000 a year to work a three-day week, or £700,000 to work a five-day week."

"It's all there in front of you, what would you like to know more about?"

"Any of it. I don't really care."

But at this small firm I would be an individual. I'd have a chance to grow, to learn, to be a future captain of industry. I accepted their job offer.

The induction day when I joined should have set off alarm bells. There were 20 of us new kids on the graduate scheme and we were all sent into a room to await our training manager. None of my new colleagues said so much as a single word as we waited.

There is an old joke that you can spot an extroverted accountant because they look at *your* shoes when they talk to you. Here they weren't even talking. But people get shy, I understand that.

The girls I'd fallen semi-in-love with on the assessment day weren't there. Very few girls were.

Then our training manager arrived and put on a VHS narrated by Jeremy Clarkson to explain something about the chemicals industry. I remembered reading that this firm did a lot of work in the chemicals industry. We practised some double-entry bookkeeping. If I'd known it was going to be important I probably would have paid more attention, but it's a lot less exciting than it sounds. In fact, after three hours of it I'd picked up just two facts, one of which, it transpired, was wrong:

1. Bookkeeping (and its derivations) is the only word in English to have three double-letters one after the other.
2. A debit is the number closer to the window.[†]

[†] If this makes no sense to you, you're not alone. I've spent a long time wondering why my training manager thought that the best way to explain debits and credits was by using the spatial relationships in that particular room. Just in case you're interested (though don't be remotely ashamed if you're not), you *debit* something you have and you *credit* the reason you have it. So if a business sold something, a bookkeeper would record this as debit: cash, credit: sales. Bookkeepers have *wild* work-chat.

Then I was taken to my desk, and given my first ever job in tax:

"One of our clients has recently refurbished its offices and has purchased 300 new computers. It wants to make a capital election for each one, so we need you to record the serial numbers of each computer in this spreadsheet."

I asked why they were making the election or, indeed, what a capital election was. It seemed like what I should be asking. But I got a blank stare in return. Apparently it didn't matter.

But everyone has to do tedious stuff in their jobs, I thought. I mean, I suspect Day 1 in the Oval Office is just getting security clearances and signing endless documents. It's probably Day 2 when the fun starts.

Day 2 was mostly photocopying. So were Day 3 and Day 4. On Day 5 I discovered that they served mid-morning soup in the canteen and it was seen as a legitimate reason to be away from one's desk. Day 6 was a little better, but then it was a Saturday, so I wasn't at work.

And after three months of this I was sitting in an ill-fitted rented tuxedo, staring at a featureless curtain, between a vacant seat and Mr and Mrs Norman VAT. Someone had just proposed a toast to the Queen. She wasn't there, of course.

So it hit me. The charm and flattery of the assessment day was a trick. This was the reality, and would be for the next 40 years.

But then the evening took an unexpected turn, and with it my career.

It began when Mrs Norman started to cry.

—

Here's what's weird about any sales tax, like VAT. Because the format of the tax is so simple – all you do is add a percentage onto your sales price, and then that percentage gets paid over to the government – you'd think there wouldn't be too many fiddly rules.

But if there weren't fiddly rules there would be nothing for accountants to do. And it's accountants who advise the government on how to write the rules, so they make damn sure that the rules are as complicated as they can be.

For instance, in the UK, we have a 20 per cent tax on clothing, but there's an exception for children's clothes. Buy your kid a hat, and the tax rate is 0 per cent. But there's an exception to that exception – if the kid's hat is fur-lined, the tax rate is 20 per cent again. But there's an exception to the exception of that first exception. If the fur in the hat is *goat* fur, then we go back to 0 per cent. But I kid you not that there's an exception to the exception of the exception's exception. The rate goes back to 20 per cent if the goat fur comes from goats raised in Yemen, Mongolia or Tibet. Which is how VAT partners at mid-sized accountancy firms get paid £600 per hour to enquire into the provenance of a toddler's goat-fur beret.

It's not just goat fur. People go to court to argue whether their crisp is really a crisp (Pringles claimed otherwise) or whether their cake is really a cake (ask Jaffa) or their *bread* is really a cake (Subway's bread has a lot of sugar in it) or, amazingly, whether pizza is designed to be consumed hot (apparently not, if you're Domino's – it's just a coincidence).

My favourite case of all time – and one I tried to share with Mrs Norman VAT in an attempt at dinner chat – was settled by the Supreme Court of the United States. A company called Toy Biz, Inc. had purchased the right to make the figurines of the X-Men superheroes. Under US law, sales taxes are not applied to toys, but they are applied to humanoid dolls. So Toy Biz, Inc. labelled their action figures as toys, only for an X-Men fan at the IRS to launch an inquiry.

In the X-Men stories, the X-Men are *mutants*, gaining their superpowers due to mutations in their DNA. Some have grown claws, some can manipulate metal with their minds, one or two have wings, that sort of stuff. Consequently, many normal people fear them, and treat them as outcasts. So the X-Men try desperately to gain acceptance – to make people realise that they are not to be feared. They may have dangerous powers, but they are just like us. They are *humans,* too.

In which case, the IRS argued, we need to whack on a sales tax, as they're dolls, not toys.

It went through a tribunal and a court hearing and the appeals process until the Supreme Court of the United States found itself having to make a decision about whether Wolverine and friends were humans or not.

I love the image of senior judges holding an action figure of Magneto and saying, "Well this guy sure looks human, but that lizard-y one over there's got four arms, sheesh, I dunno – Ginsburg, what d'you reckon?"

Mrs VAT didn't laugh at my accent. She didn't smile. If I'm entirely honest (which is not something my profession is always known for), I think she might not have been listening to me. Her husband had left the table. It was just us. She mumbled something.

"I'm sorry, what was that?"

"I said he's bought a Porsche. He thinks I don't know, but he's spending it all on her."

"Sorry, who's bought a Porsche?"

"He's taken all our money – yours too, I'm afraid. I don't suppose I'll see him again."

Finally, I thought, *this night may be about to get interesting.*

———

Actually, there's two other things about VAT I want to share with you. As they're both in some way related to sex this seems like as good a point as any to mention them.

You don't have to charge VAT unless your business makes a certain amount of money. As customers don't like paying VAT, there's an incentive for businesses to, ahem, under-report how much money they earn, especially if they're very close to the threshold above which they have to charge it. Tax inspectors sometimes go undercover, posing as customers, to try and estimate whether a business should be registered for VAT but isn't... but it's not much fun for them to pretend that their sink is broken or their windows need cleaning to try and catch some dodgy handyman out, so instead HMRC launched an undercover investigation into Spearmint Rhino.

Now obviously when I first found this out I had no idea what Spearmint Rhino was and had to google it, while at work and with my boss standing behind me. If you're pretending that you don't know either, I'll tell you – it's a strip club.

You see, a court ruling had said that all Spearmint Rhino did was provide a workspace to self-employed strippers, which left open the question of whether the strippers themselves were earning more than the threshold at which they should be charging VAT. As in "Would you like a dance? That will be £20 plus VAT."

I admire the resilience of the undercover tax inspectors, forced to spend night after night monitoring the number of sexy dances these sole traders (to use the lingo) were performing. If the strippers *were* over the threshold (some were), then at least if you went to Spearmint Rhino on a work jolly you could ask for an invoice detailing the services provided and claim back the VAT.[†]

[†] In case you're wondering, the threshold at which you have to charge VAT has been hovering around the £85,000 mark in the UK for a while, meaning that any businesses (including individual strippers) that charge more than this amount per year have to add VAT to their prices. As it's based on turnover rather than profits, if you have relatively low profits it's possible that *growing* your business could force you into bankruptcy, as once you're over this threshold you would have to give a sixth of your turnover to the taxman.

Ex-Prime Minister Gordon Brown also got involved with people's sexy times by tweaking a bit of VAT (sorry, there's probably a better way to phrase that). Back when he was in charge of tax rules – in the early Noughties – he was informed that the UK had the highest rate of teenage pregnancy in Europe. What follows is an extraordinary insight into how his mind worked.

Clearly, he thought, condoms were too expensive, otherwise teenagers would be using them – so he lowered the rate of VAT on contraceptives to 5 per cent. In Gordon's imagination he must have seen some horny kid saying, "£1.20 a condom?! I'm not paying that! Oh wait, £1.05 . . . brill, slap it on!"

In fairness to Gordon, it worked. The teenage pregnancy rate has halved since his intervention.

—

It transpired that Mr Norman VAT, the partner from Heathrow who had just joined our firm, whom I'd written off as possibly the most boring man alive, was both stealing from what I guess were now *our* clients and having an affair with his secretary. Mrs Norman VAT only gave me part of the details – I'm not sure a 23-year-old trainee she'd just met at a work party was the ideal person to share the worst revelation of her life with – but I resolved to go digging for as much dirt as I could the next time I disappeared for soup in the office.

What I was told was that Norman had created elaborate tax scams known as "carousel frauds".

Remember that you charge VAT on what you sell, but you can also *reclaim* it on what you buy, provided you've bought it for business reasons. There's also an exploitable exception (of course): you don't have to pay VAT when you export something.[†]

At its simplest, a carousel fraud works by setting up three companies, – an importer, an exporter and a foreign company – all ultimately (but secretly) owned by the same person. The three companies then sell goods to each other in a pointless circular transaction (hence "carousel") like this:

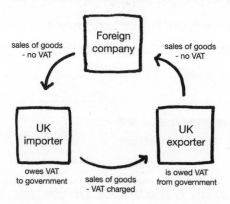

The importer buys some goods from the foreign company, then sells them to the exporter. At this point VAT gets charged – so the importer owes money *to* the government, but the exporter can claim the same amount of money *from* the government.

The exporter then sells the goods back to the original foreign company.

So far, this isn't actually a *fraud*, but neither is it making anyone any money. The goods have ended up back where they started and the VAT owed by one company exactly matches the VAT reclaimed by another.

[†]   There's a whole load of rules about VAT when you *import* something, but it doesn't affect this fraud so I've excluded them from this diagram.

The fraud happens when you make the importing company just . . . disappear. It owes a fortune to HMRC but it doesn't pay it. When HMRC start investigating, it turns out that the listed directors are fictional and the registered address can't be found.

All we've done is remove one of the companies from our carousel, like this:

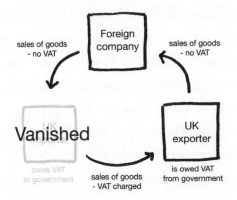

What we're left with is a UK company that is owed a lot of money from the government. That's definitely fraud, but the UK company doesn't *appear* to be connected to the other companies in the chain (even though it really is), so just happily pockets the cash.

Indeed, the actual *goods* never even need to change hands. In fact, they don't need to exist at all. All you need to make this work is the paper trail. And it's the paper trail that Norman was good at.

Carousel fraud is big business. In 2016 the UK government convicted eighteen people of the same mobile-phone fraud and confiscated almost £115 *million* in criminal profits. In 2012 another gang was convicted of a £176-million fraud, also based on fictional sales of mobile phones. In 2008 there was a £138-million carousel fraud. This doesn't include all the gangs who simply don't get caught, or the dozens of smaller scale operations, like Norman's. The European

Commission estimated that the VAT lost across the EU due to fraud was over €130 billion in 2019 alone.[†]

But Norman wasn't as clever as he thought. Too many of the "legitimate" companies – the exporters – were in some way connected to him. One of my managers thought that Norman must have got either too lazy or too greedy. Each new (fictional) "client" looked like revenue he'd brought into his firm, justifying for him a larger share of partnership income. Perhaps realising that the tax inspectors were on to him, he decided to unwind some of the frauds, paying over the VAT due by the importers. But as he didn't have that kind of money (I assume having spent it on the Porsche and the secretary), he dipped into the firm's client accounts to pay for it.

Clients tend to be better at noticing that their money is missing than the government is, so many of them started asking impossible-to-answer questions about where their cash was. Apparently Norman realised he'd been rumbled the very night of the party at which I had been sitting next to him and his wife. The rumour was that he had now gone on the run – with both his secretary and the client money.

Of course, I was appalled when I heard all of this. I'd sat at that dinner all night and missed a golden opportunity to hear about this elaborate subterfuge first hand.[‡]

[†]   Every country in the EU has some form of VAT, but outside Europe this fraud is harder to pull off, as sales taxes don't normally get refunded to businesses in the same way.

[‡]   I mentioned this tale to an accountant I met recently, who laughed and said, "Yeah, my employer started out doing a carousel fraud with mobile phones, but then realised there was more money to be made from actually selling the phones."

In the early days, whenever I was interviewed for an accountancy training contract I would always be asked the same question:

"Why do you want to become an accountant?"

I suspect most job interviews have some variation of this question, but it's different in accountancy. The way it's asked is like this:

"Why *the fuck* do you want to become an accountant?"

I'd rehearsed my answer:

"I want the opportunity to be creative."

Working in the music-video industry had taught me that the creative industries are anything but. They are built on a pyramid structure – just have a look at the credits at the end of a film. Of the 400 people who spent a year of their lives on a blockbuster movie, how many of them actually used their imagination? The director? Maybe a producer, definitely an editor, probably not a cameraman. Perhaps a couple of lead actors. But everyone else? It's not like the make-up artist suddenly decides to apply mascara to an actress's elbows, or the key grip tessellates the camera equipment in a novel way. But keep reading down past the gaffers and caterers and you'll get to the accounting team. In the old days there'd be one accountant listed, who had the job of recording the expenses. Nowadays it'll be a whole team. They're less concerned with where the money *goes*, but rather where it *comes from*. That takes some creativity.

Or so my spiel went. The partners interviewing me would nod in agreement. I was complimenting them, telling them that they were cooler than film directors. They all offered me a job.

And then at the induction at the firm that I actually joined, during a break between a PowerPoint presentation about the seemingly millennia-long history of the firm's many mergers and the issuing of our "irreplaceable" staff ID cards (I lost mine after two weeks), one of the other trainees asked me why I'd become an accountant. I said the same thing to him – that the *real* creativity was behind the scenes, following the money, not pointing a camera at a pop band or pretty actress in exactly the same way it's been done a thousand times before. When I finished he breathed in slowly before he spoke, weighing up the benefits of being honest with me or making a good first impression. He went with honesty.

"That's the stupidest fucking thing I've ever heard."

After three months of data entry and photocopying, I was starting to think that he might be right.

But then I met Wilhelm.

—

There are accountants and then there are accountants. And then there was Wilhelm.

There are a quarter of a million accountants in the UK, and five times that number in the USA. There are over three million accountants worldwide.[†]

Would it be fair to stereotype all these people? Well, here goes . . .

In Hollywood movies the accountants are usually socially awkward mathematical geniuses. But in the real world the banking industry pays so much better than accountancy that the actual savants aren't going to be auditing your small business.

[†] Though oddly only a few thousand in France. I mean, the French love their bureaucracy, so why are there so many more accountants in the UK? Though as my sources on this are in French this may be more a reflection on my failure to master the language. Despite five years of studying it, I'm so shockingly bad at French that when I was recently approached on the Tube by a French woman who asked, "La ligne rouge est la ligne central?" I thought about it and replied, "Sí."

The reality is that accountancy is a career for people who don't know what else to do with their lives. Indeed, if you are thinking about a career in accountancy, think twice before studying accountancy at university. The people interviewing you won't have done so and will wonder why on earth you did. Actually *wanting* to be an accountant is normally the only grounds not to be offered the job.

I just mentioned Hollywood, but in fairness I can only think of three Hollywood films that prominently feature accountants. One is *The Accountant*, in which Ben Affleck plays an accountant who is a mathematical savant and is inexplicably good at hand-to-hand combat. The second is *Stranger Than Fiction*, with Will Ferrell as a mathematical savant who is inexplicably attractive to Maggie Gyllenhaal. The third is *The Untouchables*, which features a relatively normal accountant. As Hollywood abhors normalcy, this accountant is brutally gunned down in an elevator.

When Hollywood features an accountant as a supporting character it normally establishes their credentials by having them wear a poorly fitting suit and saying things like, "I just like the way all the numbers balance." In reality the numbers never balance . . . sure, they're supposed to, but they never bloody do, so I can guarantee that no accountant has ever said, "I like the way the numbers balance." At accountancy college you're even taught to insert a fictional balancing adjustment into a balance sheet just because no one can ever get the damn thing to balance. If Hollywood wants to get it right its characters should say, "I didn't know what to do with my life, so here I am in the accounts department. Fuck." (To be fair, Hollywood does have the poorly fitting suit bit right.)

Some of the traditional stereotypes *can* be true. I worked with a junior manager I'll call Durukan who joined my firm shortly after I did.

I was told he had moved to London from Turkey and it occurred to me that he might be lonely. So I tried to befriend him.

"What do you like doing when you're not accounting?"

He thought about it, then gave me an answer:

"I like TV."

"Any particular TV?" I tried.

"No. Just TV."

I accept that I could have tried harder.

There are some articulate and charming accountants out there, but you probably won't realise you've met them because they've learned to say anything other than "accounting" when you ask them what they do for a living.[†]

But mostly it's a career for people who picked a job by going alphabetically through the list of career options and didn't want to work in an abattoir.

And then there's Wilhelm, in a category of his own.

—

I want to tell you about Wilhelm in some detail because it's through him that I learned what deep down I suspect you want to know: *how to avoid paying tax.*

He was also one of the brightest, weirdest and consistently inconsistent people I've ever met – a man who mirrored the tax rules he knew so well.

Wilhelm hadn't followed a conventional career path. He had left his rural Scandinavian school at 16 and found his way to the Bahamas, where he worked on a yacht belonging to an Italian billionaire.

[†] I've read that the pop band Blur had the opposite problem. When they told people they were in a band they got too much attention, so to deflect it they would tell people that they were accountants. I can see how that would work.

Though as he put it, "I didn't do much work, but I got paid a lot of money."
I can only guess what he meant by that. He became friends with one of
the billionaire's four personal assistants. There were four because one
was for the billionaire's business, one for his domestic life, one for his
social life and one who controlled the calendar. This last one was the PA
who simply wasn't allowed to get it wrong. He was the one Wilhelm
befriended.

The great advantage of yachts is that you can live on them and not be
living anywhere else. Most countries only tax people who live in their
countries, so a billionaire can avoid a lot of tax by just, well, not living in
those countries. America is the big exception. If you're American the
IRS will follow you *anywhere*. It's one reason that American billionaires
own fewer yachts than European ones.

Wilhelm learned this from the PA, but he didn't have the sort of
mind that just went, "Oh, OK", then forgot about it. Instead, while still
in his teens, he read up on international tax rules. He realised that it was
information that was important to billionaires, so he figured it was a fast
track to getting their attention – and their money.

The issue, he learned, is how long you can be living somewhere
before you count as being there long enough to owe taxes. You can
always get away with staying somewhere for a short while, otherwise
every tourist would become tax resident in the place they're visiting and
be slapped with a massive tax bill, so every country has what are called
residency rules. It was these rules that the calendar PA had to know, and
it was these rules that Wilhelm mastered at an age when I was still
playing with my Warhammer.[†]

[†]   If you've never heard of it, Warhammer is a tabletop-strategy game involving
       miniature fantasy figures, a kind of toy soldiers, where you win by mastering
       complex rules – so not a million miles away from the world of tax (only with
       more dragon-slayers and, possibly, more ogres).

From there he ingratiated himself into the company of the Italian billionaire's friends and acquaintances, teaching himself any skill that he thought would enable him to advance his new career. He knew more about wine than anyone I've ever met, yet didn't drink it. "Trust me, you know the story of Scylla and Charybdis? You don't want to be drunk on a boat between an ageing predator and a stormy sea."[†]

He told me that in his mid-twenties, when he was already running a tax-consultancy business, he had a sudden panic attack. He had always treated taxation as a *game*. There were rules – very, very, complex rules – and whoever played them best, won. But then he wondered if that was true. What if what he was doing was *morally* wrong? We only ever discussed this once, but he told me that he lay in the bath until it turned cold and refused to let himself get out until he had an answer. Eventually he did. What he decided would nowadays be seen as a bastardisation of what has become known as *Modern Monetary Theory*.

Wilhelm reasoned that taxes did not actually pay for things, like schools or hospitals. His view was that the teachers and nurses in, say, England, are paid with *pounds,* and the British government has a near monopoly on making *pounds,* so can pay for as many teachers and nurses as it wants. The only catch is that if it pays for too many, then if the private sector has not made enough products there will be too many pounds chasing too few goods, and prices will go up. So whenever the government pays for something, like a new school or a policeman's salary, it is pumping money into the economy, and so to stop the economy from overheating it must withdraw some money too – as tax.

[†]   In case you've forgotten, in *The Odyssey*, Charybdis is a whirlpool and Scylla is a multi-headed sea creature that literally eats sailors. I don't know how literal Wilhelm was being, but he did love his allusions.

Which means that tax doesn't pay for stuff. And this, to Wilhelm, was the foundation of his belief that there was nothing immoral about not paying taxes. "All taxes do is limit inflation – but on whose say-so? I want the roads built, so build them. Print some pounds and build them. If you are worried about the economy overheating, then I'll shift my wealth offshore if you like. Let the Cayman Islands suffer the inflation if you care so much – they don't mind it. And if the government wants to redistribute wealth, they can print some money and give it to the poor. I never voted to have my wealth redistributed. Besides, inflation redistributes wealth even better than taxes do. The more in debt you are, the more you need inflation. I am helping the indebted and the poor. I am a moral crusader!"[†]

He brought this attitude with him to the firm where I worked, merging his consultancy with the personal taxes department.

His beliefs endeared him well to what were known as our UHNW clients. That's *Ultra High Net Worth*, a club you can join if you've got at least £20 million burning a hole in your pocket. Wilhelm soon became the head of the whole department.

The detail about him being in the bath I'm not sure I believe. A lot of his anecdotes seemed to require me picturing him naked.

But all of this I discovered later. Back then I was three months into my new job and trying to find a way to work on something interesting. A team was being put together to unpick the tangled mess of Norman

---

[†] Modern Monetary Theory is a good one to throw into any argument you're having in order to support your position, whatever that position may be. Not only does it propose a radical reassessment of what taxes are *for,* at the other end of the political spectrum it has been used to justify vastly increased government expenditure. In other words, it can mean pretty much whatever you want it to mean, which, let's be honest, is the best type of theory to whip out mid-debate. Most economists are a little sniffy about it, incidentally, but that may be because it overturns over a century of economic thought.

VAT's carousel fraud. The team was headed by what were called our forensic accountants. This sounded sufficiently *CSI* for me to want to join it.[†]

My chance came in an elevator. I found myself almost alone with my staff partner – i.e. the person with complete power of life and death over me. I asked him if there was any chance I could get some experience working with forensic accounting. He said he would think about it, then got out of the lift a floor too early. He was the kind of staff partner who didn't like talking to staff.

I say I was almost alone, because there was one other person in the lift. I knew he was Wilhelm, the head of personal tax. It would have been hard not to know. Besides a moustache, he wore a fuchsia polo shirt and dark jeans. No one in accountancy wore jeans – at least not back then. The trainees in personal tax bragged about how he took them out for long (and, for them, boozy) lunches every Friday, and some of his philosophies had drifted their way down to the soup-time conversations, but it hadn't occurred to me to go and work in his department. *Personal* tax sounded just as dry as *business* tax.

"You don't want to work in forensic accounting," he said, having had no choice but to listen to me pleading with the staff partner. He had an accent that I'm pretty sure was affected.

"No?"

"No. It's horrendous."

I was expecting him to say, "You should do *such and such* instead," but it never came. The lift doors opened.

[†] If you've never seen it, *CSI*, or "Crime Scene Investigation", is a TV show about forensic scientists. Though in real life forensics is probably a painstaking process of comparing skid marks to pre-prepared charts, in *CSI* it's all bullet casings and drug deals, then having sex with your colleagues. I had assumed forensic *accounting* was similar.

—

I have a real problem with the movie *Sliding Doors*, in which one life takes two different paths depending on whether someone gets on a train or not. I don't think our decisions are ever made in isolation. I know mine wasn't.

If it hadn't been for this firm's sales pitch I never would have joined it. Had my date turned up at my work party I never would have spent so long chatting to the Normans of VAT. I never would have learned about his VAT fraud or asked my staff partner if I could join the investigating team. I never would have held the door of the elevator open and asked Wilhelm directly, "So what should I do?"

"Today?" he said, looking bemused, maybe irritated, again the moustache hiding the curl of his lip. "Today it's nice and bright outside. So dump your time on 31468 and spend the afternoon in the park."

—

If you have a job where you have to fill in timesheets, feel free to jump right ahead to the next section, as you already understand the pain.

If not, let me ask you a question: what did you do between 10.06am and 10.12am last Tuesday? And the six minutes after that? And after that? And after that? Imagine this is your life – converting every activity you've done into a five-digit code, recording it for eight hours each day, in six-minute increments. Now imagine that you have a job that consists of entering seemingly random numbers into a barely comprehensible software program, printing out the results, getting them signed, then photocopying them in triplicate. Tell me truthfully, would it break you? Would it lead you to cheat?

It didn't take me long to realise that when filling in timesheets it was easier to round up time to the nearest hour, meaning five minutes' photocopying became "Client 13765 research – 1 hour". More slowly I realised that a few of our clients were so huge that no one would mind me adding a little chargeable time to their records. I'm still not sure if that's fraud – timesheets bore little resemblance to what our clients got charged. Technically all timecodes were either "billable" or "non-billable", but the arithmetic of what clients got charged was simple. I once saw a senior manager absolutely delighted when a client phoned him to complain that his fee was too high. "That means we've charged him just the right amount!" he said.

Just to make that clearer – if you have ever paid an accountant, they have charged you what they think they can get away with, not what the work is worth. Always complain about your fee.

Timesheets are a genuine opportunity for a little *creativity*. Spending an afternoon in the pub could become "reading tax periodicals" (41788). Having a tactical sleep in a toilet cubicle could be recorded as three hours of "filing closed client accounts" (18121). There was even a code for "I hate this job so much I've decided to stay home": "sick or other absence" (90001).

I had assumed that non-billable time just disappeared into the fabric of the building, like laughter and hope. I was wrong.

—

One of the partners in the department was an objectionably tall, fake-tanned, sweaty sixty-something called Stewart. He'd taken a liking to one of the few girls in my department and having once seen me with my arm around her had decided that he would be my enemy.[†]

[†]　It's equally possible that he noticed that I did almost no work despite him paying my wages, but I'm going to stick with the jealousy conjecture.

Unfortunately, it turned out that he also had the job of reviewing the juniors' timesheets.

One morning, shortly before my brief but fateful meeting with Wilhelm, and shortly after a particularly bold timesheet submission, he summoned me to his office.

He had a habit of rolling up his sleeves in front of junior staff to show off a dagger tattoo on his arm which he claimed he got in the navy. He liked to make me stand in front of his desk while he pretended to finish an email. I wondered what the timesheet code would be for *this* meeting. I figured I could round it up to at least half an hour.

"I asked you to correct a spelling error in a letter and I see *one and a half hours* attached to the client. Care to comment?"

I couldn't tell him that to avoid the tedium of data entry I had invented a game called Six Degrees of Wikipedia, where you pick two random topics and using only the links in each article try to get from the first topic's article to the target one. It had consumed most of two mornings the previous week.

"Well, I had to check the whole letter to see if there were any other spelling errors . . ."

"It was a three-line letter."

"I included a break for soup."

Stewart told me, firmly and coldly, that at least 80 per cent of my time had to be billable, and that he would be keeping an eye on my timesheets.

Other than his acknowledging that I could faff around for the remaining 20 per cent of my time, this was just about the worst news imaginable.

Which is where Wilhelm's cryptic code came in. I appreciate that I'm talking about five-digit numbers in a trainee's timesheet, which is perhaps not the rollercoaster ride through international subterfuge you may have thought you'd signed up for when you bought this book, but if we could just pretend for a moment that his code had some sort of dry-ice and choir-of-angels qualities to it I'll get into the "A" material in just a moment.

I'd never heard of Wilhelm's recommended code before, but when I typed it into our timesheet software the choir broke into their Hallelujahs.

31468: UHNW – CONFIDENTIAL ("Billable")

In other words, I could spend my mornings trying to find the links from the Wikipedia page on the poison dart frog to the page on Jean-Paul Sartre and dump my time on this billable code.[†]

It was the closest a number has ever come to giving me an erection.

After letting me get away with billing his Ultra High Net Worth client team for a fortnight, despite me not knowing who was actually in that team, what the team did, why their work was confidential or even which floor of the building they were based on, Wilhelm dropped me an email:

You work for me now. Don't tell anyone.

Looking back on it, I saw in Wilhelm not so much a philosophy to adhere to as a chance to escape a life of data entry. What he saw in me was a bit more obvious. I was a 23-year-old man who looked a bit like a girl. Just his type.

[†] Poison dart frog links to French Guiana, which links to France, which links to Jean-Paul himself. Honestly, it's hours of fun.

2

HOW TO GET RICH
(IF YOU'RE ALREADY RICH)

In November 1799 Napoleon Bonaparte orchestrated a coup that directly led to him being crowned Emperor of France. It *indirectly* led to Wilhelm being able to save his clients *millions* in tax.

In response to the rising militancy of Bonapartist France, William Pitt the Younger introduced the UK's first ever income tax. The tax was a temporary measure, so in order to ensure it lasted only as long as Napoleon remained a threat, it had to be renewed every year by an Act of Parliament.

Think on that. Income tax is a temporary tax to help the fight against Napoleon. And sure enough, every year a new Finance Act is passed to extend it *just one more year*. Y'know, just in case Napoleon escapes from St Helena and comes back for one more stab at European domination.

But to get the new tax through a Parliament dominated by the super-rich (unlike Parliament today, of course), and specifically to help "the official carrying on the Empire abroad" who might, nonetheless, pay an occasional visit to Britain, an exception was made that meant there was no income tax for *offshore* income made by *non-domiciled* people.[†]

But what does *domicile* mean? It isn't where you live – otherwise the wealthy colonialists of the British Empire would never move back to the UK, as their plantations would fall into the clutches of the British taxman. So what is it?

I'm going to get a tiny bit technical here, but it's the main insight into how the really, really rich get out of paying taxes, at least in Britain, so bear with me. I'll make it worth your while.

First, there's a concept called *residence*. This refers to where you *live*. Or at least, it refers to the country where you live the most. It's meant to be a question of fact, but it gets rapidly rather complex, and can be changed by all sorts of things that might seem none of the taxman's business, like, say, if you suddenly discover that you've got an illegitimate child from a one-night stand at the Isle of Wight Festival 15 years ago.

The main test for residence is that if you're physically in the UK for more than half the year, then you count as a UK resident. If you're not

---

[†] In fairness, there were a good hundred years of back and forth on this issue. Pitt's successor Henry Addington actually abolished income tax, then almost immediately reintroduced it under a different name and in a manner that meant twice as many people had to pay it (though he reduced the tax rate for the richest people). Both Gladstone and Disraeli promised to abolish it, but didn't (though Gladstone promised to phase it out over seven years, which is a plan currently running more than 160 years over schedule). It was a similar story in America, where income tax was introduced by Abraham Lincoln to help fund the Civil War, then abolished as the war was won . . . then re-established a few years later (despite there not being a war on). Interestingly the Supreme Court of the US ruled that (some) income taxes were unconstitutional, so Congress passed the 16th Amendment to put income taxes solidly into the Constitution. The domicile rules as they are today in Britain were largely introduced in 1914, and were only possible after the Parliament Act of 1911, which limited the ability of the House of Lords to veto tax rules (because prior to that Act the Lords had a habit of vetoing any new tax that affected – you guessed it – lords).

a *resident* of the UK you only pay tax on money earned in the UK, not anything earned elsewhere. And if you're rich enough and your accountant is talented enough, everything you earn should be from *elsewhere*.

So if you want to avoid paying any income tax, jetting off to Majorca for two weeks in summer's not good enough, but doing a season in the Alps and another on your yacht with a couple of days at the Monaco Grand Prix should do nicely.[†]

There are secondary residency tests if your situation isn't so clear cut – say you spend a few months in Scotland, but also a few months in Sweden and some more in the Bahamas, so you aren't obviously resident in any of them. These tests involve establishing how "tied" you are to the UK, by looking at things like whether you've bought a house here or have any children living here. Hence needing to know about the music-festival love child.

But what if you want to live in England, but don't much fancy paying taxes? For this, we have our second concept: *domicile*.

Domicile can generally be thought of as where you're from – officially it's your place of origin. Normally you might expect this *domicile of origin* to be the country in which you were born. But this needs exceptions (of course), as otherwise every child born a couple of weeks early while their parents were on a last minute pre-kids sangria fest in Valencia would be Spanish.

So there's a rule that slightly fudges things, which says that if you don't really feel part of the country where you were born, you can take the domicile of your *father* instead (the politicians who drafted the

---

[†]   If I was your accountant, which for legal reasons I should stress I am most definitely not (at least, not yet, we'll talk), I would advise you to spend a lot of time in Monaco. I mean, seriously, go nuts. Don't ever leave. It would make my job so much easier.

rules weren't so fussed about their mothers, and no one's updated it since).

But surely even this needs exceptions. I mean, what if you were born on the tarmac to a single mother while on a stop-over in Singapore mid long haul? For just such an eventuality, Parliament inserted one of the biggest tax loopholes of the lot: *the domicile of choice*.

Actually *loophole* is probably the wrong word, as it implies a gap or ambiguity or mistake in the legislation, whereas the legislation was clear: if you wanted to, even if you were born in Britain and lived in Britain, you could *choose* not to be British (at least for tax purposes). And if you aren't British, you only have to pay tax on money you make *in Britain*. If you transfer all your wealth offshore it will stay there – offshore – untouched by the British taxman.

This was a rule specifically crafted to reward the backers of Britain's Empire, but times change, and so has the face of non-domiciled people with offshore wealth. After decades of immigration the government realised that there were now millions of UK citizens who could make non-domiciled claims. We're not talking about people with vast wealth – perhaps only a small apartment in Hong Kong, or a bit of cash in a Nigerian bank.

To deal with this change both Gordon Brown and David Cameron came up with the same idea for a reform, which they eventually enacted as law (first in 2008 and then reaffirmed in 2012 and 2019, meaning it's still the rule in force today). The more I think about this rule, the more suspect it seems. The law is this: you can only access this non-domicile scheme – the one that lets you pay no tax on your offshore wealth – if you pay at least £30,000 to do so.

To make that clearer, British law says that you can only reduce your tax bill relating to offshore wealth if you are already rich. Specifically, that you have at least £30,000 to "buy" a reduced bill.

This means that if you earned £20,000 a year renting out your Hong Kong apartment, you would have to pay UK tax on that rent, but if you earned £2,000,000 a year renting out an entire Hong Kong apartment block you would just hand over a £30,000 fee each year to pay no UK tax at all (which is a bargain, when the tax on the income from that apartment block would have been around £900,000 per year).

This is the kind of thing I mean when I say that our tax laws are specifically designed to reward the wealthy.

But you have to wonder who would take advantage of such a law? Surely the stain of using so morally ambiguous a ruse would prevent anyone in the public spotlight from actually putting in such a claim?

Nope.

Let's say, hypothetically, you were, I dunno, a Conservative MP and one-time London mayoral hopeful called Zac, born in London and educated at Eton, and currently living, very comfortably, in England.

Now imagine you'd inherited a huge amount of (mostly offshore) wealth. Actually I don't quite mean that. I mean *you* didn't inherit the wealth, but an offshore trust did of which you are a named beneficiary. Were you just a normal Brit without an offshore trust you would declare your worldwide income on your tax return and find yourself with a tax bill that took away almost half your income.

How beastly.

To avoid this frightful state of affairs you could make a visit to someone like Wilhelm.

You could explain to Wilhelm that you had a foreign grandparent (I don't mean the 8th Marquess of Londonderry – that's your mother's side) and that your father, despite having been knighted by the Queen, was actually born in France, so maybe you're not quite as British as you first appear?

Wilhelm would ensure that you owned a foreign house (or put you in touch with the right sort of agent if you happened not to own one). If it really were Wilhelm you were dealing with (and for the record, Zac Goldsmith was *not* one of Wilhelm's clients), as a final flourish he might also suggest that you make it known that you never support England when they play cricket, and much prefer Gaelic football to the other kind.

Then suddenly, with the stroke of an accountant's pen, you would be deemed "non-domicile".

And your tax bill? Your tax bill could fall to next to nothing. Why? Because, just on the very off chance that you glossed over the technical bit a couple of pages back, there is no income tax for *offshore* income made by *non-domiciled* people.

Zac Goldsmith, incidentally, didn't actually need to visit someone like Wilhelm. Because his father, Sir James Goldsmith, had been born in France, Zac was allowed to claim he was non-domiciled in the UK. Remember that you can take the domicile of your father, which Zac did. He could have chosen not to and paid his taxes like the rest of us, but he didn't – that is, until he discovered a previously unsuspected love of Blighty and decided to become an MP.[†]

Apparently it was David Cameron who persuaded him to give up his

---

[†]   What Zac did was entirely legal and I'm not accusing him of anything illegal at all, or indeed of not supporting the English cricket team. And he has paid UK income taxes on his income earned in the UK (though who on earth gave him that advice?). He's also not especially unusual, even in Parliament. Former Chancellor of the Exchequer Sajid Javid has admitted to claiming non-domicile status during his tenure as a banker, during which time he parked his offshore earnings in an offshore account. This is the same Sajid Javid who said it would be "morally wrong not to raise taxes to help the NHS". Interestingly, the tax rises he was referring to would not have affected non-domiciled bankers with offshore income.

non-dom status, which must have been a hard sell when even the Deputy Chairman of the Conservative Party was claiming to be one.

And of course, as an MP Zac got paid a decent salary, meaning we all started paying *him*. He did, at least, offer to donate part of his parliamentary salary to charity (though if he did he would have been allowed to reclaim 45 per cent of it as a tax break). He has since been ennobled and is now Baron Goldsmith of Richmond Park. Richmond Park being, of course, very much part of Britain.

—

Wilhelm arranged similar non-domicile claims for a suspiciously large number of his clients. Broadly, anyone earning more than about £200,000 per year from overseas income could benefit from making a non-domicile claim. Poorer people could in theory benefit too, but Wilhelm wasn't interested in them. The reason it was (and still is) such a loophole is that lots of other countries don't have similar rules. If you're French and usually live in France, for instance, you're taxed on a residency basis. So if you then move to the UK you don't have to pay much French tax. But the amazing thing about being in the UK is that, being French, you can claim to be non-domiciled and not pay much UK tax either. *Et voilà!*

But a claim to be non-domiciled still has to be accepted by HMRC. In theory a non-domicile claim is meant to indicate that you intend to one day leave the UK and return permanently to your true domicile, but in practice you might someday simply change your mind.

As I got to know Wilhelm, I realised that he knew all the buzzwords that the authorisers at Tax HQ were looking for (really it just had to start with "foreign" like *foreign* business interests, *foreign* real estate, *foreign* personal relationships, *foreign* emotional ties), but to be sure of sign-off you needed a foreign ancestor. Just one grandparent would do.[†]

If you couldn't get non-domicile status, which for Wilhelm's clients was rare, he still had a trick up his sleeve. Marry a non-dom instead, then transfer them all your money.[‡]

This trick wasn't fool-proof and led to one of the most difficult letters I ever had to write.

Wilhelm was being sued. For Wilhelm, this happened perhaps unsurprisingly frequently.

Wilhelm's client was British, right down to his domicile, but had a (much younger and, frankly, hotter) non-domiciled wife, who lived most of the year in Monaco. Wilhelm had advised his client to transfer most of his wealth to his wife, for tax reasons. I should stress that, for tax reasons, this was very good advice.

And then what did his wife do, once the money was hers? Yup, she divorced him.

So the husband then wrote to Wilhelm and blithely requested that we "transfer the money back to him" and the letter I got called in to draft was Wilhelm's reply along the lines of, "Um, sorry, we really *did*

[†] You might wonder whether Britain's non-domicile rules are uniquely British, and broadly, the answer is no. Ireland, Malta and Cyprus have similar rules. Spain and Portugal used to. And a fair few countries allow you to pay a lump sum to be ignored by the taxman, though the mechanics of their schemes work a little differently. For instance, if you buy the Thai "Elite Visa" you not only pay no Thai taxes, you also get a limo service to pick you up from the airport and free spa treatments, courtesy of the Thai government.

[‡] In most countries you can transfer as much wealth as you like to your spouse without it triggering any tax. Until recently, this was also the case if you were British but your spouse lived offshore and wasn't British. I can't be certain that Wilhelm never *arranged* a marriage to a non-resident, non-domiciled spouse to effect the transfer.

transfer the wealth to her, so, erm, it's hers now, we can't transfer it back."

So, yes, he sued Wilhelm, but he lost. They always lost. Wilhelm had given him great *tax* advice, not great *marital* advice. You only get what you pay for.[†]

—

The client who sued Wilhelm was luckier than Lord Clore's family.

Charles Clore was a businessman and philanthropist who decided to relocate to Monaco in his twilight years (there's a theme here, isn't there?). Inland Revenue (as it was called back then) got suspicious about his motives and queried his claims to have severed all ties with the UK and become Monacan domiciled.

So in court his private correspondence was called as evidence and was found to be filled with homesickness and regret for leaving. He had also professed a wish to be buried in England. Well, if home is where the heart is, then choosing your heart's eternal resting place to be this green and pleasant land does hint somewhat that you're not really Monégasque.

So it was with Lord Clore. On his death he was ruled to have been British domiciled all along and as a result his worldwide estate became taxable in the UK. This must have made his funeral one of the most expensive in history. I imagine his bereaved and now substantially poorer relatives must have been gritting their teeth, thinking, *You couldn't have just found a nice little churchyard in Monaco . . . ?*

[†] Former BHS Retail boss Philip Green famously arranged for a £1.2 *billion* dividend to be paid to his wife (who lived in Monaco) rather than himself, saving the couple about £400 *million* in income tax. I worked with one manager who used to say, "Just get the client to Green it", but it was not an expression that caught on – I imagine because it required people to think about Philip Green.

And so it's come to pass – there are now churches in tax havens all around the world making a killing (so to speak) selling their burial plots to billionaires, just so those billionaires can say to the tax authorities, "Look, of course I'm Panamanian, I've even arranged for my eternal resting place to be there . . ."

So these are the things I began to learn from Wilhelm:

If you're a Brit, the easiest way to avoid paying tax is to shift your wealth offshore, then declare yourself non-domiciled. It helps if you have a foreign grandad, a *lot* of foreign wealth and you're willing to understate your love for the country you live in.

That said, I couldn't see how *I* was going to benefit from this. It was clear that, if ever I made good on my plan to spend a few weeks in Australia helping out on a 'roo farm, HM Revenue & Customs would be allowed to take a slice of my pay. They wouldn't see it as *Australian* income, but as British income. But if instead of earning a few dollars shaving wallabies I could earn a few *million* from an offshore investment, then I could legitimately pay nothing by claiming non-domicility.

Perhaps it wasn't the rich non-doms that were a bit morally iffy. Perhaps the fault was with the *law*. It seemed like it was specifically designed to reward the very wealthy, and stiff the little guy.

But let's return to the morality of the law later, because Wilhelm had barely got started.

—

If you're not the child of a foreign father, internationally rich and/or willing to claim you're somehow not British even though you went to Eton and plan to become an MP, you can always work around these rules the other way – by becoming *non-resident*.

Remember that "domicile" is *where you're from*, so it can be a bit tricky to change (unless you're willing to sign a piece of paper saying your maternal grandmother is Polish and although you've rarely been to Poland you think you're not really "from" England).

"Residence", though, is *where you live*, which you can change by, well, just living somewhere else.

Very broadly, if you're in the UK for less than half the year you don't have to pay UK taxes on your offshore earnings. This probably doesn't help *you* all that much (if you're British), but it does help anyone rich enough to live more than half a year outside the UK and who *earns* a lot outside the UK, such as sportspeople or hedge-fund managers.[†]

For instance, the humongously wealthy financier Guy Hands (said to be worth $500 million) has decamped to (the tax haven of) Guernsey in "protest" at the UK's tax rates, and stated that he doesn't visit his children in England because it would be too expensive to do so (i.e. if he did it too much he may be deemed UK resident and have to pay UK tax on his worldwide income).

One accountant I know pointed out to me an odd consequence of Guy Hands's stance. If either of his daughters announced she was going to get married, it could make more sense for Guy to refuse to walk her down the aisle in England, but instead offer to fly the entire wedding party out to the Caribbean, because it would be cheaper to do that than have his worldwide income become taxable in the UK.

I don't know whether that particular father–daughter conversation ever had to happen, but it's true that once you get to a certain level of wealth it really could be cheaper to pay for an offshore celebration than

---

†   Some of the residency tests involve being out of the country *at midnight*, and I've heard a few rumours about spectacularly wealthy Brits sleeping on private planes while the planes nip out of British airspace for the night.

to come onshore yourself. Think about that the next time you read about a celebrity's Caribbean wedding extravaganza.

And this leads me on to an important question, one which I'm sure you've asked yourself from time to time:

How rich do you have to be to make buying a yacht a sensible investment?

—

A little too early on in my time working for him, Wilhelm invited me to join him at the Monaco Yacht Show. I was in two minds about whether or not to go.

On the one hand, this was a level of glamour several rungs above photocopying invoices in a windowless print room.

On the other, it was so apparent I had nothing to add to Wilhelm's professional world that I was pretty sure I'd end up having sex with him. My girlfriend would be furious.

I decided to ask Wilhelm why he wanted me there. For a man excelling in the art of obfuscation his answer was surprisingly matter of fact.

"Because Stephen will fancy you!"

He laughed hard as he said it, like we were sharing a good old joke. But I was genuinely, completely, lost for words. *Stephen's* real name is not *Stephen*, but I don't even want to hint at his real name, both because he's shockingly famous and because he would have no hesitation in having me beaten to a pulp.[†]

[†] His choice of film and TV roles means he's known as a bit of a softie, but I've heard two stories that suggest otherwise. One is that he once threatened to garrotte a commissioning editor who refused to renew his show (though I've heard that tale about a few other celebrities) and the other is that he once, in a fit of rage, killed a horse with a single punch. I assume it was a small horse.

Wilhelm explained to me that a good part of his income came from commissions from a yacht maker. Wilhelm's job was to convince the super-rich to spend more than they were planning, by pointing out to them that, the more time they spent on their yacht, the more likely they would be able to claim for *non-resident* status.

He also understood that no matter how sensible an investment he could make buying a yacht sound, what the buyers really wanted to be able to do was impress some young skirt or, in Stephen's case, trouser. I was to be the trouser.

"Don't act impressed by the boat until it costs at least £25 million, but north of that start swooning."

I told Wilhelm I didn't feel comfortable with the idea.

"I'll pay you five grand," he said.

For £25 million you can buy a pretty decent superyacht. Obviously you could spend more, but the one Wilhelm, Stephen, the bronzed yacht salesman and I found ourselves swooning over had six bedrooms, a decent-looking pool and a power boat that came out of the side of the hull Bond-villain style. [†]

I realised that my naivety had value. I was genuinely gasping at the hot tub that sank down into the deck and the indoor glass lift that ran up from the master suite. When the salesman said that they had another yacht where the helicopter landing pad could be retracted to reveal a

---

[†]   I learned that when you're told how many bedrooms a yacht has it's usually only half the total. This particular yacht actually had 14 bedrooms. I struggled with that for quite a while. I couldn't imagine an estate agent showing me around a six-bedroom house and telling me it had two bedrooms. It seemed like poor salesmanship. But then I realised – these rich bastards don't care where the crew sleep.

swimming pool underneath, I was uttering very unprofessional "wows!" I also looked great in chinos.

Looking at the brochures, I figured out that the real expense lay in the running costs. Not just the diesel and the crew, but the monogrammed towels for your guests, the fridges of cocaine, the adornment girls. I didn't even know that cocaine should be refrigerated. Does it go off? And *adornment girls?* Apparently that was a job. Rich yacht owners paid to have attractive women sunbathe on their yachts, just as a status symbol. The yachts could even be owned by a Cayman Island company which hired the adornment girls and then leased the boats back to the actual owner, making the girls a *tax-deductible* status symbol. Not that anyone in this process had much intention of paying tax.

The cocaine was usually described as "flowers" on the invoices (which is something it's said Guy Hands discovered when his investment company purchased the music label EMI and found they were spending £200,000 a year on, ahem, *fruits and flowers*). Ever since I learned that, I've had to cock an eyebrow whenever I read about a celebrity spending thousands per month on *flowers*. I assume that lets the celebrity reclaim the "flowers" as expenses and someone else write off the expense as a tax deduction. Wilhelm and I didn't go near the stuff, incidentally. His take on it was that "drugs and helicopters were invented to kill millionaires".

Wilhelm told me that the five-year running costs of these yachts tend to be about the same as the purchase cost, so Stephen was looking at spending £50 million over five years. Though in fairness the industry average ownership period of a yacht is just three years. Because who wants an *old* yacht?

But the money didn't matter to Stephen, because Wilhelm could explain to him that buying the boat would actually make him *richer*. Both Stephen and the yacht salesman were delighted.

I'll try to do Wilhelm's argument justice.

For simplicity, let's say Stephen was looking at a cost of £10 million per year to own and run his yacht. He already spent a couple of months in the USA each year, and at least a month skiing. If he could rack up another three months living on his yacht (or at least claiming to – those towel boys aren't snitches), then he could just about get away with being *non-resident* in the UK.

So what? Well, apart from going completely stir crazy (not Wilhelm's words), how much does Stephen have to be earning offshore for the yacht to be actually *saving* him money?

"Let's say most of your income comes from an offshore company. If you're tax resident in England you would pay tax at a rate of just under 40 per cent. So, a quick bit of maths . . . you could earn up to £25 million per year in foreign dividends and what not and actually be better off if you splash £10 million per year on the boat."

In other words, Stephen would avoid paying £10 million per year in tax if he became a non-resident, so why not spend £10 million on the boat?[†]

But the best was yet to come. Wilhelm knew exactly what he was doing. He let Stephen think about it, to work it out for himself – if there's a stereotype about self-made multi-millionaires it's that they all think they're one step ahead of everybody else.

"But I earn at least *double* that!" said Stephen. I think helping him say that was almost the main reason I was there.

[†] Wilhelm was careful not to mention that the residency rules are also a bit more complicated, and Stephen didn't actually *need* the yacht to become non-resident – he could have just lived onshore anywhere but the UK, as long as he didn't stay in one place for too long. But Wilhelm wasn't about to ruin anyone's fun.

"Well, then," said Wilhelm, "you should probably buy the boat with the retracting helicopter pad."

And that's how Wilhelm earned his 1.4 per cent commission.

If you're interested in this method of tax avoidance, I understand that liveable yachts start at about fifty grand.

—

I want to come back to the issue of ethics again. Waiting in line for a coffee a few weeks ago I heard three men having a conversation about their university days. I would guess that they were in their thirties, and they had the 'suit, no tie' outfit that suggested that they were professionals. Casually, confidently, unashamedly, one of them recounted how the "best thing" he had done at university was buy a stamp in the shape of a lizard. I gathered that he didn't mean a postage stamp, but the kind that you use to put ink on someone's wrist to show that they've paid entry to a nightclub. The nightclub in question was called the Lizard Lounge. He and his friends used the stamp to scam free entry and skip the queue each night.

His colleagues both laughed. They admired his chutzpah. Using a bit of imagination and ingenuity, he had beaten the system and saved himself some money. Without irony, he ended his nostalgic digression by saying, "The Lizard Lounge has shut down now, it's a real shame."

I wondered if he worked in tax.

Of course, all accountants are *meant* to abide by a set of fundamental ethical principles, it's one of those things that's drummed into us from Day 1 of our training contracts. When most laypeople think of ethics it tends to be about doing what's right for society. But the accountant's version of ethics is doing what's right for your client.

So with that in mind, I want to put you in someone else's shoes for a moment, just so that we are sure to judge this from the right perspective. Let's pretend that you were born and raised in Stevenage, a town so lacking in glamour that its Wikipedia entry states merely that it's sited between junctions 7 and 8 of the A1(M). But you, you're special. Named after a famous explorer, from an early age you sought out speed and adrenaline. You had the reflexes of a cat and the determination of a – actually, screw this, let's just say your name's Lewis Hamilton, you're the world's most famous Formula One driver and one of Ernst & Young's more famous clients.

Who could blame you for wanting to live somewhere other than Stevenage? But where to pick? Where in the world has the right mix of dizzying parties and celebrity night clubs, heady excitement and 24-hour globalism?

Lewis Hamilton moved to Switzerland. And then, when that got too fast for him, he moved to Monaco. I say "moved to", but the nature of his job is that he travels around a lot. His job, incidentally, is based in Guernsey (not exactly famous for its racing circuit). And because of all this work-related travel, he obviously needs a private jet. Sorry, a *business* jet, which it has been claimed was purchased by a company in the British Virgin Islands and leased through another company in the Isle of Man. And while I'm listing famous tax havens, as a bonus his image rights are owned by a company in Malta.

Stevenage, Switzerland, Monaco, Guernsey, British Virgin Islands, Isle of Man, Malta. There's definitely an odd one out here.[†]

Let me unpick all of that for you.

A move to Monaco (via Switzerland) is easy to explain (at least from

---

† One of my colleagues claims that Stevenage is actually quite nice. She calls it St Evenage.

a tax perspective). Monaco has no income tax. Lewis Hamilton has been estimated to be one of the highest earning sportsmen in the world, with *Forbes* putting his income at over $50 million in a good year (which for Hamilton is most years). If all of that was routed through Monaco (I'm not saying it was, though he has acknowledged that tax considerations "definitely add" to Monaco's appeal) instead of being paid into an account in Stevenage, then he could have saved around $23 million per year.

Guernsey does have income tax, but only if you live there. It doesn't have corporation tax except for a few types of businesses that Lewis Hamilton isn't involved with. It doesn't charge any tax on moving money out of Guernsey and, as Monaco doesn't have a tax on dividends received, Lewis could get paid into a Guernsey account and if he wanted to would be able to redirect his money into his tax-free Monaco account. I'm not saying he did, though if he did I suppose it would just be another case of "I'm so rich I can live somewhere other than England, channel my wealth through layers of offshore corporate entities and not pay any tax, unlike you tax-paying peasants."[†]

But then Lewis did something that in Formula One might be referred to as creating *dirty air*.

I mentioned his private jet a moment ago. Buying a jet can be as straightforward as buying a car. You pick the one you like and then buy it. Think about the last time you bought a car. Did you set up a series of companies in tax havens to lease it in a giant circle while claiming it was a legitimate business expense? You did?! Then I wonder if Ernst & Young helped you buy it.

[†] This is not a quote from Lewis Hamilton, just to be absolutely clear. He says he pays tax in 20 different countries, which is more than I do. Nor can I imagine he's called anyone a peasant. Slum-dweller, maybe. But not peasant.

Lewis Hamilton's jet was a £16.5 million Challenger 605, painted bright red. Or rather, I don't mean *Lewis Hamilton's* jet, I mean (according to reports) *a jet owned by a company based in the British Virgin Islands which Lewis Hamilton owned.* This company was alleged to then lease the jet to a company based in the Isle of Man (also owned by Hamilton). The Isle of Man leasing company's business was renting the jet to "business users". And as the jet was for business purposes, the company could reclaim the VAT they had suffered on the purchase – a total of £3.3 million.

But it's also been alleged that Lewis Hamilton was the only "business user" and, just to really ensure this scheme was a *polesitter* (that's more F1 slang), that he leased it through his Guernsey-based company.

Let's put this together. The claim was that Lewis Hamilton owned the British Virgin Islands company and the Isle of Man leasing company, and the jet was allegedly leased only to Lewis Hamilton. So every time Lewis used the jet he would pay the leasing company for his use. There's no corporation tax in the Isle of Man, so every penny could be paid back to Lewis as a dividend to his bank account in Monaco (where there's no income tax).

In other words, Lewis could pay himself to use his own jet, but claim that other people could hypothetically rent it too, so it wasn't really his own private jet but was instead a business asset, so he should be allowed to reclaim £3.3 million of tax.

But then the scheme had a *tankslapper* (I'm literally googling F1 lingo as we go along here, and desperately trying to get *bottoming* into a sentence about tax).

Or, in non-racing lingo, there was one thing Lewis's accountants didn't think of, and it scuppered the scheme.

You might think it was this:

In order to be a genuine business expense, the jet would have to be used almost exclusively for business – say, flying out to a Grand Prix somewhere. But unfortunately Lewis Hamilton loves his social media, and loves his lifestyle brag. He posted pictures and messages to Instagram and YouTube, along the lines of, "Here's my dog on *my* plane", "Here's me with my mates on *my* plane", "Lucky I've got a private plane to fly to America to see my girlfriend" and "Here's me bottoming on my plane."[†]

In other words, "This plane is mine. It's not for business purposes." I'm paraphrasing a bit out of necessity, as most of his posts on the subject have mysteriously been deleted.

But no, that's not what scuppered the scheme, though it would be reasonable to think it might. I mean, if you're going to deprive the government of over three million quid in tax, you'd think a decent accountant would tell you not to brag about it on social media. But even with it plastered all over Instagram, his accountants still claimed it was a *business* jet. The accounts of the Isle of Man leasing company weren't being examined. For all any authority knew, it really was a genuine leasing business.

What the accountants didn't consider was that their secret scheme might get exposed. And exposed it was, by the Paradise Papers data leak and some incredible journalism by the *Guardian* newspaper (ironically no stranger to avoiding tax itself). In the fallout, the tax partner responsible at Ernst & Young was arrested and charged with fraud and Lewis Hamilton was fired by Mercedes.

Oh, no, wait, I got that wrong. Nothing illegal had taken place because the intention all along had been to set up a legitimate business.

Ernst & Young's profits went up and Lewis was knighted by the

---

[†] Yup, clearly I made that one up. It's not even about tax. Sorry.

Queen (and awarded the title BBC Sports Personality of the Year for a second time).

—

There's actually an interesting postscript to the Lewis Hamilton saga. What I've just described were the allegations made by pretty much every news outlet from *The Guardian* to *The Sun*, *The Daily Mail* to the BBC, after the Paradise Papers were leaked. Lewis Hamilton didn't deny them, but what does that prove? I wouldn't expect him to understand his own tax affairs any more than I understand how a car engine works (my A-level physics teacher told me it goes "Suck, squeeze, bang, blow", but I think he may have been pulling my leg).

You see, what was much less reported in the press was the conclusion of an extensive enquiry by HM Treasury into the Isle of Man's treatment of private planes (and yachts) in 2019. Our inspectors reported that they found no evidence of VAT fraud in the Isle of Man.

So that settles it. All the papers got it wrong.

Except . . . the Treasury report said only that at the point of importation the Isle of Man followed the correct procedures. Which is a bit like saying, "Before he shot his gun he hadn't murdered anyone." The whole point of these schemes is that a business buys the jet with the "intention" of running a leasing business. That allows them to reclaim the VAT, entirely legally and with a clear conscience. If it just so happens that after the VAT is reclaimed the business changes its mind and provides the jet for the exclusive use of the business's sole owner then, well, whoops. Who could have predicted it?

The Treasury report says of this possibility that the Isle of Man's "post-registration procedures are a concern" which, to take my gun metaphor a step further, is a bit like saying, "The fact that he shot his victim six times in the face is a concern." The UK government didn't say, "We're going to investigate this further", just it's "a concern". It's almost as if our government is turning a blind eye to having a secrecy jurisdiction a couple of miles off the coast.

However, for Lewis Hamilton, this means his slate is clean. He was just unlucky to get fingered in the Paradise Papers, but it's important to acknowledge that doesn't make him unique. He was only doing what countless other UHNW individuals are doing all over the world right now – just look at how difficult it has been for Western nations to seize the yachts of sanctioned Russian oligarchs. The yachts aren't owned by the oligarchs, they're owned by companies in tax havens.

But a simpler fact is that nobody really cared that Lewis may or may not have been paying his taxes.[†] Nobody wants to be paying their taxes. There are even advertisements in the UK for cars that make you think you can avoid VAT too. You may have seen them – they say things like:

BUY NOW PAY NO VAT

What's weird is that when you read the small print it turns out that you *are* paying VAT, it's just that the car dealership will give you a discount that results in you paying an amount equivalent to getting the car VAT-free.

[†] And for the record, he is said to be one of the 5,000 top taxpayers in the UK. He's also said to be one of the top 1,000 richest Britons. I'll let you do the maths on that.

That's a bit strange. The ad could say:

BUY NOW GET A
16.67% DISCOUNT

It would work out mathematically the same, but would clearly not be so appealing. There seems to be something in so many of our psyches that views tax avoidance as something clever, devious, even admirable. Look at how Donald Trump's supporters bought into the idea of it being evidence of his genius.

But are tax-avoidance schemes works of genius? And if they are, do they work? This was what I wanted to find out, and not necessarily for the sake of my clients.

3

LOSING IT

Becoming an accountant is easy. It's a bit like becoming a writer. You just decide it's something you're interested in and then you start boring people at parties about the books you're working on.

Becoming a *chartered* accountant is different. To get a charter you have to pass a lot of exams. You also have to serve some time at an accountancy practice, but as there's no actual obligation to do anything in particular at the practice, it's pretty hard to fail that part of the requirement. A lot of people fail the exams, though.[†]

You might think that given how important it is for chartered accountants to actually know stuff about, well, *accounting*, the exams would ensure that any junior accountant who makes it through the complete exam cycle would have a detailed understanding of how businesses actually work, how accounts are put together, how

---

[†] Weirdly, the definition of being *chartered* is that you have a charter. But that charter doesn't give you any particular rights, other than being able to say that you're chartered. i.e. having a "charter" really just means that you have a charter, though I guess that is how the entire Western education system operates.

to check whether a financial director is being dishonest, the best practices for running an organisation, how to raise finance to fund the expansion plans of a business and, the big one for me, how taxes work.

The exams I sat did, indeed, have titles that suggested that I was on my way to being a master of the business universe. I had to pass exams like *Financial Management* and *Business Strategy* and *Corporate Reporting.* My institute liked to boast that only one of the exams I sat had "accounting" in its name.

"Accountants aren't bean counters any more. They're vital business strategists."

That may have been true for the senior partners. My reality as a trainee was somewhat different. The closest I got to strategising was wondering if I could save on ironing time by wearing the same shirt all week.

But at least studying for exams was an opportunity to get away from the office for a while. Each exam meant at least two weeks in college, plus a few days of study leave, and given how many exams there were this almost felt like a justification for the mindless tedium that was my day job.

To begin with, I only really had two official tasks in the office.

The first was to copy numbers from a set of financial statements into a computer program, which could then calculate the client's tax automatically.

The second, and marginally more glamorous, task was to print out the computer program's calculation, attach it to a pre-written letter, photocopy it three times, then hand the bundle to a secretary who reprinted most of it on slightly fancier paper.

I wasn't entirely sure what value I was adding to the process, least of all because I didn't know what financial statements were, or what they

were telling me, or how I was meant to find out. Very occasionally I tried
to read them, which is a sign of just how bored I was.[†]

I did notice a few patterns in these statements, like how many of the
directors had Russian names but had registered offices in Ireland. And
how a disproportionately large number of companies seemed to have
profits of exactly £300,000.

I tried asking my manager, Penelope (*never* "Penny"), if she could
help me understand any of this.

"I'm a little busy right now – but you'll learn all about financial
statements in college."

—

I imagined accountancy college would be pretty much like university,
i.e. more an excuse to drink heavily and flirt awkwardly with girls than
an actual exercise in learning anything, so I turned up late on the first
morning with a crossword tucked under my arm, assuming I could
finish it off while the lecturer did their thing, then copy someone else's
notes. As a result I missed the first lecture, which was called "An
Introduction to Financial Statements".

The lectures were unceasing. They lasted for seven hours each day,
with another few hours of homework. At university I'd rarely had more
than seven hours of lectures a *week*. To make it worse, the lecturers
assumed we had a level of knowledge several rungs above what I actually
had. In a course called "Audit and Assurance" the lecturer's opening

---

[†]   The only consolation I had at that time was that one of my best friends from
    university, whom I call Kititi (for one of those stupid reasons best left at
    university), had just started at Google and he said that his job was mostly data
    entry too. In his case, he was typing lists of "key words" that people searched
    for that hadn't otherwise been assigned advertisers. Mostly these words were
    common typos. Apparently the most "searched for" typo he found was "pron".

sentence was "I assume you're all auditors, so I don't need to explain to you what an audit is."

I knew what an *Audi* was (it's a car), and I knew what *reassurance* meant (as in, "Don't worry, I'm sure you won't fail this exam"), but neither seemed to be relevant.

I decided against the drinking heavily, but I did try the flirting awkwardly. It was even harder with accountancy trainees than it had been with university students, and not just because they were accountants. It was also the stress. Many firms had a policy that if you failed an exam you would have your contract terminated.

In one course I spent four days sitting next to a girl called Rosie from a Big 4 firm and on the fifth day I greeted her by saying, "Do you come here often?"

I thought it was funny. She started crying.

It occurred to me that I didn't know what my own firm's policy was on letting us fail exams. I asked one of my colleagues.

"It's different for everybody. You'll have to ask your staff partner."

So I did. I got this reply:

The partners have decided that to demonstrate your continued commitment to this firm we expect you to pass all your exams first time.

In other words, fail an exam and I was out.

I had mixed feelings about this. Clearly it had only taken a few months for the partners at my firm to realise that I spent most of my time at work devising ways not to work. (I'd recently taken to simply going for long walks around the office. I figured that as long as I had a file under my arm it looked like I must be working, and to complete the charade I'd swap files on a different floor, so no one would comment that I'd just returned with the same file. A lot of client files went missing this way.) On the other hand, I'd never failed an exam in my life, so what was there to worry about?[†]

The first two exams were Accounting and Audit and Assurance. This is what I was *meant* to know:

Financial statements tell you how wealthy a company is. The profit-and-loss account tells you how much the company is earning, and how much they're spending. Confusingly, the profit-and-loss account is also called the income statement, or the statement of financial performance, which you would think should abbreviate to SOFP but actually abbreviates to π/λ.

The balance sheet (also called the statement of financial position, which also abbreviates, confusingly, to SOFP) tells you what the company owns, and how they came to own it.

A cash-flow statement tells you how much cash the company used to have, and how they lost it, but weirdly bears no resemblance to either the profit-and-loss account or the balance sheet.

The rest of the financial statements, which are also called the accounts (though accounts can also mean almost anything else), are mostly either notes about how the numbers this year were calculated using an entirely different methodology to the numbers from last year, or are polite fictions about the directors' expectations for the future.

But like I say, I missed the bit where this was properly explained to me, so I had to piece this together *after* my exams.

And an audit just means, "Check these financial results aren't massive lies." Accountancy firms are notoriously bad at doing audits, but unfortunately no one else is any better. One of the main parts of the audit

---

[†] I now realise this is like saying, "I can't have broken my arm, I've never broken a bone in my life", but that didn't occur to me, then.

process is making sure that the correct systems are in place at the business being audited to ensure that financial transactions get recorded properly. These systems are normally referred to as "controls", so my exam plan was just to write "improve controls" as many times as possible.

If you're remotely confused by any of these descriptions, try doing a three-hour exam where you have to reverse engineer the cash-flow statement or suggest how you would audit a Welsh cheese factory.[†]

And none of this told me why our clients were registered in Ireland or had profits of exactly £300,000.

Luckily, and ridiculously, and it makes me genuinely concerned for the state of the accountancy profession, the exam structure was based not on attaining any deep and meaningful understanding of the topics being taught, but on simply memorising vast quantities of information, and then getting at least 55 per cent of the available marks.

In other words, saying, "I'm a chartered accountant" just means that on a series of particular days, possibly several years ago, you got up to 45 per cent of the answers completely wrong.[‡]

—

[†] This was the actual scenario in our mock exam. Our tutor told us that anyone who wrote *Caerphilly* would get a zero.

[‡] Or it can be even worse than this. In 2021 KPMG Australia was fined $450,000 after over 1,100 of its personnel were found to have cheated in professional exams (mostly by sharing answers). In the US, KPMG was fined in 2019 after its employees and partners were caught cheating in training exams (some employees had even "manipulated an internal server hosting training exams to lower the score required for passing"). PwC was fined $950,000 in 2022 by Canadian and US official bodies after 1,200 of their staff were also found to be sharing exam answers. Not to be outdone, the world's third largest accountancy firm, EY, was fined a gob-smacking (and record-breaking) $100 million by US financial regulator the Securities and Exchange Commission (SEC), after it was revealed that not only had some of their staff cheated on their *ethics* exams, they had also misled the SEC's investigation into the cheating.

It always took a month or two before exam results were released, which meant a month or two back in the office, with the threat of sudden termination if it turned out there weren't 55 marks available for writing *improve controls* over and over.

I still hadn't really learned much about tax, so I still wasn't really any use to anyone.

Penelope was in a bad mood because some of her files had gone missing.

"We need to improve controls on the filing system," I suggested.

"That's a really good idea," she said.

—

It was at least six months before I finally got to start studying tax. Like Pavlov's dogs, the mere word *tax* was making my eyelids flicker. I was ready to be bored. Instead I had my mind blown.

You may wonder how anyone would go about learning 32,000 pages of tax legislation, plus the thousands of individual cases, and then understand the consequences well enough to create a scheme to wriggle out of a little tax.

The answer is that no one does. Not a soul. This is kind of obvious when you think about it. If you include all HMRC's guidance and extra-statutory concessions and all that case law and international treaties, you'd probably get up to a good 100,000 pages or more of tax rules. And these aren't nice, neat pages with a few hundred words on each, the occasional witty aside and some useful diagrams, like a certain other work on tax that will remain nameless.

Instead, these pages are densely written in legalese. If you've never had the joy of reading legalese, try this, from one of the most basic rules on how much income tax you have to pay each year:

the amount of the excess (the relevant amount) is not less than such amount as may be prescribed by regulations made by the Board, and the proportion which the relevant amount bears to the assessed amount is not less than such proportion as may be so prescribed.

To which you might add, *Well duh, what else would it be?*

Sometimes it feels like the people responsible for writing these rules don't want laypeople to understand them. Every time we hear about some celebrity shirking their tax bill their excuse is "My tax advisor said it was okay." And a *little* bit of me thinks that's reasonable.

Most of my lecturers were young women who talked fast and made lots of jokes. This in itself was a shock, as although it's a demographic that obviously exists in wider society it was one that seemed entirely absent from my firm.

One of my favourite lecturers had a wonderfully lilting South African accent, and wore large square glasses that were on the exact threshold between hipster chic and accounting stereotype. She would say outrageous things but soften them by adding, "Just joshin'."

She began our tax course, and decided to start by finding out how much we already knew. We had been accountants by this point for more than half a year.

"Let's start with an easy one. How much tax do you pay?"

There was a general murmur. I scribbled *20%?* on a piece of paper and showed it to my buddy next to me. He shrugged.

"Twenty per cent?" said a cocky-sounding boy near the back.

"What?" asked our lecturer, her eyes squinting towards the back of the hall.

"I said 20 per cent," said the boy again, a bit cockier. A few people sniggered a bit. No matter how old you are, being back in a classroom always brings out the little schoolboy or schoolgirl in all of us. The lecturer was probably also in her twenties, and I wonder if there was a bit of macho bravado going on too, though, as I've mentioned, this was a roomful of accountants, so that seems unlikely.[†]

"No, I heard you," she said. "Someone always says *20 per cent*. It's just such a freakin' daft answer."

We gasped a bit, so she added, "Just joshin'."

My buddy nudged me, indicated the *20%?* I had just scribbled and whispered, "You idiot."

—

One of the problems with writing a book about tax is that the *numbers* that are used – the rates and thresholds that determine the actual tax you'll pay – get changed all the time. Sometimes twice a year. More in a year with a government U-turn. So actually more than twice a year. Sometimes the lingo changes too. And of course these rates and lingos are slightly different in different countries. But the *gist* of it never changes. And the gist of it, as explained by our lecturer, was this:

There are three main types of tax:

- *Income taxes,* which are levied on how much you earned during a year;
- *Capital taxes,* which are levied whenever *assets* (like artworks or shares or houses) change hands;

[†]   Most of our lecturers were only a few years older than us, but simply by being in charge of the class they were awarded a degree of respect. For instance, one unwritten rule was that the lecturers were *men* and *women*, but the students were *boys* and *girls*.

- *Sales taxes,* which are added onto the price of a product or a service when it's sold.

So you would think there would be just three taxes to learn, but on our syllabus there were more than a dozen.[†]

Our tutor's take was that the government's task was to take as much tax as possible off us without us noticing, and the main way it did this was by overcomplicating the system as much as it possibly could. She said it was telling that whenever she asked how much tax we're all paying, someone always replied *20 per cent.* But what we'd all forgotten about was all the other taxes we pay, not least other payroll taxes, which in the UK is primarily *National Insurance.* She showed us how we actually paid more in National Insurance than we did in income taxes.

In fact, let me show *you* this, too. This is mostly a British example (actually, it's an English and Welsh example, because it's even more complicated in Scotland), but the logic holds anywhere that has a payroll tax, which is almost everywhere.

In the UK (and, indeed, in most countries) we have a tax on employing people. If that sounds crazy, it's because it is. It should be one of those "Wait, this makes no sense, what?" taxes, yet somehow most people don't give it a second thought (until they employ a nanny).

You would think that the government would want to encourage businesses to either employ more people or pay the people they do employ a little more, but no, it turns out that is not the government's intention at all. If it was, it wouldn't slap a tax on employing people.

You would think it's so crazy that no one else in the world would

---

[†] I attended a work quiz recently where one question was "Name the 20 new taxes introduced since 2000." I'm still annoyed with myself for forgetting about the Economic Crime Anti-Money-Laundering Levy. I mean, I bet it's all you ever talk about.

copy it. But they do. The USA (normally) calls it social security contributions (Medicare contributions are another type), Australia calls it payroll tax (and Medicare, too), and France calls it nine different things, each with their own *petit peu* of bureaucracy. But whatever it's called, and however it's justified ("Oh, but this is for pensions"), it's just another income tax.

In the UK, rather than being called something apt like "Extra Income Tax" it's called Class 1 Secondary National Insurance Contributions. By the time you read this sentence it will probably be at a rate of just under 14 per cent.

Here's what my tutor sketched on the board (I'll use more recent rates):

Imagine your boss unexpectedly has £100 available and decides to pay you a bonus. For the sake of argument, let's imagine that you're not earning a spectacular income (perhaps it will help to picture yourself as an accountancy trainee). That 14 per cent payroll tax has to come out of the £100 that your boss had available to pay your bonus.

That means your boss can only set aside just under £88 to pay you with.[†]

Already this is getting confusing. It's designed to be. It's officially a tax that employers pay. But if your bonus is paid out of the cash available to pay you, and that available cash gets diverted to the taxman, leaving you with less money, then aren't you the one suffering the tax?

I think you are (so did my tutor). Though that means that maybe this isn't a tax on employing people after all. In this situation, it sounds like

---

[†]   You have a choice here. You can trust me on the maths or follow this dry proof. Your boss will pay you £87.87. 13.8 per cent (the NIC rate) of £87.87 is £12.13. £87.87 + £12.13 is £100. This footnote is a little taster of what most tax books are like, so not only will it be out of date as soon as the rates change, but for authenticity I'm also leaving it joke free.

the employee is really paying it. It sounds like the employee (that's you) is just getting less cash than they might have expected. That would make this a stealth tax – a tax that you don't realise you're paying.

This snappily named Class 1 Secondary National Insurance Contribution (or indeed, any social security or payroll tax) is calculated by multiplying your salary by a percentage (just like income tax is), it's collected on your behalf by your employer (just like income tax is) and it's used to pay for general government expenditure (just like income tax is).

If it looks like a snake, slithers like a snake and bites you like a snake, then for how long can you claim it's a tasty sausage? Once again, this is a tax that *you* suffer.

Anyway, you still don't have your cash.

The £88 will be your actual bonus. But unless you're really low-paid – so low-paid that you don't have to pay any income tax at all – a British boss will take at least another £28 of taxes off, leaving you with just under £60 (after a bit of rounding).

In other words, despite a headline tax rate of 20 per cent, most Brits have to pay more than double that in tax. And if you're not British, stop smirking. Your payroll taxes aren't as swingeing as ours (unless you're French), but they're still out there.

If you had the audacity to go to a British university you'll have to fork out another 9 per cent to repay your student loan (and the extortionate interest on it), because obviously taxes don't pay for the education that was free for the politicians who decided to make you pay for it, and that was a prerequisite of getting your job. Though if you're American the nine grand a year that Brits have to pay for their university courses probably looks like a bargain.[†]

[†]   Though wait 'til you hear how much we pay for healthcare . . .

And you probably have to pay another £4 out of that £100 into your pension, because otherwise the state would have to look after you when you're old. Technically paying into your pension isn't making you any poorer – it's just deferring your wealth until you're retired – but the stats aren't on your side. Someone in their twenties has between a one in four and one in eight chance of not making it to retirement.

All this means that you'll be left with between £48 and £60 out of the original £100. So the tax rate (or other compulsory charges) on a trainee accountant's bonus (not that I ever got a bonus) – or broadly anyone in Britain earning less than about fifty grand a year – is between 40 per cent and 52 per cent.

Come on, seriously, but what the fuck? Is this not crazy?[†]

We should be out on the streets, manning the barricades, ushering in a revolution of the proletariat. We've had the wool pulled over our eyes.

And it gets worse.

All the students in that class were working for partnerships, and doing their exams as part of a training programme. That meant our employers were the partners at our firms. A typical partner will be earning in the hundreds of thousands of pounds.

That means the partners are what is known as "additional rate taxpayers". They pay an effective tax rate of 47 per cent on everything they earn above £150,000. And we just made them a bit poorer.[‡] The £100 that was spent on the bonus is an expense for the partnership. In other words, that is £100 of income that the partners are now not

---

[†] These were not the *exact* words my tutor said.

[‡] The equivalent rate in Australia is similar, whereas richer Americans currently pay significantly less. Globally this percentage varies enormously, from a lot of places with no income taxes, to Finland and Japan with rates above 50 per cent.

getting, because it's heading our way instead. But that means that the partners will now not be paying their 47 per cent tax on that £100. So the government is going to collect less tax from the partners. Specifically, £47 less.

It can be tricky to spot what's going on here. Perhaps a picture will help:

Effect of a richer person paying
a poorer person a £100 bonus

Poorer person   Richer person

Pays £40.25 tax   Pays £47 less tax

It is a golden rule in accountancy that everything has two effects. Here, one person's income is another person's expense. As the person with the expense pays a higher rate of tax than the person with the income, the net effect is for the government to get poorer. So not only has the poorer person suffered more than double the "headline" rate of income tax, but all that tax hasn't gone to help pay for hospitals and schools and pensions; instead it's been handed as a tax break to the pretty darn decently well-off partner.

The only way in this situation for the poorer person to contribute to the Exchequer is to ask for a pay cut.

Now do you want to join the revolution?

—

The "additional rate" tax that I just mentioned was the brainchild of Labour Chancellor of the Exchequer Alistair Darling, in the late Noughties. The professed logic was that the tax would bring in an extra £3 billion a year and be paid by only the highest earning 1 per cent of taxpayers. So far, so typical Labour policy, you might think. Except . . .

Tony Blair brought Labour to power in May 1997. Labour left power on 12 April 2010. Want to guess when during that 13-year run they decided to introduce this new extra-high tax rate for rich people?

The answer, amazingly, is 6 April 2010.

So for 4,726 days Labour didn't have an additional rate tax, and then for six days they did. Or if you prefer that as a percentage, there was no additional rate tax for 99.96 per cent of New Labour's time in office.

But the best bit is this. Shortly after the Conservatives came to power in 2010, Chancellor George Osborne lowered the additional rate tax rate from 50 per cent to 45 per cent. At which point Labour's attack line was, "Typical Tories."

—

I remember reading an article by a famous TV presenter in which he said that a 50 per cent tax rate was the absolute maximum that he was prepared to pay. Any more and he would up sticks and leave Britain.

There was also a 2 per cent National Insurance charge. So he would have been paying 52 per cent.

I don't know if he left.

—

Our tutor seemed genuinely cross about how much tax we had to pay. She even found time to have a dig at the BBC licence fee, *and car parking charges*, even though they weren't on our syllabus, and possibly aren't even taxes. But then, the licence fee costs Brits £3.75 billion per year (and has to be paid if you own a telly) and English councils alone make about £900 million each year from parking charges, with the NHS making almost another £300 million.[†]

We were just genuinely cross about how much we had to *learn*. It seemed ridiculous that to get our heads to a place where we could scrape through our tax exams took over three weeks of lessons. But just when it seemed like I couldn't cram in one more tax fact, the tutor abruptly stopped writing on the board and, I guess noticing that our attention was waning, said, "Right, who wants to know how to not pay *any* tax?"

I'd always imagined that learning about tax avoidance was more clandestine than this. I stopped chewing my pen and got ready to write some notes.

"There's one big concept you need to understand if you want to avoid paying taxes."

She had every single student's attention now. It was remarkable.

"You need to get your head around tax losses."

—

In 1997 the alternative rock band Mansun released a song called "Taxloss". The accompanying video featured £25,000 in five-pound notes being thrown from the upper concourse of Liverpool Street Station, in London.

The idea was that footage of commuters scrambling around to pick up the notes would symbolise human greed. It struck me as a very

---

[†] These parking charges are roughly the same amount raised by a levy that's charged on banks' profits. When he was Chancellor, Rishi Sunak announced that he would like to reduce the banking levy, as it makes the banks less competitive. You still have to pay to park to visit your dying mum in hospital, though.

strange location to pick – the commuters at Liverpool Street must be some of the wealthiest in the entire world. Indeed the video doesn't really give you the impression of the people in suits being greedy money grabbers – most of the people diving around on the floor after the notes are the station staff.

Because what self-respecting banker would bend over for just five quid?

The song has very little actual tax in it, incidentally; it's mostly about kinky sex.

—

A monetary loss is a bad thing. It means you're poorer. You've lost money. But a tax loss doesn't have to mean that at all. The holy grail for an accountant is to create a situation with real world *income*, alongside a *tax loss*. There can be genuine reasons for this to occur, but it usually needs a convoluted tax-avoidance scheme. One scheme that was being actively marketed at the time (and I half-suspected my lecturer might have had some involvement in, given the glee with which she described it), was known as Working Wheels.

Caught up in the spokes of the scheme was the self-confessed "Saviour of Radio 1", Chris Moyles, host of BBC Radio 1's flagship *Breakfast Show*, which at its height around 2010 almost one in nine Britons listened to each morning. Chris was rewarded with a reported salary of at least £630,000 per year.

But there's a problem with having a salary this large. I don't want to trivialise anyone's life problems, but his were clearly worse than most: almost half his salary would disappear as tax.

To solve the problem, Chris Moyles did what any of us would do. He became a used-car salesman.

And to be a used-car salesman he would need a small loan to get started. Just £5,000 would do. He borrowed this sum from a company set up by a small, but notorious, accountancy firm called NT Advisors. The NT is rumoured to stand for "No Tax".

Now as you'll know if you've ever taken out a mortgage, it's not unusual to pay a loan-arrangement fee to procure your loan. So there was nothing suspicious in the fact that Chris Moyles was asked to pay a fee for his £5,000 loan.

The fee though, on his £5,000 loan, was £1 million.

The first clever part of this scheme was that the fee qualified as an *expense* of operating as a used-car salesman. Expenses can be deducted against the revenue of your business, so Chris Moyles deducted this million-pound expense from his second-hand car business's revenues.

Now unfortunately for Chris Moyles he wasn't very good at selling cars, so he didn't actually manage to sell any. This meant his £1 million fee became a £1 million *loss*.

Losses can be used to reduce the amount of your income upon which you pay tax. But crucially, the losses could be used to reduce *any* type of income, including your salary. So because he now had a huge loss, he no longer had any *taxable* income, of any description.

So by paying the ludicrous arrangement fee, the Saviour of Radio 1 had saved himself at least £300,000 in tax.

But this, you may have spotted, is insane.

If you've managed to follow this so far, you may be wondering why on earth anybody would pay a million quid to save a few hundred thousand in taxes. It doesn't seem to make sense. That's where the next part of the plan comes in.

So far, all we've seen is something that looks like this:

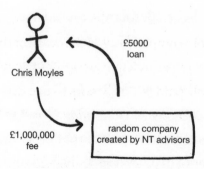

I'm going to simplify this next bit, because NT Advisors used five different companies, plus something called a Bare Trust, and a total of 20 different transactions.

But in short, the company that received the £1 million fee promptly paid it over to another company as a tax-free dividend. That second company then loaned £1 million to Chris Moyles. So ultimately the cash went round in a circle, like this:

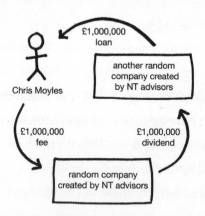

The longer you stare at this, the harder it becomes to work out who the prime mover was. As in, where in this circle did those £1 million payments originate?

Suddenly paying a million to avoid a few hundred thousand doesn't seem so illogical. I mean, technically Chris Moyles still owes a million quid to some random company, but in the detail of the scheme are some legal mechanisms to ensure that he never has to pay it.

Over 400 people paid NT Advisors to use this scheme, reducing their tax bills by a collective £290 *million*. When HMRC dragged it to court (some years after my lecturer told me about it), they decided to pick on just three of the users of the scheme, one of whom was Chris Moyles. This was not random. HMRC have had a policy for a long time of picking on the most famous person they could find, as a cheap way of marketing their efforts to fight tax avoidance, and Chris was the most famous person who was using the scheme. I don't know whether or not he was flattered.

In court NT Advisors were quite frank about the scheme being designed to avoid tax, but their argument was that the motive didn't matter. It was legit. Unfortunately, there was one small detail they had overlooked.

Chris Moyles hadn't actually sold any cars. He hadn't sold any, he hadn't tried to sell any, he hadn't even told his millions of listeners about his new-found vocation.

As such, he wasn't *actually* a used-car salesman. So he didn't have a *trade* so couldn't have a deductible *loss*. After all, just spending money on something doesn't mean you've got a tax loss, otherwise every trip to the pub would be tax-deductible.[†]

And no *loss* meant he did, after all, have to pay all his taxes.

I believe Chris Moyles is no longer with the BBC.

—

[†]   Well, for you. I run a popular blog about pubs in my area, so all my beer is tax-deductible. Well, I say *popular*, but I'm the only one who reads it.

My reaction to Working Wheels wasn't thinking, *What an outrageous attempt to avoid sharing the burden of taxes* but rather, *That's clever. I wonder if I could create a scheme like that too?* I clocked that the advisors got paid their fees whether the scheme worked or not. They also got a bonus fee if the scheme succeeded. That sounded to me like my ideas could be *rubbish,* yet people might still pay for them. It seemed amazing that any customer would agree to that.

Here was an incentive to do my homework. If I could come up with a scheme – which didn't seem such an outrageous proposition, given how relatively simple the Working Wheels one was – then I knew just the man to take it to.

—

A rather more famous individual than Chris Moyles who may have used losses to avoid paying his income taxes is Donald Trump. I say *may* because, as you probably know, he is the only US President since 1976 to have refused to release his tax returns, on the grounds that he wasn't able to release them due to an ongoing IRS audit, which is a worse excuse than when my son claimed he hadn't had a bath because his sister had drunk all the bathwater.

The New York Times reported that they had a copy of Trump's 1995 tax return, which showed a loss of over $900 *million.* Under US law, that loss could be legitimately offset against his income in later years. But, if the *New York Times* story is true, it would have to mean *either* that the loss was somehow contrived, or that Trump is a terrible businessman.

—

My first idea for a tax-avoidance scheme didn't make it past Penelope, my manager. I had drawn up a convoluted web of sham marriages to get around inheritance tax, and I think somewhere in the middle of it someone had to marry their aunt.

There were always a few weeks between the *taught* phase of a course at accountancy college (in which financial rules were explained to us) and the *revision* phase (when we practised exam questions). These two phases were just far enough apart for most students to forget everything from the taught phase by the time we started the revision stage.

One of the things we weren't taught, incidentally, was what taxes actually *are*, or where the idea of them came from. Perhaps this was an oversight by the professional body that wrote our exams, though I suppose a tax accountant could go their entire career and not once need to stop and ask whether this whole tax idea made much sense.

I do wonder, though, whether a person's attitude to paying their taxes can be assumed from which of two historical narratives they prefer.

Either the origin of taxes is in the violent exploitation of the weak – a literal *give me that or I'll kill you* – or, alternatively, taxes are the sophisticated modern version of the tribe sharing their bounty, working together in peace and harmony for the betterment of everyone.

There are engravings from 5,000 years ago of Egyptian rulers demanding (or happily being given, depending on your view) grain and cattle and pottery and pretty much everything else you can imagine from the people they ruled over. Now it's true that some of this was kept safe for redistribution in leaner times, but it's also true that the Pharaohs used this wealth *just occasionally* for personal enrichment – the evidence that they did so is still there to see.[†]

As for whether these taxes were gratefully accepted by society or

---

[†] I say "there", but a lot of the more gilded stuff is in the British Museum.

not, the Greek historian Herodotus claimed that the punishment for tax evasion in Pharaonic times was being burned alive. Though Herodotus also claimed that Northern Europe was awash with griffins guarding pots of gold from Cyclopes, so it's just possible he was wrong about the immolations. Other historians claim the punishment was more a light caning.

There's a similar combination of violent threat and mutual benefit, ultimately leading to the enrichment of the ruling classes, in just about every ancient historic example of taxation. The English used to pay a "Danegeld" – a tributary payment – to stop Danish Vikings from attacking England. When the Danes conquered England in 1016 the Danish kings kept the Danegeld going, with the justification that it might be needed if England got attacked *again*. But then it was attacked again, so maybe the Danes had a point?

Many ancient kings subcontracted tax collection to their barons, who of course exempted themselves from paying tax on account of the military service that they provided, which is another way of saying that the people who were *armed* didn't have to pay tax, only the peasants did.[†]

On the other hand, there are a *few* examples of early taxes having some semblance of fairness. In England, the Poll Tax of 1379 was designed to be paid by *communities*, with the richer members of the community paying the poorer members' share. Though an attempt by the government of the day to actually *collect* the Poll Tax led to a massive revolt that ended with the sacking of the Tower of London, the killing of royal officials by angry peasants, and the eventual execution of over 1,500 potential taxpayers.

[†]   In France this system lasted up until the 18th century, with one aristocrat, the Duc d'Orléans, allegedly bragging about a tax he was meant to be paying by saying, "I pay more or less what I like". *Plus ça change*, and all that, I guess. Though you may know that it didn't end well for the nobles.

It was more common in medieval times for tax exemptions to be given not for the *poor*, but for a select few, via the granting of "privileges" (literally "private laws"). Often these privileges were granted to powerful supporters of the government. Sound familiar?

In fact, in England at least, you probably have to wait until the Liberal Party's "People's Budget" of 1909 before you find a genuine attempt at funding tax cuts for the poor by raising taxes on the landed gentry (the House of Lords vetoed it).

Now I come to think of it, maybe there was a good reason why we were never formally taught about the history of tax. There was enough tax to get our heads around in the *present*, without delving with too much detail into the past. And besides, I wasn't using my time between college sessions to read Herodotus, I was honing my avoidance skills.

During our break from college, one of the junior managers I worked with announced that she was quitting. The firm had sponsored her for a UK work visa, so it was a little controversial that she was leaving, as normally you had to pay the costs of the sponsorship back if you left before a certain number of years. But she had successfully argued otherwise, due to her unusual circumstances.

Her first love was acting, and she had been offered a training contract at the Royal Academy of Dramatic Art. She was going to quit accountancy and become an actor.

We all gathered round her desk for her leaving speech. She had a beautiful voice, but joked that if we wanted to see her perform we'd have to go to the National Theatre. We joked that only the partners could afford to do that.

Back at our own desks I remarked to Penelope how peculiar it was to move from accountancy to acting.

"Oh sweetie, you're so naive," she said. "She's not joining RADA. She's going to Hitch & Limmermans."

This was a profession that rewarded people who were willing to lie.

My second avoidance scheme was a little better. We had learned in college how if a company pays interest on a loan, that interest is deductible against the company's general income. So say the company had profits of £100, but paid £25 interest on a loan, it would only pay tax on the net figure of £75.

This in itself is a slightly peculiar rule, because it incentivises companies to borrow excessively in order to claim tax-deductible interest payments.

We also learned about what happens when the company *lends* money, rather than borrows it, and how in some rather niche situations (mostly lending money to the government), there was no tax on the interest it received.

This seemed to open up a loophole, and I took a plan to exploit this loophole to Wilhelm. I did ask Penelope first, but she told me she was too busy to look at it.

It starts like this. Imagine there's a company earning £100 of profits. Say the corporation tax rate is 30 per cent, then without any shenanigans they'd have to pay £30 tax.

But what if they borrowed £2,000, upon which they paid £100 per year of interest? Now their profits would fall to zero, so they'd save tax. Of course they'd also have no profits, which isn't such a great result.

But they could then lend the £2,000 (that they'd just borrowed) to the government (by buying Premium Bonds or National Savings

Certificates), earn £100 per year in tax-free interest and use that interest to pay off the tax-deductible interest on the original loan.

Wilhelm looked at me like I was making no sense, so I sketched a diagram:

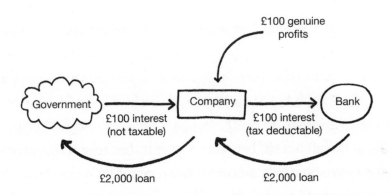

Wilhelm bobbed his head up and down a little bit, not quite nodding, but definitely thinking.

"Well, your first problem is that the interest rates won't match up. There's no way the interest this company *earns* will be the same as the interest it *pays*."

My heart sank a little.

"The second problem is that most of the loan products that pay tax-free interest are only available to individuals, not companies."

I could see the old adage about knowing only a little bit about a subject being a dangerous thing.

"And the third problem is that this has already been done."

I perked up a little.

Wilhelm explained that what I'd stumbled across was a pretty standard avoidance ruse back when he was getting started in tax.

Instead of the company being in the middle of things, a person would be.

"All the big names did it – The Beatles even sang about it."[†]

And they wouldn't borrow from a bank, they would borrow from a firm of tax advisors, who ensured that the interest rate they paid exactly matched the tax-free interest they were earning from their government bonds.

"But you know what?" said Wilhelm. "Perhaps you and I should revisit this idea?"

———

I like the distinction between the Noughties and the Tens (or 2000s and 2010s) as being that the Noughties were the decade of the internet and the Tens were the decade of the smart phone.

It's easy to forget now how much paper used to be on desks or how incommunicado you could be if you left the office. I would put my email on "Out of Office" and then disappear back to college for a few weeks without ever once checking in with my firm. And while at college I had nothing more distracting on my phone than Snake, and rereading the ten text messages the phone could save.

So a couple of weeks passed before I spoke to Wilhelm again, by now after I'd actually sat my tax exam. He strolled into my cubicle area and sat in Penelope's seat (she was busy looking for a file).

"Good news!" he announced. "I've sold your scheme to a client."

This, it turned out, was not good news.

The red flag should have been that he'd described it as *my* scheme.

[†] Technically, The Beatles' song "Taxman" is more about the sky-high tax rates they had to pay than the mechanisms people used to avoid them. Interestingly, most people seem to be on The Beatles' side on this one – either because, hey, they made great music, or because the 95 per cent supertax rate they paid seems a little unfair, even for the super-rich. It was also a remarkably prescient song, predicting both the tax on heat (the climate change levy) and on going for a walk (VAT on shoes).

4

A THREE-LETTER WORD ENDING IN "X"

Things didn't go really wrong for me for about another year.

I'd progressed to a level where rather than just put numbers into a software program I could query the clients if any of the numbers needed clarification. This was quite the promotion.

Usually it just meant checking that all the client's expenses were genuine business expenses. I had one client shout at me after I told him he wasn't allowed to deduct the cost of his children's school fees from his consultancy company's profits.

"Of course it's for business purposes. If I had to look after the brats all day how would I get any work done?"

The issue for him was that expenses have to be what's called "wholly and exclusively" incurred for the purpose of running your business. So while it might *help* to have the kids at Eton rather than under your feet all day, their schooling had another purpose too. This catch is known as the *duality of purpose*.

One of the most famous cases involving the duality of purpose featured a barrister who purchased a black trouser suit to wear in court. She argued that she was required to wear black in court, but wouldn't be seen dead in such plain business attire in a normal social setting. As such, she argued, her clothes were wholly and exclusively for her business as a barrister, so she should be allowed to write them off as a tax deduction.

The judge disagreed.

In his view the clothes did serve a duality of purpose. They weren't just for work, they were also for "warmth and decency".

And so this decision would have rested, were it not for an enterprising accountant who some years later realised that he could take advantage of this ruling for one of his own clients.

This client had to spend a lot of money on her work clothes, and like the barrister was unlikely to wear her clothes in a normal social setting.

The client was a stripper. Her clothes were not designed for warmth, the accountant argued, and were definitely not designed for decency.

He won his case. So the law now is that if you go to work in just your knickers, then, provided they're indecent, you can write the cost of them off against your taxes.

Anyway, it wasn't the chap with the kids at Eton who complained about me. I had another client whose phone lines had been hacked and redirected to call some premium-rate adult chat lines. Legally you can't deduct any costs that result from criminal activity (even if you're the victim), so I *disallowed* the cost of all these calls, of which there were thousands of pounds' worth. As the corporation tax rate at the time was over 30 per cent, this *disallowance* would have pushed up the company's tax bill by about the same amount I earned in three or four months.

A client always has to sign the final tax return to acknowledge that it's correct (as legally, if the tax accountant screws up, it's still the client's fault), and this client refused to do so. He went further and complained to one of the tax partners about the mistake I'd made in disallowing the cost of the calls. The partner told me to resubmit the return without the disallowance. I was adamant that my disallowance was correct.

It was Penelope who explained what had happened.

"You idiot," she said, "the phone lines weren't really hacked."

—

But the dubious phone calls were a long way from being the most serious issue I had to deal with. Rather, two situations arose at around the same time that made me question my career choice. One involved the, ahem, *arrangements* Wilhelm had devised, and the other centred around a client called Daniel.

The first thing you do when you get a new client is google them to see how rich they are. That way you know how much to bill them for your work.

The second thing you do is something called Know Your Client, or KYC, to "prove" your client isn't a money-launderer.

These days the rules have been tightened up a little bit, but back when I picked up Daniel's file it seemed to consist merely of getting a photocopy of their passport. Half the time the clients just emailed us a copy of their identity papers, most of which were in Russian. I think Photoshop hadn't been invented back then, so no one had a problem with this process.[†]

[†] Despite saying that a lot of the legislation on this has been tightened up, I was still laughing recently at a friend who told me that his entire firm had an emergency meeting after the Pandora Papers data leak exposed how many of their clients were (potentially) money-launderers. He said the partners' reaction to the revelations were like the scene in *Casablanca* when the French cop has to shut Rick's Café and says he's *shocked, shocked* to discover gambling is taking place on the premises (before being handed his winnings for the night). My friend's firm is not one of the small ones.

Daniel's photocopied passport was the only one we'd used the colour copier for. There were also a couple of newspaper articles about him in the file. He ran a production company in the film and TV industry and was famous for having dated a couple of actresses.

One of my colleagues, a tax senior called Aarti, was the niece of Daniel's business partner, and Daniel used that as an excuse to come and say hello whenever he'd finished a meeting with a tax partner.[†]

Aarti sat opposite me, and Daniel would sit on my desk with his legs wide apart and his tight trousers far too close to my face.

"I just came to congratulate you on your upcoming wedding," said Daniel, to Aarti, but also to the small crowd of accountants who had formed around him. We didn't get a lot of clients in our side of the building, or strikingly handsome people, so this felt like a special occasion. "I hear you're having it at the Clouden Park Hotel?"

"Yes," said Aarti, "that's right."

"You know my business partner owns that place?"

"Yes. That's why we're having it there."

"You know they've got a helicopter pad there?"

"I didn't."

"Maybe I should fly in to say hi on the day?"

Daniel wasn't the first multi-millionaire I met who assumed that other people must have similar preoccupations to him – like where to land their helicopter. At one business tax dinner I sat next to one of the senior

---

[†]   "Senior" denotes that she was only one rung above me – i.e. less than halfway through her training contract and not even close to having any actual responsibility. My title at the time was "Semi-senior", which sounds like a joke, but isn't. My friend Kititi's job title at Google, incidentally, was "Creative Maximiser". I don't know what title they give their accountants, but I dread to think.

(in age and rank) partners, who, clearly supposing he had nothing in common with someone 110 years his junior decided to ask me where my parents played golf.

"Well, they live in Central London, so I don't think they have many opportunities to play golf."

He thought about this.

"So . . . do they sail? Do they shoot?"

I was sitting next to him because of a mentoring scheme in which a senior partner would take a junior accountant under their wing. Over lunch I learned about the foolishness of keeping a rifle cabinet in the cellar, because the moisture does terrible things to firing mechanisms. This, apparently, was sufficient mentoring, and I didn't see him again for two years.

Once Daniel had gone, the office chat was all about how good-looking he was. Penelope went as far as to say she'd like to *lick his fingers*, which is one of those comments I can't now unhear. Aarti, on the other hand, rolled her eyes at me. She was horrified at the idea that Daniel might try and upstage her on her wedding day by landing a helicopter outside the reception.

I laughed, and it was like our shared joke – that we both felt the same way about Daniel, and from that moment on we were friends.

Aarti had divided our colleagues up into two groups: "accountants" and "not accountants". She never really explained this distinction, but she told me that I was in the "not accountants". I think that was a compliment.

—

I'd just about finished my last round of accountancy exams (a good couple of years after I'd started) when I learned from Wilhelm that

HMRC had taken an interest in "my" tax-avoidance scheme – the one loosely based on borrowing money to claim tax-deductible interest while simultaneously investing in something else to receive non-taxable income. What Wilhelm had created bore very little resemblance to what I'd suggested to him, not least because there was now a company based in the Isle of Man doing something incomprehensible with a loan that seemed to have been made between two entirely fictitious entities.

An inspector had written to the firm asking for more information about the transactions involved, and Wilhelm jokingly asked if I wanted to reply. The letter from HMRC was very specific, and asked a series of well thought-through questions, with follow-on questions and detailed lists of transactions that they wanted to review.

"Don't worry," said Wilhelm, "I'll show you how to respond." Then he dictated a letter:

Dear Mr ——

Thank you for your letter dated ——
    All the transactions you referred to were part of routine commercial activity and have been correctly treated in the appropriate accounts.

Yours sincerely

And then he suggested I write my name.

I was about to ask if he was serious when he burst out laughing,

"Never put a name on these things! Just write the firm name. And put a second-class stamp on it."

Apart from the obvious stalling tactic, there was more than meets the eye to this response. All the Big 4 firms, and most of the medium-sized ones, like mine, had managed to get lucrative gigs for themselves advising the government on everything from Private Finance Initiatives to tax reform.[†]

As the chartered accountants were the experts in all things number-crunching, the partners at top firms were on first-name terms with many government ministers. Putting the firm name – instead of an individual partner's name – on a letter to HMRC was thus a subtle way of saying, "You mess with me, you mess with my whole family" and someone in that family would have the young tax inspector's boss's phone number.

A few months later I was to see just how integral this was to Wilhelm's plan.

—

Early one morning around the time of Daniel's visit to Aarti, I returned from a half-hour stroll around the office with a random client file under my arm to find Wilhelm sitting on my desk reading an article from *The Financial Times* out loud to Aarti (Penelope was busy looking for a file).

"What's so funny?" I asked, as they were chuckling.

[†]   "PFI" schemes were the darling of Tony Blair's government – effectively a private company paid (with borrowed money) for something, like a hospital, and then the government bought it from them over a few decades. It was meant to be a way to build a lot of hospitals and schools and suchlike without paying for them upfront. Of course, they had to be paid for eventually – and the private companies charged the government through the nose for what had been built. PFI has been referred to as "Pay for two hospitals, get one." But worse, many PFI companies then took those payments they'd received offshore. One PFI company admitted to Parliament that 72 per cent of its shares were held by investors in Guernsey.

"One of my ex-clients has been arrested," replied Wilhelm.

"Why's that funny?"

Wilhelm looked at me sideways, like I was asking something idiotic.

"Have you ever had an ex-girlfriend?"

As it happened, I had. I'd managed to date the same girl all the way from my last term of school, through university and up to getting a job in accountancy. But then she had ditched me for a chap called Xavian who directed perfume commercials. I was devastated, and was rather wishing we might get back together, but I didn't want to reveal that to Wilhelm. So I shrugged and said, "Sure", though probably in a way that suggested I wasn't sure.

"And how would you feel if she got arrested?"

Aarti enjoyed my forlorn inability to answer the question while Wilhelm folded his paper away. He could charge £1,200 an hour, and he knew it, so he hadn't just come by for a chat.

"What do you know about *poos*?" he asked.

He had a strong accent, and I'm partially deaf, and this was a weird thing to be asked by a senior partner (or by anyone, for that matter), so I hesitated for an uncomfortably long time, wondering if I'd misheard him.[†]

The only connection I could make was with what more than one of my colleagues referred to as *poo chicken* – the social awkwardness of being in a toilet cubicle alongside another engaged cubicle. I'm sure

---

[†]   I don't think the deafness is a genetic thing. I think it was triggered by listening to the album *Aquarius* by the pop band Aqua (of "Barbie Girl" fame) on a trans-Pacific flight. For some insensible reason I thought I'd give the album a try, and because I was seated behind the engines I whacked the headphones up to full volume, then promptly fell asleep. I woke up 12 hours later with the album still playing on a loop. The only silver lining was that I was able to identify their hit single "Cartoon Heroes" from its lyrics alone in a pub quiz nearly a decade later.

no one likes to share this literally shitty experience with colleagues, but accountants are so bad at dealing with social awkwardness that a couple of the junior accountants I gossiped with at soup time had confessed to 40-minute-long stand-offs fuelled by scatological dread, with neither defecator willing to risk flushing lest it be the exact moment the other did, and they found themselves face to face with a partner and forced to make small talk as they both ignored the small horrors they had unleashed.

One colleague said it was a stand-off (or sit-off) that was only resolved by feigning a light snore, at which point the other chap made a run for it, not even washing his hands.

Was this what Wilhelm was asking me? Did he want to know who he'd lost poo chicken to? I mean, Wilhelm was a little eccentric, and more than a little competitive, but I assumed his pride rode a bit higher.

He was waiting for an answer. I could think of nothing else to say.

The pause grew longer. He was still staring at me. I wondered if this was one of those career-defining moments. A chance to bond over a secret acknowledgement of some social anxiety. I'd helped him sell a boat, maybe I could help him with his toileting anxieties too.

I had to say something. So quietly, almost a whisper, conspiratorially, therapeutically, I asked,

"Poo chicken?"

There was a very, very long pause until he spoke.

"A Purchase Of Own Shares," he said. And then, when (in an effort to hide my mortification) I didn't react, "When a company buys shares in itself from one of its shareholders."

Aarti shook her head at me.

"You're very weird," she said.

—

Daniel was one of Wilhelm's clients and had told Wilhelm that he wanted to release some of the cash tied up in his production company to buy an estate in the South of France, but getting the cash from the company's bank account into the director's pockets would trigger a tax charge – quite a sizeably big one. Or it would have, if Wilhelm hadn't found a solution.

Rather than pay Daniel a dividend, the production company would instead buy some of the shares Daniel owned in it. In other words, the company would purchase its own shares. The company was owned and run by just two people, and Daniel was one of them.

"If there is an irreconcilable breakdown in trust between the two directors, then the purchase of own shares by the company is treated as a *capital disposal*, as it will benefit the company's business for the company to purchase this director's shares. Otherwise, the purchase of own shares will be treated as income. If it's *capital*, the tax charge will be much, much smaller."

"Has there been a breakdown in trust?"

"Not yet," laughed Wilhelm, "but this is why I need you."

—

One of the significant aspects of our tax system (and indeed, most tax systems) is that there is a major distinction made between "income" and "capital".

Capital is the stuff that you own – your car, your house, your clothes, your pristine collection of Pokémon cards and so on.

The UK's Office for National Statistics does a lot of analysis of how much of this stuff there is. As of 2018 there was enough of it in the UK for £564,000 of it per person. Of course, that doesn't mean that the average person has £564,000's worth of stuff. To be exactly halfway between the poorest person and the richest you only need £286,000.

In other words, a lot of this *stuff* is owned by not a lot of people. It was those "not a lot of people" that Wilhelm was interested in.

Many people have a big gripe that so much wealth is concentrated in the hands of the "1 per cent". At first glance this seems a pretty reasonable complaint. The richest 1 per cent of Britons own (depending on who you ask) about 25 per cent of all the wealth in Britain (though some commentators have pointed out that quite a lot of the top 1 per cent's wealth isn't in Britain – it's in tax havens).

But delve a bit deeper and it turns out that you can get into the top 1 per cent if you have a net wealth (i.e. what you would have left after you'd paid off your mortgage) of about £2 million. This might seem like a lot of money – and of course it is – but given that it includes your pension pot and your home, you only have to have spent a lifetime paying off a mortgage on a house in suburban London, as well as putting a chunk of a modest salary into your pension, to reach these dizzying heights. If you split the wealth by age bracket it becomes less striking.

About a quarter of 60–69-year-olds are in the richest 10 per cent of Britons, and one in ten of these older folks are just shy of being one-percenters themselves.

So at a second glance begrudging the one-percenters is really just being cross about old people.

I'm not saying inequality doesn't exist – far from it – it's just that there wasn't much Wilhelm could do with a retiree's pension pot and their semi-detached house in Pinner.

It's not the 1 per cent that gets tax accountants excited. It's not even the 0.1 per cent (a club you can get into with about £5 million). Wilhelm only really held his doors open for the 0.01 per cent. Those are people who might be increasing their capital by £5 million each year.

That's where the real inequality is. That's where lifestyles (and outlooks) start to fundamentally change. If you join the 1 per cent you might have a slightly bigger house in a smarter neighbourhood. You might have a nanny and send your kids to private school, but fundamentally your day-to-day won't be much different than if you're in the top 50 per cent. But get into the top 0.01 per cent and normal everyday chores evaporate. I knew one client who paid £4,000 a week for a concierge service, which she only used for booking restaurants and, on one occasion, ordering some new towels (because she didn't know how else to buy towels).

The top 0.01 per cent doesn't trip off the tongue so well, but there are still a good six or seven thousand people in this 0.01 per cent in the UK alone. That's a lot of potential clients.

When your capital goes up in value you get richer, but it's only when you sell something for more than you bought it for that you have a *capital gain*. And when you have a capital gain, you *might* have to pay capital gains tax.

I say "might" because some things are exempt from this tax, depending on what those things are and where you live. In the UK your house, your car, your clothes and (probably) your Pokémon cards are exempt, which does make me wonder whether I should have come up with some better examples of "capital" earlier. I'll deal with houses being exempt later on, because it gets pretty complex, but cars being exempt is actually a little micro-injustice, masquerading as a tax exemption for us all.

If you sell something for less than you bought it for you have what's called a *capital loss*. This loss can be deducted from your capital gain, meaning you pay less capital gains tax on those gains.

But the one big capital purchase we're all likely to make in our lives that actually *loses* money – our car – is exempt from capital gains tax.

Meaning that *loss* – the fall in value of our car – cannot be used to reduce our capital gains tax bill.[†]

So why is this an injustice? It's because not all cars lose money. Sure, your Ford Kuga does, but not your Ford GT40 (one of which sold at auction for $9.8 million).

So if you buy a car to, you know, drive it, the car will lose its value and you get no benefit from that loss. But if you buy a car as an investment, and stick it in your climate-controlled garage alongside your McLaren F1 ($19.8 million) or Ferrari 250 ($78 million) or 1955 Mercedes Benz 300 SLR Coupe (a record-breaking €135 million), you can sell it at a profit and not pay any tax at all.

This sticks in my throat a bit when I read about celebrities like Chris Evans (the media mogul and ex-*Top Gear* presenter, not Captain America) saying their hobby is "collecting classic cars". Apparently Chris Evans has bought a dozen such classics (including one as a gift for a teenage girl he had a crush on), almost all of which are now worth more than what he paid for them.[‡]

So he can sell them, make millions in *gains*, but not pay a penny in tax. He doesn't even need to get an accountant to use a loophole, it's simply how the law is written.

[†] Capital gains tax rules are pretty similar in different jurisdictions, but the USA has more idiosyncrasies than most places – including that you sometimes pay tax when you sell your car, but get no tax benefit if you sell it at a loss. Sorry, guys – you've got the worst of both worlds here. At least cars aren't a big part of your culture.

[‡] To be fair to Chris, I had a crush on her too. She was the pop star Billie Piper and she did marry him not long afterwards. If only I'd known that the way to win a teenager's heart was to buy them a silver Ferrari I would have had ~~so much more~~ the exact same amount of success with girls.

But anyway, if capital is the stuff you *own*, and it's different to income, and that difference makes a huge impact on how much tax you have to pay, then it raises the big question, what is income?

Income is surprisingly hard to define. I'm tempted to say it's the stuff you *earn*, but a lot of income isn't earned in the sense of "Well done, mate, have a beer, you've *earned* it." It includes your salary, but also the rent you get from tenants, dividends you receive from investments, payments from trusts and bank interest, and a host of other things that you don't necessarily have to get off your fat backside to *earn*.

It's pretty much all the money you receive *every* year, because there's some contractual reason why someone has to pay you something.

To have a top 1 per cent income in the UK you need to earn about £120,000 per year. Though to be in the top-earning 1 per cent of middle-aged men in London you need about £650,000 per year (i.e. most of the UK's top 1 per cent are middle-aged men in London). The average partner at Deloitte reportedly took home £1 million in 2021, which was the highest share reported by any of the Big 4 firms that year. There are over 1,000 partners at Deloitte.

The richer you are the more likely it is that your wealth comes from capital, rather than income. And indeed the more likely it is that you've got richer due to your capital increasing in value, rather than your income going up.

Capital and income are taxed very, very differently. Can you guess which one has the higher rates of tax?

When your capital goes up in value you don't actually have to pay any tax. This is probably fair – if you own a house and it goes up in value it would be a bit harsh to make you pay tax on that increase, as you'd usually have to sell the house to get your hands on the cash to do so.

Owning something that has gone up in value is known as having an *unrealised gain.* The Democrats in the USA briefly toyed with the idea of introducing a tax on unrealised gains (as it would raise some colossal sums), but the idea never got much traction, partly because almost half of the poorest 20 per cent of Americans have unrealised gains and partly because it could trigger a mass sell-off of homes and shares.

More recently, President Biden suggested a tax on only the unrealised gains accrued by *multi-millionaires,* though his suggestion seems to be more political theatre than having a chance of passing through Congress. A senator needs to have more than $30 million just to be in the top 10 per cent of rich senators, which might make passing a tax on the unrealised gains of multi-millionaires tricky.

In June 2021 the Pulitzer Prize-winning investigative journalism outfit ProPublica analysed the tax returns of some of America's wealthiest businessmen. Their headline was that the "true tax rate" of people like Warren Buffett, Jeff Bezos and Elon Musk was as low as 0.1 per cent. But their logic was that, say, Jeff Bezos's wealth had grown by $99 billion over a period in which he'd paid tax of just under $1 billion (i.e. about a 1 per cent "true" tax rate in his case).

This a little messed up – but not for the reason you might think. During the same period Jeff Bezos was claimed to have reported $4.22 billion in income, so was paying an *actual* tax rate of about 25 per cent. To my eyes, that's the scandalous bit – that even on his *reported* income Jeff Bezos could pay a lower tax rate than "ordinary" people.

There's no need to invent some headline-grabbing measure of assessing "true tax rates", as ProPublica did, to highlight how unequal the tax code is – otherwise we'd all have to reassess our own true tax rates. If you live in an apartment that has gone up more in value than you've earned over the last five years, that doesn't mean you're somehow paying less tax than you should be.

The main reason, it seems, for this lower rate was that Jeff's *income* wasn't income at all, but capital gains. And for reasons that remain inexplicable (unless somehow wealthy people are able to dictate tax policy), capital gains are taxed at lower rates than income.[†]

The issue here is so obvious – wealthy people don't need to use convoluted tax-avoidance tricks to pay lower rates of tax, because capital and income are already taxed at different rates.

Of course, I'm not saying that they don't use convoluted tax-avoidance tricks, too.

Once you get to a certain level of wealth you no longer need to use your own money to buy stuff (because what kind of pauper would do that?), which means you no longer need an income (or to make capital gains) – which means you no longer need to pay income tax (or capital gains tax).

One of the easiest ways for the really ridiculously wealthy to avoid paying taxes is to use the wealth they already have as collateral and *borrow* money instead.

Elon Musk, for instance, is said to have never accepted a pay cheque from Tesla – though he was offered minimum wage (for legal reasons). And yet, he's still doing all right. If he finds himself needing a bit of cash,

---

[†]   I say "inexplicable", but one of the arguments put forward by rich people for taxing their gains at lower rates than your income is that their capital can move offshore more easily than your income can. But that argument only works because government policy is designed to ensure it works. i.e. government policy could just as easily say, "If you make offshore gains you have to pay tax on those gains here, at high rates." Depressingly, when income taxes were first introduced, "unearned" wealth *was* taxed at higher rates than incomes from jobs, as this was seen to be fairer. But slowly, bit by bit, such policies have been turned upside down, so that now, like in feudal times, it's the poor that get shaken down the most.

he can borrow it. Borrowing money doesn't make you richer – you still owe the bank, after all – but it does mean that you now have cash in your pocket, *and* still own all your Tesla shares.

You read that right. Elon can get cash to buy things *without earning anything at all*. And where there are no earnings, there's no tax.

This tax-avoidance tactic is sometimes called "Buy, Borrow, Die".

Occasionally, this tactic can go badly wrong. *The Financial Times* reported in 2022 that six top executives at Peloton, the indoor exercise-bike makers, had borrowed against their shareholdings, only for Peloton's share price to crash by 80 per cent. They would have been much better off if they had just sold their shares in the first place.

The "Die" part of "Buy, Borrow, Die" goes like this: when a billionaire dies, the borrowed money reduces their taxable estate, so their heirs pay less tax too (though also inherit less). But their heirs also inherit the, say, Tesla shares, without inheriting the "unrealised gain". This means that all that tax that was not paid by Elon or Jeff or whoever *will never be paid*.

This might seem scandalous, but what they're doing is effectively what lots of old people do when they get an *equity release* mortgage – borrowing cash using their (in the old people's case) house, spending that cash and then letting their kids inherit anything that's left, (but not the unrealised gain).

I'm not advocating dying to avoid your taxes, by the way, though it is bloody effective.[†]

—

[†]   That is, bloody effective for everyone except Australians, who very cleverly (and almost uniquely) don't allow unrealised capital gains to evaporate on death. I'll remind you about this when we get round to talking a bit more about death later (which I appreciate is a slightly unusual way to set up a cliffhanger).

There is another reason why a select group of gazillionaires pay so little tax, but it's ethically a bit trickier to get your head around: you can reduce your tax bill by giving to charity.

Warren Buffett is said to have given away over $41 billion of his wealth, a great deal of it to the Bill and Melinda Gates Foundation. Since charitable donations are tax-deductible, he could earn $41 billion and not pay a penny in tax (which kind of makes sense, as he wouldn't have a penny to pay it with, if he'd just given it all to charity).

But this is one of those issues that gives me an ethical headache. Giving to charity is a good thing, surely? But so is paying tax . . . And the richer you are, the greater the tax saving you make from donating (since you "save" the tax you would otherwise have paid).

Indeed, when the UK government announced that they would change the law to limit the tax breaks on charitable donations to just 20 per cent of the amount donated, there were such howls of protestation from big charities which depend on the (tax-efficient) largesse of the super-rich that the government promptly U-turned.

Effectively, the richer you are, the more you get to decide whether you'd rather pay tax or give to charity (or, in some cases, neither). A charity might name a hospital wing after you, or invite you to a lavish ball. To my knowledge the IRS is yet to offer that, so you can see the attraction. Maybe they should?

—

Anyway, let's get back to Daniel, Wilhelm's client. He had two options for extracting cash from his media company. The same transaction – money being moved from the *company's* bank account to *his* bank account – could be deemed to be *income* or it could be *capital*. The tax rate was four times higher if it was treated as income. But the law said it could be treated as capital only if the payment was due to *a breakdown of trust between the directors*.

So there was a snag. The directors adored each other. They holidayed together. They played tennis together every Thursday morning. One of them was godfather to the other's daughter. And Wilhelm couldn't just email them and say, "Make sure you have a breakdown in trust" because that's just the sort of thing an HMRC investigation would pounce upon.

This is where I came in.

Wilhelm handed me a document.

"I seem to have lost a copy of the client's *authorisation of agent* form. So unfortunately I need to get the client's signature. I would like you to go to his office and get it for me. Perhaps you could explain the POOS rules while you're there."

"How much will a capital treatment save this guy?" I asked. He shrugged, as if the numbers were less important than the principle. The principle being that he won this game.

"A few million."

"Why don't you send Aarti?" I asked.

"Are you kidding? She hates Daniel's guts."

I assumed that Wilhelm didn't just phone Daniel to tell him the POOS rules himself in case his phone record was used as circumstantial evidence at a tax tribunal.

Wilhelm was cleverer than that. I wasn't. After all, he could have just used my phone if my assumption about a tax tribunal had been correct.

Wilhelm knew what he was doing. If Daniel were ever asked where this advice came from, it wouldn't be from Wilhelm. It would be from me.

—

It also didn't occur to me until many years later that it's a bit weird that companies can buy shares in themselves. I mean, if Tesco buys Tesco shares, then who owns Tesco? Why, *Tesco owns Tesco*. It's all a bit *Black Mirror*.

Luckily, most of the time the company cancels the shares – meaning those particular shares no longer exist, so all that happens is the remaining shareholders own a greater proportion of the company. But that "most of the time" still gives me the creeps. [†]

—

Being back in the lobby of a media business, I was reminded of just how gorgeous everyone was. I'm not saying accountants are ugly, just that there's no need to look good in accountancy. The receptionists at the production company looked like they could be catwalk models, and they seemed unimpressed with my meek suggestion that I was there to get a signature from the director.

"You can leave that form with me, I'll see it gets signed."

"I really need to get it signed in person."

"Do you have an appointment?"

Well, no, that was the whole point. I'd got it in my head that this was all supposed to be a little clandestine. I'd even paid for my tube ticket in cash just in case some tax inspector ever queried my movements that day.

The receptionist suggested I wait in the lobby, as Daniel would be heading out to lunch soon.

Daniel did appear after a while, striding through the lobby, with a wink at the receptionists. I rushed up to him as he reached the doors and explained that I was there to get his signature on a tax form.

[†]   I can imagine my old man reading this and thinking, "What's a Black Mirror?" The answer is that it's a bit like *The Twilight Zone* for people who spend too long on Facebook.

"Sure!" he said, signing with his Mont Blanc, but barely slowing down to acknowledge what he was signing.

"And while I'm here, can I quickly talk to you about POOS?"

He stopped, put his pen away and looked me up and down.

"You're a very weird kid."

And then he got in a taxi and left.

I gave the signed (but unnecessary) forms to Wilhelm's secretary, and avoided Wilhelm for the next couple of weeks. I felt pretty down about my job. It was crushingly boring at the best of times, but made worse by the glimpses of glamour from rich clients' lives, and it turned out I couldn't even do the conspiring-with-clients bit right.

As it happens Daniel did get his capital treatment, but it was nothing to do with me.

Aarti told her uncle that she didn't want Daniel landing a helicopter during her wedding day, and her uncle promptly disinvited Daniel from the wedding. Daniel threw a very public strop about this at a fancy restaurant in Soho, shouting about how disrespectful it was to him and vowing not to work with her uncle ever again. The argument was overheard by some journalists who happened to be dining in the restaurant at the time.

Later that week Aarti showed me and Penelope a new watch she was wearing. It looked expensive.

"Daniel bought it for me as a wedding present."

"I thought he had fallen out with you over not being invited to your wedding?" I asked, having read about the row in the paper.

Penelope laughed.

"Oh, sweetie, you're so naive," she said.

—

I realise I've not really taken the time to explain what tax avoidance actually is. I think I've been avoiding the subject (so to speak) because there's no really good definition.

When I was at college I was told that "avoidance" was legally rearranging your affairs to minimise your tax bill, and "evasion" was a filthy, horrible crime that would put you in prison.

The official guidance has evolved a bit since then. Avoidance has been split in two, or rather a new category called "planning" has been added.

Weirdly, both "planning" and "avoidance" are defined as rearranging your affairs to minimise your tax bill, but *planning* is doing it in a manner that isn't controversial, whereas avoidance is controversial.

Controversial is defined as something unreasonable.

Unreasonable is defined as something that other people might not approve of.

And what people might not approve of is doing something controversial.

Glad we cleared that up.

Let's try this instead.

When the US state of Minnesota banned smoking in public places, they made an exception for theatres. If it was necessary for a character to smoke a cigarette, then it was OK for the actor to really light one up.

But bars across the state realised that this left open a pretty big loophole – for who was to say what was and wasn't legitimate theatre? Over 100 bars were suddenly "transformed" into makeshift theatres, putting on nightly (and all-nightly) plays with titles like *The Smoker, The Tobacco Monologues* and *Before the Ban*. The props were ashtrays and cigarette machines, the characters were the bar's attendees. The Health Department threatened the bars with fines – but which laws were they breaking? Their actions were strictly within the letter of the law, albeit far, far outside the spirit of it.

Irrespective of what you think of smoking, whose side would you be on? Were the bars just being clever, inventive, resourceful, sticking it to the man? Was it the legislature's fault for not thinking through the consequences of the exemptions to their law? Are we all obliged to assume the law's true meaning, even when it's not obvious (or even when it is, but the law's badly written)? Is it better to be legal and unethical or ethical but illegal? *Can* you be ethical but illegal?

In other news, a lot of people in Minnesota have died of smoking-related illnesses.

—

HMRC eventually lost patience with Wilhelm's single-sentence replies to their inquiries into the tax-avoidance scheme he'd sold and insisted on a meeting at our office, where they wanted to run through the particular transactions in person.

I assumed that I didn't need to be in that meeting. I may have been the progenitor of the scheme, but only in an academic, accidental way. Wilhelm saw it differently. I had *fall guy* written on my forehead.

I imagined a tax inspector from HMRC would be a fierce, stern character, a bit like a policeman outside a nightclub, accepting no bullshit, demanding answers.

Instead he was about 25 and looked terrified. I recognised this look – it was the same one I used whenever I was out of my depth.

I guess there are two explanations for why he was so young. Either someone more senior than him was a little nervous about taking on Wilhelm, or the staff cuts at HMRC were really biting – apparently a third of their workforce was being made redundant. Perhaps this chap was all they could spare.

Wilhelm, by contrast, was flanked by a silver-haired man whom he introduced as the QC who signed off the legality of the commercial transactions, and a woman in a power suit who said nothing during the meeting but shook her head slowly from side to side whenever the poor sap from HMRC said anything. On the table between those three and the inspector was a goldfish bowl, in which, swimming in circles, was a goldfish.

The meeting had clearly already started when I arrived, and seemed to be in full swing, though I'm sure I turned up when Wilhelm had told me to. Wilhelm made such a show of stopping the meeting to greet me that I quickly realised he was wasting time. He then suggested I take a seat that was against the wall, behind the tax inspector.

The inspector had a stack of papers in front of him, and had circled a few numbers with a pen. "I'm just trying to understand why these loans were needed in the first place." He sounded like he was pleading.

The QC sounded like – well, I think the correct description is that he *scoffed*.

"Look, I don't mean to invoke the Human Rights Act, but Article 1 quite clearly states that our client is entitled to the peaceful enjoyment of their possessions, which would plainly be encroached if they had to reveal the nature of these very commercially sensitive transactions."

"I'm sorry, are you saying this is a human rights issue?"

The woman in the power suit tutted. The QC sighed.

"I'm just saying that in the absence of a corporate structure there can't be a shareholder to pursue a claim against in the UK. So the nature of this enquiry is invalid under Section 270. I'm not saying we'd claim legal costs against HMRC just yet, but there's clearly nothing in Section 6 that warrants an investigation."

"Well, yes, but, these loans . . . ?"

Wilhelm sat back with his arms crossed. "We're going round in more circles than Starbuck."

"Starbuck?"

"The fish."

The meeting continued in this vein for the next half-hour, with Wilhelm doing his best to ensure that nothing of any real substance was actually said, while the QC continued to invent section numbers. Wilhelm still hadn't played his trump card.

A secretary knocked on the door, and pushed inside. "I'm sorry to interrupt, Wilhelm," she said, "but Sebastian Fowley is on the phone . . . he wants to know if you're intending to bring a plus one to Downing Street tonight?"

Sebastian Fowley is, of course, a fake name. But the real Sebastian was a government minister, quite a senior one.

Wilhelm stood up. "I'm so sorry, I'll have to take this call. It may take a while – you know politicians, they like to talk . . . perhaps you could give a list of your queries to my assistant here and then we could continue this meeting another time?"

To my knowledge, there never was another time. I didn't understand half of the inspector's queries, but I'm not sure he really did either. It struck me that tax avoidance was less about devising some complicated set of transactions and more about ensuring your team had more money, time and inclination than the taxman did.

Sometimes cases took a decade to get to court, with HMRC having no certainty that they would win them. It was all just a game, and the accountants were winning.

But was it a game I wanted to play? And if it was, was this the firm I wanted to play it with?

My friend Kititi (the one who worked at Google) invited me to visit him not long after he had transferred to San Francisco. He took me for lunch at Google's global HQ in nearby Mountain View. The sprawling campus had something astonishing at almost every turn. There was a giant swimming pool with a constant current, so all the swimmers remained in one spot as they thrashed their beautiful Californian arms; there was a full-size tyrannosaurus rex skeleton draped in pink flamingos (the flamingos were fake, but I'm not sure the T-Rex was), and hanging in an atrium was the original prototype of SpaceShipOne (i.e. an actual spaceship).

My office in London, by contrast, was a 1960s nine-storey concrete and, very occasionally, glass building, with three slow lifts, a basement canteen and lots and lots of cubicles.

At Google they had sleep pods, ping pong and masseuses who would rub your shoulders as you typed.[†]

I had a swivel chair that had lost a wheel.

Perhaps it was time for me to move on.

[†] One of Google's first masseuses was also one of their first 40 or so employees, and received not just a wage of $450 a week but also *stock options* in the then unknown start-up. I'm guessing that someone rubs *her* shoulders these days.

5

AN OFFER HE CAN'T REFUSE

When I was 14 I went on my first ever date with a girl. We went to see a film called *Spy Hard*, a James Bond parody starring Leslie Nielsen as an ageing and bumbling secret agent. The poster featured Nielsen with his trousers round his ankles, and I must have assumed that that was exactly the kind of thing that gets a girl in the mood for some teenage snogging. After the film we went for a pizza. I figured I'd wait until after the pizza before I made my moves. That, in retrospect, was a mistake.

Being new to this dating malarkey I wasn't entirely sure what I should talk to her about, so asked about her taste in music, pretty much ready to acknowledge that whichever band she liked, I, too, thought they were amazing. You would think this was a pretty foolproof plan. It wasn't.

In the February of that year the pop band Take That had split up. This was news so devastating to my date that the mere thought of it made her burst into tears. Apparently she had been so upset that her father had had to phone the "Take That helpline" – for parents struggling to understand why their daughters were so sad, which I must admit was pretty thoughtful of their record label.

Spy Hard came out in the summer. Despite Take That's split having been a few months earlier, this girl was in floods of tears just talking about it. She explained that Take That's lead singer, Gary Barlow, was the love of her life. Just on the off chance that you think I've just exposed something front-page-worthy, I should stress that she had never met him. All the same, he had somewhat ruined my plans to get a little smoochy.[†]

A few years later, Gary would be apologising – not to me, nor to my date, but "for anyone who was offended by the tax stories earlier this year". Other than being about as vague a non-apology as it's possible to make, it may take some digging to know what he had actually done. Get ready for it.

—

Actually, before we shine a light on Gary Barlow's tax avoidance (while playing a game of *how many Take That song titles can you spot in this chapter?*), I think we left things at the point where I had decided to move on from my job. Let me go back to that for a minute, because it's kind of relevant to Gary.

With the expiration of my training contract imminent, and with it the chance to slip away from my firm, I managed to line up some interviews with some companies that promoted film partnership schemes.

One of the reasons I did this was that I'd met a girl called Sasha at a nightclub called Infernos and we had started dating. I had told her I worked in chemicals, she said she worked in films. About four dates in I confessed I did tax returns for companies in the chemical industry,

---

[†] Though now I come to write about this I realise it's always possible that these tears were an act. I can think of four separate occasions when a girl burst into tears at the prospect of kissing me. They can't all have been thinking about pop groups breaking up.

and she confessed she was about to complete a training contract at one of the Big 4 accountancy firms, but she "audited a lot of film companies".

Her experience of accountancy seemed more exciting than mine, and she suggested I take a look at some roles in film financing.

Thanks to a recent government initiative to give huge tax breaks to thespians (and their enablers), there had been a rush of start-ups trying to cash in by acting as the middlemen between investors and film companies.

I like to think that it was my background working in film and TV that helped me get a foot in the door, but really it was only because I was an accountant. Companies that sell tax breaks need accountants, and it seemed like these companies were madly scrambling for accountants to keep up with the demand from investors for these new, *glamorous* tax breaks. It didn't really matter what sort of accountant I was. Or, indeed, whether I was remotely competent.

Foolishly, I wanted to make the point to my interviewers that this was an industry I knew about, so I prepared for my first job interview in a slightly unusual way. I decided to dig out some interesting trivia that I could throw in, to show my future employers that I wasn't just an accountant, I was *fun*. I doubt this is a good idea in any industry. It's definitely not in accounting. I know that now.

I should have had an answer for their first, and in retrospect pretty obvious, question.

"What do you know about how film partnership schemes work?"

"Well, I know you helped finance a film that was directed by Jon Favreau, who used to be best known as the actor who played Monica's boyfriend in *Friends*."

A long pause.

"But do you know about how film partnership schemes work?"

"I do not."

I did not get that job. It probably didn't help that I was wrong about Jon Favreau. He did play Monica's boyfriend, but he had not directed a film they'd financed.

That may hardly have been my greatest day, but it was not my most disastrous job interview ever. I was once asked in an interview how I thought I would be at managing people.

These days I know that the correct answer is, "Amazing."

Instead I went with, "Not great, to be honest. I'm still young and I don't have much experience of managing people."

"You're interviewing for a management role."

Luckily he was very good-humoured about it, but I didn't get that job either.

Eventually, I learned my lesson: say exactly what the interviewer wants to hear.

In among the film finance interviews, a recruiter had lined me up an interview with a very well-known Japanese engineering company, for a job in their international tax team. The recruiter told me that I was going to be interviewed by the company's International Head of Tax. This gave me shivers. I was still struggling to get my head around UK tax, though thanks to Wilhelm I knew a lot about some very niche areas of international tax avoidance. But international tax rules generally? That would be a tough one. I spent the week before the interview desperately reading up on foreign tax rules, on cross-border transactions and, especially, on Japanese tax. I was also told that I was expected to bow at the interview rather than shake hands, which made me surprisingly nervous, as apparently there's a whole etiquette surrounding how low you go, and I haven't yet really mastered the etiquette of hand-shaking.

The day of the interview with the International Head of Tax arrived. I was ready, my head crammed full of facts about Japanese *double tax treaties* and *offshore subsidiary rules.*

After a lot of awkward bowing with some members of the London team (who I don't think were Japanese), I established that the International Head of Tax was not going to be joining us in person – I was not worth flying halfway round the world for. He would, instead, be joining us by telephone.

"So, tell me," he began, with a strong Japanese accent, "how did you learn tax?"

I wasn't really expecting that. I guess he was warming me up, just making polite small talk.

"Well, some of it I learned in college, some of it I learned from my colleagues and some of it I taught myself."

"Very good," he said. He paused before his next question. I braced myself for something especially challenging. I half hoped he would ask me about film partnerships, as I'd now read up on those, too. It seemed unlikely that he would ask me about Jon Favreau, but you never knew.

"So, tell me, do you like tax?"

How to answer this? Was it a trap? Was he probing for my take on the morality of taxation?

"Yes, I like tax a lot, it's very interesting."

"Very good. I have no more questions."

That was it. I must have said the right thing because they offered me a job.

—

Actually a lot of companies offered me a job. For all the bitching about my time as a trainee chartered accountant, in terms of career prospects everything changes when you get a charter. I didn't necessarily know much more than I had three years earlier about anything that was actually useful, but now that I had a CA after my name, prospective employers assumed I did.

In fact, such was the demand for chartered accountants that one of the big recruiting firms handed out flyers outside the exam hall in which we took our last ever exam (a case study about the photocopier industry, of all things). The flyers were an invitation to a party that Saturday night at a high-end nightclub in Soho. The flyer promised free drinks, free entry, free cash (in the form of casino chips) and an iPod for everyone who attended.[†]

There was only one thing they wanted in exchange: our email addresses. My email address was worth tens of thousands of pounds to them, as they got a commission of at least 20 per cent of the starting salary of any job they found for us.

I took a job at a small company in the West End that specialised in financing major films. I'd been away for three years and I wondered if I was now back for good. The company's offices were spread over two warren-like floors, sandwiched between TV production companies, in a building that housed a nightclub in the basement. I was told I didn't

---

[†]   My friend Kititi at Google told me about a lecture he'd been to in which some global head of something technological had pointed out that computer memory was developing so quickly that by 2020 your iPod would be able to store every piece of music ever made and that by 2030 it would be able to hold every TV show and film ever recorded too, but that the best minds in tech were more concerned with how they could *monetise* such a thing. There were two competing business models: you could have an item in your pocket that stores every single bit of music ever made, or you could pay a monthly fee for the rest of your life to access that music instead. Guess which model the accountants suggested? Oh, and if you're under 30 so don't know what an iPod is, it's like a phone that can't make calls, take pictures or connect to the internet. They were (briefly) very desirable.

have to wear a tie, which might sound like a small thing but it felt like I was joining the punk rockers of the accountancy world.

My first day at the film finance company contained more glamour than the three years combined at my old accountancy firm and not just because the first person I met was an *actual* punk rocker. Admittedly all he did was hold the door open for me. But, hey, that counts.

My new boss looked a bit like a Viking but spoke like a vicar. He was called Hugo and he seemed to be enthusiastic about everything – he talked more than I did in my interview, telling me several times how they were "helping films get made". He said that particular phrase a lot. It took me a while to realise that it wasn't *me* he was trying to convince.

He suggested I shadow him "to get a feel for things". *Things*, it turned out, meant opening random doors in the office and asking the occupants what they were up to.

I recognised one of the occupants – he was about 50 and had an unruly mop of hair and I was pretty sure he had delivered a talk at my school during Literature Week. Not that he was especially literary – I think the school was sufficiently satisfied that he was famous.

What he was famous for was directing films. Hugo gushingly said his hellos and introduced me. The director, in that cool way that famous people do, introduced himself. Actually I guess all people do that, but it sounds cool when you know their name already. Hugo asked if we could help.

The other person in the room, who I would later learn was called Mike and who was to last at this office for even less time than I would, explained that they were only up to *15 points*. For almost the first time in my accountancy career I knew what they were talking about before they explained it to me. It was a good feeling.

—

Despite trying really rather hard, there had been some meetings at my old firm that I couldn't avoid, even by hiding behind the large pot plant at the end of the hallway. There was one meeting, though, that I'm glad I didn't miss.

We had "tax update" lectures pretty frequently, and the trick was to avoid sitting on the front row, lest you had to pay attention for two hours to news about how the capital allowance regime for energy-efficient hand dryers was being slightly modified to accommodate the findings of the All-Party Parliamentary Group's research into the efficacy of paper towels.

But then, at the beginning of the third and final year of my training contract, we had been introduced to the government's latest, and ridiculous, wheeze: *Film Tax Relief.*

The government decided that they needed to do more to support the British film industry. This seemed less to do with targeting those areas of the economy that genuinely needed help, and more to do with politicians wanting to attend movie premieres. I guess hanging out with actors was more fun than hanging out with miners. But no matter the logic, the Film Tax Relief scheme was born.

The relief was amazingly generous. Pretty much any film that qualified as British would get up to a fifth of its budget paid for by the UK taxpayer. You'd think that British taxpayers might prefer, say, free cinema tickets, or to pay less tax, but no, subsidising movies was seen as the preferable policy.

Now of course a major problem with supporting the *British* film industry is that one of the fun features of films is that they can be set pretty much anywhere – or any time. So how do you assess whether a film is British? Luckily, we already had an institute that could answer that question: The British Film Institute. They were tasked with analysing Britishness using a points-based scheme.

Which leads to the question – when is a Hollywood movie really a British one?

Actually let's make this into a quiz. Which of the following films do you think was British?

a) *Slumdog Millionaire*. An adaption of a novel by Indian author Vikas Swarup about a boy growing up in India and entering the Indian version of the gameshow *Who Wants to be a Millionaire?*

b) *Metro Manila*. A Tagalog-language crime thriller set in the Philippines, about a rice farmer who relocates his family to the Philippine capital.

c) *12 Years a Slave*. An adaption of the memoirs of an American who was kidnapped in Washington DC and sold into slavery in 1841.

d) Obviously all of them.

To count as British, and consequently get the British government to pick up a hefty share of the production's costs, a film has to get 18 points out of a possible 35. Points are awarded for fairly understandable things like "Was the film made in Britain?", but also for more nebulous criteria like does the film "reflect British heritage", does it have an "approach which values diversity", is it based on a "British story" and does it portray "British culture"?

In case that sounds like a difficult thing to prove, especially for an Indian biopic, a Filipino crime caper or a shameful slice of American history, the official guidance to the tax relief uses the 1986 film *The Mission* as an example of a film that might have "strong resonances for the development of British history, ethnicity and culture".

If it's been a while since you saw *The Mission*, it's about a Spanish

Jesuit priest attempting to convert the Guarani community of Paraguay to Christianity.

In other words, a classic bit of British heritage.

But even if your story isn't as British as the tale of the Guarani's reluctance to embrace Catholicism despite the interventions of Robert De Niro as mercenary and slaver Rodrigo Mendoza (though it's hard to imagine how it possibly couldn't be), you get six points just for getting your characters to speak English.[†]

You also get one point if one of your lead actors is British and one point if a character is British, so you're almost halfway there if you can get Judi Dench or Jason Statham to play themselves (or each other, even). Actually that might take it to nine points if you can argue that Statham's East End geezery is an example of attaching value to the experience of people of diverse backgrounds.

—

Hugo (my new boss), Mike (my new colleague), the director (who was British, which made him worth a point) and myself (British if I needed to be, but not worth any points) spent a good 20 minutes trying to squeeze a couple more Britishness points out of the director's script.

"Could a main character be British?" asked Hugo.

"It's set on the planet Wirovia," replied the director. He'd been over this with Mike already.

"Could it be on the *British* part of the planet Wirovia?"

"There isn't a British part."

"So . . . have the character listen to old recordings of British pop songs?"

_____

[†] Which is probably why so many Hollywood films are in English. I mean, what other reason could there be?

The director seemed affronted.

"This is an adaption of one of the most famous science-fiction novels of all time, set in an alternate universe, featuring ambisexual inhabitants of a distant planet – we can't just add a British colony or have the main character listen to Gerry and the Pacemakers on a Walkman."

"Even for £20 million?"

There was a long pause as the director let that sink in.

"Okay, let's do it."

—

Perhaps the most famously British film series to take advantage of this particular tax break is James Bond. It would be hard to argue that any Bond film isn't quintessentially British, what with the hard-drinking and overinflated sense of self-importance, though the intellectual property rights are owned by a company that was formerly resident in Switzerland and is now based in the US state of Delaware.

Sadly, though, Bond is not a British success story – at least not as far as can be told from looking at the accounts of EON Productions, the company that makes the films. The investigative think tank TaxWatch has pointed out that since the film scheme was introduced, EON has paid no corporation tax, as it has made no taxable profits.[†]

Indeed, the company has actually been subsidised by the UK taxpayer with at least £122 million given to it since Film Tax Relief was introduced in 2007. That seems peculiar – this is a film franchise that doesn't recognise its profits in the UK, has been running successfully

---

[†]   TaxWatch is easily my favourite tax think tank (I'm sure you have your own). Not only did they thoroughly dissect Bond's accounts, they did so under the titles *Dr No Tax* and *No Time to Pay Tax*. I've struggled to top them. *Muckraker? Windfall? A View to a Bill?*

for over 60 years, yet somehow the government thinks we should be subsidising it.[†]

The government's argument seems to be that unless the taxpayer pays for Bond films to be made in Britain, they won't be. It's all about *jobs*, you see. But that argument could be applied to literally anything. Why don't we go back to subsidising shipbuilders and steelworkers? Why doesn't the government pay for a fifth of every plumber's wage, or every lawyer's? Hell, I reckon tax authors deserve a decent subsidy.

It's not unusual for governments to subsidise certain industries that are essential to daily life – farming, energy and public transport all typically receive a little help – but are Bond films essential? Or rather, is it essential that they're made in Britain, especially if the *profits* aren't recorded here?

Daniel Craig was reported to have been paid around £18 million for each of his last two Bond films. If a fifth of that was paid by the government it seems a little peculiar. He's one of the world's richest actors, but is it the British taxpayer who's paying him?

Even more peculiarly, we only know so much about Bond's finances because the North Korean secret service hacked into the email server of Sony (which had the rights to release some of the Bond films) and published commercially sensitive documents online in revenge for Sony releasing the comedy *The Interview* (which was less than flattering about North Korea).

Sorry, I should probably add the North Korean Secret Service *allegedly* hacked into the email server, as I'm not sure the North Koreans ever admitted it.

[†] On the other hand, £122 million would get you only about 125 yards of high-speed rail built, so maybe it's great value for money? Though I have a suspicion that the Bond films would have been made even without the assistance of the British government.

—

It's not just films that get the tax break. There are similar subsidies for musicians, orchestras, theatres and "high-end" TV. I would say that this surely reflects the aesthetic tastes of the politicians who introduced the rules, but there's also a tax relief for video games.

Arguably one of the most successful products made by any entertainment company ever is the computer game Grand Theft Auto V. When it was first released in 2013 it made over $800 million in sales in just – get this – *24 hours*. Since 2013 it's thought to have made more than $6 billion. For comparison, all 12 *Star Wars* films between them have made about $10 billion, and that is over a period of 45 years.

If you're not familiar with the game, the gist is that you guide a character through a fictional American city, generally on a series of adventures, but with a free-flowing gameplay that allows you to do pretty much anything. Popular activities involve stealing cars, shooting bystanders and, if the mood takes you, murdering prostitutes. It's sold over 155 million copies.

I say Grand Theft Auto V ("GTA" to its fans) is *arguably* one of the most successful products, because another way of looking at it is that, like Bond, GTA was a failure.

GTA is published by an American company called Take-Two Interactive Software, Inc. but was developed in the UK, first by a company called DMA Design and then by Rockstar North Limited, based in Edinburgh.

Just as with films, if a computer game is culturally British its makers can claim up to 20 per cent of its development costs from HMRC. So if a game cost £10 million to make, HMRC will pay for £2 million of this amount. In theory, this £2 million will be given as a reduction on the company's corporation tax bill. But if the company is unfortunate enough to be in a loss-making position, then HMRC will simply hand the company some cash.

Rockstar North, maker of the most lucrative computer game in history – and probably the most profitable entertainment product of any description, ever – was handed more than £80 million by HMRC. And I don't mean "their corporation tax bill was reduced by £80 million", but rather, as Rockstar North paid no corporation tax, HMRC paid *them*. Those murdered prostitutes weren't going to pixelate themselves, after all; they needed a subsidy, as pretty much all the profits had been transferred outside the UK.

You might, reasonably, wonder why HMRC would help fund this game. But computer-game ethics aside, the law was that – sorry, *is* that – provided a game is culturally British then the government will pay for up to a fifth of it.

And as you may have gathered from my description of this game as one in which Americans drive around an American city, killing other Americans, it is, obviously, culturally British. Now it's possible that the British Film Institute (which also assesses games) thought that killing Americans was a sufficient part of Britain's heritage that a couple of points could be picked up from the gameplay, but it's more likely that they were swayed by Rockstar North's residence in Edinburgh. If the creative input is in Scotland, then culturally the production of the game – if not the game itself – is British.

But here's the thing. If GTA is a British game, why are none of the profits in Britain? Under international tax law, payments made to a parent company, like Take-Two Interactive Software, Inc., should be at "arm's length". So if the game was sufficiently developed in the UK to receive cash from the British authorities due to its Britishness, then a suitable amount of British profits should be declarable in Britain. But they're not. Instead, British taxpayers have subsidised the company.

It's enough to make you want to shoot some innocent bystanders.[†]

—

You might think that the Film Tax Relief scheme would be a sufficient incentive to make films in the UK, but it was actually only the *third* best tax scheme available to the film industry.

Most of my day-to-day at the film finance company wasn't vetting scripts for sufficient Britishness, much as I might have wanted it to be. Most of it was making sure that our investors lost their investments.

The film industry is perhaps uniquely ill-suited to making money, which might seem like an odd thing to say, when it clearly makes a colossal amount of cash. But whereas in pretty much every other industry the name of the game is *business*, the film industry is filled with artists, auteurs, visual poets, actors and other general poseurs (no offence). Many a cinematographer might lie awake at night imagining the rays of a morning sun dappling through autumnal leaves onto the faces of their leading actors, but few are thinking, "We should film it in Bromley to save a few quid." That's where the suits come in. It's also where I need to relight my fire about Gary Barlow.[‡]

The scheme Gary Barlow invested in was, on the surface, about

---

[†] Most of these allegations were also first made by TaxWatch UK, and neither they nor I are accusing Rockstar of doing anything illegal. Rockstar responded to the allegations by saying that the Video Games Tax Relief scheme is "forward thinking" and has helped Rockstar support over a thousand jobs. Well, yes, I imagine that if I was given 80 million quid I would say it was forward thinking and I could support over a thousand jobs too. You'd also think that the $6 billion in sales the game made could pay for a few jobs without the government's help.

[‡] I might stop trying to sneak in Take That song titles at this point. I've smuggled in 11, though I'm struggling with "Could It Be Magic?", and I'm worried that things will get weird if I try and include "Once You've Tasted Love".

helping to fund struggling musicians (rather than films, but the mechanics of the scheme are the same). For every pound Gary invested of his own money, he would invest another four pounds that he borrowed from an offshore bank. These five pounds would be mixed with other investors' money in a partnership that then paid all the invested money (after a fat fee to the organisers and the offshore bank) to a company to exploit the intellectual property of a struggling musician. It also paid a tiny bit to the struggling musician. The offshore bank at this point got nervous that their money was being used in so risky a project, so the company tasked with exploiting the intellectual property deposited the four pounds they'd received from Gary back with the first bank.

Were you following that? Gary puts in one pound of his own money into a partnership that then pays five pounds to a company, and that company gives four pounds back to the bank that had lent those four pounds to Gary.

So the partnership has spent five pounds, but received nothing back. As a partner in the partnership, Gary now has a *tax loss* of five pounds. If he was paying close to half his income as tax, he could get close to half of this tax loss back as a refund. So for every one pound he put into the partnership, he could get almost £2.50 back from the government. Or, more accurately, from all of us.

Only of course it wasn't one pound he put in. He, his bandmates Howard Donald and Mark Owen and their manager Jonathan Wild reportedly invested £66 million. Allegedly, Olympic athlete Colin Jackson, former England football manager Terry Venables and TV presenter Gabby Logan were also co-investees, as were a surprisingly large number of orthodontists.

Interestingly, not only did some of the users of this scheme claim to be the *victims* (as they'd been tricked into using a scheme that wiped out their tax bills), Prime Minister David Cameron actually defended Gary Barlow despite his party claiming to be clamping down on tax avoiders.

It happens that Gary and David are friends who have campaigned for the Conservatives together, so rather than call for Gary's OBE to be returned (as some people suggested), Cameron said that while "this scheme was wrong", Gary had also done "a huge amount for the country". By which, I think he meant, helped Cameron get elected.

One of the consequences of investors in these schemes using artificial losses to reduce their tax bills was that anti-avoidance measures were introduced to the tax rules, restricting the use of losses if the investor wasn't "active" in the business.

Hugo asked me to help make sure our clients were sufficiently active.

"They have to spend at least ten hours per week making the film, otherwise they won't be actively involved for tax purposes."

"What can they be involved *with*?"

"I don't know," said Hugo. "Didn't you say you used to work in this industry?"

I thought back to a poster that used to be on the wall of my old TV company's office. It explained what all the people on a set actually did. Only, I *think* it was satirical, as it said:

Executive Producer:	Decides where to have lunch
Assistant Producer:	Books table for lunch
Associate Producer:	Decides who to invite for lunch
Supervising Producer:	Decides where people should sit at lunch

This gave me an idea. I rang one of our clients, who was putting a lot of money but not sufficient time into a film that was destined to flop (for tax reasons).

"How would you like to have lunch on set?"

"That would be great," he replied. "Who with?"

I phrased my actual response carefully, but the real answer was simple:

"Another investor."

Hugo put his hand on my shoulder and smiled encouragingly.

"We're helping films get made!"

—

There were other ruses. It used to be common practice to buy the rights to a film (using borrowed money) and then lease back those rights to the actual film producers over a period of 15 years. In theory this didn't save any tax – it merely deferred it. But if it got a client out of paying a million quid now they were usually keen to sign up to it – as they could invest that million into something that would actually make money, and use the income from the investment to pay the original tax bill as it came due, with a bit left over.

The main thing my company marketed, though, were Enterprise Investment Schemes. To understand what these are, we really need to go back to 1985, and at the risk of sounding weird, to 88mph.

By the time *Back to the Future* was released in cinemas, the DeLorean Motor Company had already gone bust. This was obviously embarrassing for John DeLorean, who had set the company up only a few years earlier, but it was more embarrassing for the British government (both James Callaghan's Labour administration and Margaret Thatcher's Conservative one), as they had sunk almost £80 million of subsidies into the company – and that's £80 million in 1980s money, when a Mars Bar cost just 15p (and was a bit bigger).

The government's logic was that the economy was in the doldrums, taxes were high and unemployment was higher. So how to raise money and boost employment? Why, by pouring money into one entrepreneur's idea for an all-steel gullwing sporty-looking car with an underpowered engine made in Northern Ireland.

John DeLorean offered to employ 2,500 people. *Wonderful*, said Callaghan and Thatcher, *have some cash*.

How's your maths? Is it better than Callaghan's? The £80 million subsidy given to DeLorean divided by the 2,500 people employed by DeLorean is £32,000 per job (or over £100,000 in today's money). And none of these jobs lasted long, as the company went bust. It turns out, shock horror, that politicians are really bad at picking the right horse (or car) to back.

It didn't help that the car was crap, either. The producers of *Back to the Future* used the noise of a Porsche's engine instead of the DeLorean's to make it sound more powerful, and swapped out the engine for a Volkswagen's when they needed it to drive in more challenging terrain.

But you can kind of see the government's logic. The engine of economic growth really is successful businesses. If you want lifestyles to improve and people to get jobs and wealth to be created you really do need businesses to grow. So it's not crazy that the government would want to support them. But most new businesses fail – by some measures 90 per cent of new businesses fail in their first three years. The question is, which businesses should be supported?

The solution the government eventually came up with was to leave that decision to individual investors. If you're going to risk your own money, the thinking went, you will probably put the effort into checking whether the business you want to back has a sound business plan (rather than, say, a plan to build a car that travels back in time at inconvenient moments).

So the British government created the Enterprise Investment Scheme. If a company qualified for the scheme the investor in that scheme could claim back some cash from the government. Currently, the most generous version of this allows any investor to claim back *half* their investment. i.e. if you bought a share in a new company for £100, the government would hand you £50. Furthermore, if you happen to have invested in the new Facebook, and your share becomes worth £100 million, you won't pay any tax on that increase in value (and nor will your heirs). Or if, as is more likely, the share becomes worthless, the government will give you another £20 or so to compensate you for your loss.

There are three things to say about these schemes.

The first is that this is an amazing, official, tax break. It really does encourage people to invest in speculative start-ups and give businesses a kick-start.[†]

The second is that the people who most benefit from this – apart from the small businesses who find it easier to raise cash – are the people rich enough to sink hundreds of thousands of pounds into speculative ventures. Because obviously rich people need tax breaks.

And the third is that this was a tax scheme ripe for exploitation. I mean, screw these convoluted loss-making film partnerships, here was an official government tax-avoidance scheme.

—

[†] I was in one pitch meeting listening to the CEO selling her new business's fantastic plans to a potential investor, when the investor interrupted her and asked, "Are you registered with the Enterprise Investment Scheme?" I told him they were. "Great" he said, "then I'll invest." He didn't even listen to the rest of the pitch. If you fancy playing *Dragon's Den* yourself, then check out seedrs.com, where new "EIS" registered companies seek funding. They're mostly companies that make yoghurt drinks and fitness apps, but maybe those are the next big thing?

I know I've been a bit cagey about the name of the company I was working for, probably for obvious reasons, but you've almost definitely seen its name more than once. When I was a kid a movie would start with something like "20th Century-Fox", or that woman in a toga holding a torch, or "Universal" swinging around the Earth (which is an odd juxtaposition, if you think about it), and then the film would start. Whereas nowadays you have to sit through a dozen or so snazzy logos – "Joyless Films Presents a PandaCoitus Production, in association with Guzzlick Films, Phlegmborough Media, Iveryacht H&H . . ." Why are they there? Why do we care about them? What are they?

Accountants. That's what they are. Accountants did that to your film.

—

Mike told me he was leaving the company. This was sad news as we'd hung out after work a few times, mostly in the nightclub in the basement of the building we worked in. We'd even had a drink on a couple of occasions with the ageing punk rocker who'd held the door open for me on my first day – it turned out he made most of his money doing voice-overs for children's cartoons.

Anyway, I asked Mike why he was leaving.

"I can't help but feel that all we're doing is saving rich people tax."

"Aren't we 'helping films get made'? I mean, I got twenty investors to be extras last week." Though I felt compelled to add, "For all of ten hours."

"I'm going to go back to university to study proteins."

I had a real pang of envy. He knew what he wanted to do with his life. He knew it wasn't helping rich people pay less tax. And he would get to go back to university, which was a lot more fun than submitting EIS forms.

"When are you going to leave?"

He'd thought about that too.

"Not till the end-of-year bonus."

His moral compass may have been better than mine, but he was no fool.

I wondered if I should leave too.

—

In the short time I worked at the film finance company, all of the films we helped finance successfully lost money. With one exception.

An obscure, low-budget film we financed had unexpectedly, and very definitely against the odds, won an Oscar. The resultant publicity suddenly meant that people actually paid to go and see it. My company didn't have much experience of dealing with real profits, and Hugo suggested that I email all the investors to suggest a meeting about what we should do with the cash.

I invited all the unexpectedly profitable investors to our offices to discuss what we should do next. I wondered if I should ask the nightclub downstairs if we could use their space, just to accommodate everyone. There were about 60 investors in total.

But basement nightclubs are a lot grottier during the daytime, so I decided as I hadn't had many responses to my email to the investors, I would simply hold the meeting in one of the larger rooms in the office.

The meeting was due to start at 11am. I was rather excited about hosting it – I'd never hosted a meeting with clients before. By 11.20am only one old lady had turned up. At 11.30am I suggested that we start.

"Do you have any ideas about what you would like the profits to be spent on?" I asked her. I had prepared a pamphlet of all the possibilities. She had a copy in front of her. So did I. I had another 58 spare.

"Could we make a sequel?" she suggested.

"I'm not sure there's enough money to do that, I'm afraid. Also all the characters died at the end of the film."

"Oh? I never saw it."

We agreed to pay a dividend and wind the company up.

—

Despite him costing me a teenage snog, I have a little bit of sympathy for Gary Barlow. The scheme he invested in was obviously a massive tax dodge, but at least it had the redeeming feature of supporting up-and-coming musical acts.

The same can't be said of a scheme called Liberty, which involved purchasing the rights to a Cayman Island company's dividends, claiming a tax loss for doing so, and then somehow arguing that the dividends subsequently received weren't part of a taxable trade – or, in layman's terms, doing some dodgy stuff with tax havens.[†]

Liberty's investors included pop stars George Michael and Katie Melua (who had previously been nominated by Christian Aid to receive their "Tax Superhero award"), consumer champion Anne Robinson, actor Michael Caine and four of the rockers the Arctic Monkeys (though the band have said they pulled out of it before they avoided any tax).

All of them have since either apologised or blamed their naivety, or their accountants, and they've all now paid their taxes in full (though that's partly because the £1.2 billion tax-avoidance scheme was defeated in court, so they had to pay up or they'd go to prison). The easy reaction, and probably the more fun one, is to think, *What a bunch of amoral responsibility shirkers.* But remember that the accountants who pushed

---

[†]   The Liberty scheme is unrelated to the pop band Liberty X, who used an entirely different scheme called Tower M Cashback.

these schemes all got paid a handsome fee – cumulatively often running into the millions of pounds.[†]

And most of these schemes got defeated in court, meaning the celebs ending up paying back their taxes on top of the fees they'd paid to join the scheme. Indeed, several hundred of them (including Sir Alex Ferguson and Lord (Andrew) Lloyd Webber) banded together to sue HSBC for misleading them (they alleged the bank played a role in developing and marketing a failed film scheme), and 500 of them decided to sue the company that had promoted the scheme to them, claiming they hadn't had the risks fully explained to them. The risk being that HMRC didn't allow them to deduct artificial losses because that's a really dodgy thing to do.

Then again, some schemes were straightforward Enterprise Investment Schemes – which the government actively encourages. And sometimes the film scheme promoters won their cases in court (sometimes *after* HMRC had made the investors pay back their tax breaks).

At the very least it's a little confusing. Again, maybe it's meant to be.

If all I was concerned about in this book was the word count, I could probably fill it with a list of names of other famous people who have been splashed across newspaper front pages for having invested in various film or music or other finance schemes that have been dragged through

---

[†]   *The Guardian* claimed that Patrick McKenna, the founder of one of the biggest promoters of film finance schemes, a company called Ingenious Media, was worth £400 million. He has brought a case against HMRC for briefing against him, after a senior executive at HMRC described film partnership schemes as "scams for scumbags". McKenna has stated that he is "not in the business of tax avoidance", that his investment schemes are wholly legitimate and that, to quote the film director Stephen Frears "the true heroes of films are the investors". And in fairness, he has won some of his biggest cases against HMRC.

the courts, like David Beckham, Jeremy Paxman, Ant & Dec (who, apparently, HMRC wrote to as "Dear Ant & Dec", before it was pointed out to them that they were two different people), Robbie Williams, Gary Lineker, three Spice Girls, Sacha Baron Cohen, Davina McCall, Craig David, Neil Morrissey, Kate Adie, Peter Gabriel and Phillip Schofield, at least one former Solicitor General and *literally* more than a thousand others.[†]

But here's the thing – they could all use the same excuse. The schemes weren't illegal and they followed the advice of their accountants. And some of them really were helping films get made. Indeed if, by the time you read this, David Beckham has been knighted, it will be because HMRC has given him the all-clear as officially not a tax dodger. Not that, if he hasn't been knighted, it means he *is* a tax dodger. For the avoidance of doubt, I'm not accusing any of the people here listed of having done anything criminal.

—

Not long after Mike had left, I was faced with a dilemma.

Sasha, the girl I was seeing, told me that she had accepted a new job.

"That's fantastic!" I told her. "What's the job?"

She was very coy about telling me.

"Well, it's actually a new *role* at my current firm," she said.

I had thought that she was keen to leave her current firm as soon as her training contract expired, like I had been. I told her so.

"I *am* leaving," she said.

"I'm not sure I understand."

So she came out with it.

[†] I'm guessing non-British readers will have heard of perhaps five of these people. But they're all irritatingly famous in the UK.

"My new role is to audit Australian companies."

I didn't quite click . . . "How many Australian companies are there in London?"

And then she looked at me the way a dog-owner might look at a puppy that had caught its leash around a lamppost.

"Oh . . ." I said.

I'd never really thought about emigrating to Australia. True, I had a couple of friends who had moved out there around the time I decided to become an accountant and whenever I spoke to them (which admittedly, due to the 11-hour time difference, was rarely) they *raved* about it. The image they projected was of surfing, and "barbies", and generally spending their whole lives in shorts. A quarter of Australia's population was born overseas, and they suggested that this created a culture of friendliness and openness to strangers.

Not that it was clear that Sasha was inviting me to join her. I asked her if she wanted me to come with her.

"If you want to." She said. I spent more time analysing those four words than analysing the entirety of the Film Tax Relief legislation.

I skyped my friends in Australia and jokingly asked if I could stay in their spare room if things didn't work out with Sasha. They agreed.

Then I rang the recruiter who had got me this film finance job and told him I was planning to move on. He was a little miffed, as I'd been in the job for such a short time that he had to pay part of the recruitment fee he had received back to the company.

To dissuade me, he decided to tell me how I might struggle to get another job.

"I never told you how bad your references were," he said, far too maliciously.

"What do you mean?" I'd given him the contact details of two people at my old firm – one was Wilhelm, and one was Penelope, my manager, so that they could vouch for me.

"The one from Wilhelm was okay. But Penelope said – I quote: 'He often turns up late, doesn't really apply himself and often looks scruffy.'"

"And yet they still offered me a job?"

"What? No, I didn't show them the reference from Penelope."

"So what did you do?"

"I told them I'd lost it."

Maybe it wasn't just my industry that incentivised people to present one particular version of the truth.

Weirdly, the next time I spoke to that recruiter he'd be much, much friendlier.

6

RORTING ON THE BEACH

When I worked in TV – back before I became an accountant – I had a conversation with a production assistant who asked me if I knew anything about a nightclub called Koko that had just opened in Camden Town. She told me that she was keen to go to it.

About two hours later the office phone rang and I answered.

The woman on the other end of the phone said, "Hello, I'm calling from a new nightclub called Koko and I'm offering free tickets to people who work for TV companies, would you be interested?"

Until I took a job in Australia that had been the biggest coincidence of my life. (I'm not counting it as a coincidence that I quit my job at my old firm almost to the day that the global economy crashed in the great credit crunch, as I suspect the two are somehow linked.)

—

While the decision to move out to Australia was a challenge, getting a job was a doddle. Even though I had zero Australian tax knowledge, and even though it was the tail end of 2009 and what had started as the credit crunch had escalated into a full-scale global depression (I suspect you remember it), with hundreds of thousands of people being laid off across every industry, one profession was still doing all right.

The global financial crash had created some giant opportunities for tax advisors, as it had created some *genuine* losses, and losses meant tax savings, and tax savings mean advisory fees. If anything, there weren't enough accountants to go around.

My recruiter was delighted to hear from me. He had never been busier – companies that were suffering in the recession needed accountants to help them cut costs, companies that were going bankrupt needed accountants to act as their administrators and liquidators. And companies (and people) with those juicy losses needed accountants to conjure their magic and create some tax savings.[†]

Talking to my recruiter felt rather like rekindling a romance with a jilted lover who had, when we last broke up, pointed out all my faults. But now we laughed at each other's jokes and shared our optimism for the future and whispered sweet nothings (though mostly these nothings were promotion prospects).

I told him I wanted to move to Australia. He told me he had just the job for me.

—

[†] You've probably heard about companies being bought "for a pound" or "for a dollar", and as a kid this always seemed crazy to me. I mean, I had a spare pound, could I buy some failing company? Of course, what was really going on was that these companies owed far more money to banks than they had available to pay, so were going spectacularly bust. The buyers were agreeing to pay off the debts. This is where the administrators and liquidators come in. Administrators have the job of keeping a company *alive*, liquidators simply of selling everything a company owns. Usually, even after selling everything, there is not enough cash to pay all debts, so there is a strict legal order that determines who gets paid first, second, third, etc. Want to guess who always gets paid before everyone else? Yup, the accountants.

Before I go on I need to ask you a quick question about morality. I'll keep it brief. How much money would you need to be paid to compromise your ethical principles? For instance, say you are vegetarian (for purely ideological reasons), how much cash would it take to make you eat a delicious bacon roll? How much would you need to vote for a political party you hated? You might instinctively think, *There's no amount of cash*, but that itself would be an immoral answer, wouldn't it? If someone gave you a billion pounds (or dollars or whatever) just to bite into that crispy, salty, succulent meat or vote for the *other* party, you could always use that billion to help an awful lot of good causes, maybe even run an ad campaign for your preferred party, or rescue some pigs.

Or what if, say, the moral issue was a bit more hazy, like would you work for a mining company with a less than perfect human rights record? We all need the stuff that gets mined, and couldn't you do more good on the inside rather than just getting miffed reading articles in the paper about a lack of mine safety in far-off countries? Again, what if you used the money you were paid to help the needy? And what if the needy were children? What if they were *your* children? What if they hadn't been born yet, but when they did get born you wanted them to have an easy, comfortable life? And what if, to get to the point where some woman thought you were the future father of her children, you needed to impress her with what an easy, comfortable life you already had? And what if the money you were offered was three times what you were making before?

Like I say, it's a moral maze.

—

For many years, large-scale corporate efforts to avoid paying tax had been mostly reliant on the advice of the Big 4 accountancy firms, often with the support of the large banks. But gradually the legal world was waking up to the fact that taxes are based on laws, and laws are what lawyers are particularly good at. It seemed daft to leave the manipulation of these laws to accountants.

My recruiter explained that there was a South African law firm that had been expanding aggressively internationally and was now looking for accountants to join its new corporate advisory team in Australia.

As I had officially worked in business taxes for a few years and had a brief stint in what was effectively one big front for tax avoidance, I seemed to fit the bill perfectly. Of course *unofficially* the only productive hours I had in business taxes were working for Wilhelm in personal taxes and I'm not sure filling out Enterprise Investment Scheme application forms quite qualified me for international tax subterfuge, but no matter. I was posh and willing to lie about my achievements. In other words, perfect corporate lawyer material.

I'd never considered working for a law firm, but I was assured that it wouldn't be much different from working for an accountancy firm. My face must have fallen because the recruiter added, "I mean it's very different. The whole culture is different. The lawyers are all so charming. You'll love it."

We both knew he was lying, but we both wanted it to work.

He told me the name of the firm and arranged an interview.

The law firm's website tripped over itself to demonstrate how they were one of the *good* law firms. They sponsored educational programmes for deprived children, hosted pro bono drop-in centres in underprivileged neighbourhoods, and supported cultural institutions in every city in which they operated (which was about a dozen). Maybe I should have stopped reading there. But I didn't want to get caught out again in a job interview. If my Australian tax knowledge wasn't (yet) great, then at least I could show an understanding of what this law firm actually did.

There was a case studies section. There were beautiful photos of rainforests, and accompanying text on the great work the law firm did on sustainability. There were smiling construction workers in hard hats, with a blurb about health and safety. And there was a photo of the stunning Australian outback, under which the website described the work the firm did on understanding the land rights of indigenous peoples, in particular a case about Aboriginal Australians claiming the rights to an area of desert that had recently been found to be very resource-rich. An international mining company claimed that the land was not, in legal fact, owned by the indigenous people who lived there (I think on the grounds that the mining company got there first).

This all sounded great. I could live in Australia, learn to surf, get paid some decent cash and brag about working on sustainability, indigenous land rights and, um, health and safety.

You may well have realised already what I only realised later – frankly, too much later.

Sustainability was the enemy. Logging companies were trying to cut costs and environmental commitments are expensive. Health and safety checks slow down construction projects, which is especially galling in those parts of the world where concrete costs more than labourers. And the indigenous people were not this firm's clients. The mining company was.

By the time it became apparent that most of the firm's clients had at various stages been Bond villains (I'm not ruling out the possibility that some of them had built space-lasers), I was already settled into a new routine of having my barista-made coffee brought to me each morning at a desk that looked out over the city from 20 floors up.

And the firm was at pains to point out that *everyone* deserves legal representation, even Bond villains.

—

You may know that Australia has long had a "points-based" visa system for immigrants. In short, a bit like proving a film is British by tallying up sufficient points, I had to prove that I was a suitable candidate to be allowed into Australia. What seemed to be worth more points than just about anything else was the answer to the question, *Do you have a skill that is on the official "skills shortage" list?* – i.e. did I have a talent that Australia lacked, or at least needed more of? Accountancy was number two on the list. That meant Australia needed accountants. That meant I was going to be let in.[†]

There was one more thing I did before leaving England – something I bet most people don't think of when they emigrate, but it was something that saved me enough cash to buy a small car. If you think that what follows is a little nerdy, and maybe a little dry, here's a sweetener: I'm going to try and save *you* a similar sum of cash towards the end of this book.

In almost every country where taxes are deducted from your pay packet by your employer (which almost definitely means in *your* country, wherever you are), your tax-free allowances are split evenly across the year. That is, the amount of your income that you don't have to pay tax on is calculated on a month-by-month basis, so that you pay

---

[†] In case you're wondering, the number one most in-demand profession – i.e. the profession that had the skillset that the Australian government deemed most lacking in Australia – was hairdressers. I booked a haircut before I left.

the same amount of tax each month, rather than paying no tax for the first few months and then loads of tax once you've lost your allowance.[†]

This is one of those fiddly and annoying and a little bit boring aspects of tax that help give tax a bad name. I bet if I gave you the choice of either looking at your payslip to work out your monthly deductions or sitting back on the sofa and watching a bit of Netflix, you'd pick the TV option every time. In fact, if it was a choice of looking at your payslip and *any other activity* I suspect the *other* would win. But this might be where you and I differ.

I not only checked my payslip, I called my local tax office.

"I'm leaving the UK," I told a friendly sounding woman who eventually picked up the phone, "so I guess I've been overpaying my taxes . . . can I get a refund?"

I wasn't actually guessing, of course. And I knew what her next question would be. I had prepared my answer.

"When do you plan on returning to the UK?"

Now, technically, I already had my return plane ticket. I knew the date of it. But in my defence the return flight was only a few pounds more expensive than a one-way ticket and I didn't *intend* to use it. I was going to live a long and wonderful life with Sasha and raise beautiful Australian children.

[†]   For instance in the UK you have a "personal allowance" of a bit over £12,000, meaning you pay no income tax on the first £12,000ish of your income, but this is given to you as an allowance of just over £1,000 per *month,* so if you received £12,000 in your pay packet in the first month of the year, you would pay tax on £11,000 of it. You could, in theory, get this tax back (but you might not). The equivalent in Australia is the tax-free threshold, which is a little over $18,000, which is lower than the UK threshold. Though I feel most for Americans, where the thresholds for where you start paying tax depend on the state you live in and your local municipality and whether you're married (and in some situations, up to a dozen other things, too).

"I have no plans to return," I said.

That's what the HMRC official needed to hear. By law, I should have been a tax resident in England for the whole tax year. But HMRC had announced that anyone who leaves permanently can, by concession, be treated as becoming non-resident the day they leave. Effectively I was telling the tax office that I had been taxed on a monthly basis and wanted to be taxed on a yearly basis instead, but I also wanted my "year" to end the day I left.

My plan to remain in Australia forever was, I should make clear, absolutely *nothing* to do with tax. But if I hadn't called HMRC, my income in Australia would have been subject to UK tax, too, at least until the end of the tax year, which would have cost me another couple of thousand. As such, altogether that one phone call saved me about £3,000 (so maybe a *second-hand* small car).

The fact that I didn't end up staying in Australia was, obviously, not something I could have foreseen at the time.

—

I've just mentioned tax years, but it may not be obvious what I was referring to – even if you're an accountant. Indeed, when, in the morning of 6 April this year, I sent a WhatsApp to my boss that said, "Happy New Year!" she replied with, "Are you drunk?"[†]

Most countries have tax years (i.e. the time period for which you calculate your tax) that are the same as calendar years. Australia – being in the southern hemisphere – has a 30 June year-end, to avoid clashing with long summer holidays taken in December.

But Britain, being eccentric, has a 5 April year-end – due to (hold your breath, this is the longest sentence in this book) the new year

---

[†] I *was*, but I was still a little hurt.

originally being in spring, then being fixed on 25 March (as this was already a festival, specifically the Feast of the Annunciation, which is the celebration of the archangel Gabriel telling Mary that she was pregnant – nine months before Christmas), but because the medieval calendar was based on a 365.25-day year and not the more accurate 365.2425-day year, Pope Gregory revised the calendar in 1582, however because (in case you didn't know) the Pope is Catholic, and England wasn't Catholic, England refused to make the switch to the Gregorian calendar until 1752, by which point there was a ten-day difference between the two calendars, which meant the UK government would miss out on ten days of tax revenues unless they moved the tax year-end to 4 April.

Strewth, that was a 157-word sentence and it still doesn't answer the question of why Brits have a 5 April year-end. The extra day is because the year 1800 wasn't a leap year in the new Gregorian calendar but was one in the Old Style calendar (which had been created by Julius Caesar), so there was a final one-day fudge to get a bit more tax revenue.

As I write there are plans to get rid of this April anomaly, but I'm guessing the government will make sure it doesn't lose out on any tax.

—

To begin with, most of the work I was asked to do in my new job was fairly routine. A lot of wealthy Australians had lost money as global stock markets tanked and they were taking the opportunity to sell their assets at a loss (usually just enough assets were sold to offset gains they'd accrued on other things), then repurchasing those same assets via a Singaporean company. Singapore charges no capital gains tax, so effectively the wealth was shifted to a regime that wouldn't tax that wealth, and shifted in such a way as to avoid tax.

In the UK there are so called "anti-avoidance" provisions to prevent a Brit owning an asset through an offshore company in order to circumvent the tricky issue of legally owning the asset, and consequently shirking responsibility for paying taxes on that asset. I asked the Australian lawyers if there were similar laws in Australian statute.

"This is absolutely fine, mate, don't worry about it."

That didn't *exactly* answer my question about the legality of what we were doing, but I followed their advice and didn't worry about it.

In truth, the main reason I didn't worry about it was that I was desperately scrambling to get up to speed with Australian tax rules.

To get the job in the first place I had to demonstrate a detailed understanding of the differences between UK taxes and Australian ones. Luckily, the Australian tax system is broadly based on the British one – as indeed are many of the world's tax systems (though an inherently corrupt tax system is hardly the worst legacy of our empire), but even more luckily there was a "featured" (meaning "very thorough") article on Wikipedia called "The Australian Tax System".[†]

A quick scan through the article was enough to bluff my way through the interview, even though, as with my interview at the Japanese firm, we were joined by telephone by a tax expert on the other side of the world – the head of department at the Australian office. Unlike the Japanese International Head of Tax who had interviewed me before, this guy actually wanted to ask me questions about, well, tax.

[†] Though now I come to think of it, maybe a tax system that entrenches wealth in the hands of a tiny minority and allows that wealth to be shifted anonymously around the world, while preventing "normal" people from accumulating capital *is* one of the worst legacies of empire? Seven out of the ten largest accountancy firms in the world are British, but we're not going to tackle inequality or undermine despots or have any coral reefs left unless they help us make capitalism a bit more honest.

"What do you think of the Laffer?" he asked.

What the fuck was a Laffer? I'd heard of the *Laffer curve*, which is the theory that if the tax rate was 0 per cent then the government would collect no taxes, but if the tax rate was 100 per cent then the government would also collect no taxes, because nobody would do any work, so there must be some sweet spot between zero taxes and 100 per cent taxes where taxes raise the most amount – which also suggests that sometimes the best thing to do for everybody is to lower the tax rate.

But I got the impression that he wasn't asking me about economic theory.

"I think it's very interesting," I said.

"D'you think it's a good idea?"

"Well, obviously it has its detractors, and it will be interesting to see any changes that occur in future."

"But do you think it's fair that you'll pay less tax as a Pom than I will as an Australian?"

At this point one of the interviewers, who was in the room with me and had introduced herself as from HR, leaned forward to speak clearly into the phone: "I think we should make clear that *Pom* is a term of endearment." She smiled nervously at me.

I still had no idea what a Laffer was, but I liked the sound of it meaning I would pay less tax.

"Well . . . I trust in the wisdom of the Australian government."

Everyone laughed. The Australian on the phone laughed the most. And then, thank the Great Dingo, the conversation moved on.

—

He'd actually said LAFHA.

There is a great rivalry between Sydney and Melbourne (despite there being a nine-hour drive between them). Both cities are a similar size (about five million people) with all the potential infrastructure to be a national capital. They're very different. Sydney – or at least, the rich, coastal parts of it – is like the handsome jock at high school: good-looking, outdoorsy, popular, not that into trendy bars but happy to get smashed at the weekend. He doesn't read many books but loves to surf.

Melbourne is the cool gal who smokes a bit of weed and knows who all the best bands are (if only they'd ever play in Australia). She dresses fashionably but as if she's not trying to, and writes a bit of poetry in her spare time.

Or at least, that's how one Australian explained this to me. He was from Melbourne, so perhaps he was biased. But I'm not disagreeing with him.

Anyway, both cities wanted to be the capital city and, unable to resolve the argument, the Australians decided to create a whole new city (and a whole new territory) just to be a seat of government, which is pretty much why Canberra exists.[†]

But here's the problem: who in their right mind would want to live there? If you're a jock you pick Sydney and if you're cool you go for Melbourne, so why settle in some newly built micro-city miles from the sea?

Tax, that's why.

To encourage people to move to Canberra the Australian government created a Living Away From Home Allowance (or LAFHA)

[†] The Australian government states that "Canberra" means "meeting place" in the local Ngunnawal language. Some Ngunnawal people have suggested "cleavage" is a better translation.

that gave generous tax breaks to anyone who, well, lived away from home.

At least, this is the potted history I was given at a conference on the LAFHA in my first week of my new job, which was held, in true tax-avoidance style, in the ballroom of a casino.[†]

The official conference title was pretty dry – it was something about new legislative changes – but the subtext was quickly made clear: "rorting" the LAFHA.

There's a lot of great local lingo in Australia. Most of it involves beer. But *rorting* was one of my favourite words. It sounds so dirty. It sounds fun. It means "engaging in sharp practice". Not quite being illegal, perhaps, but hardly being a stickler for the rules, either.

"The legislation allows any *reasonable* costs of living to be reimbursed by your employer – tax free for the employ*ee* and tax free for the employ*er*. But a strict reading of the rules means you can go a long way with *reasonable*."

The speaker explained that instead of receiving a taxable salary, I could get my employer to pay for a *reasonable* rent – but reasonable didn't mean the actual rent I was paying, but the kind of rent I might pay if I really pushed the boat out (and pushing a boat out was something I could reasonably be expected to do from the boathouse of my hypothetically rented new pad). And not just rent – food was covered too, and entertainment. The conference speaker explained that pretty much any entertainment would do. He used the example of hiring a jet ski – "salary sacrifice that too".

[†] Officially the tax break was to help servicemen returning from the Second World War to find work, and they didn't have to move to Canberra to get the tax break (just anywhere away from their usual home), though a lot of them did.

As salary sacrificing (i.e. having the expense paid for by your boss rather than receiving a salary) saved the employer payroll taxes, employers were just as keen as their staff to take advantage of the LAFHA. In theory receipts needed to be provided, but they rarely seemed to be checked – it became routine at the end of a meal for everyone present to ask for their own copy of the bill, so that they could each claim they'd paid for all of it – waiting staff would often ask how many copies were wanted when the bill was requested.

Obviously I never claimed for a bill that someone else was also claiming for: that would be illegal.

The cost of the tax break to the Australian Taxation Office rose from $162 million in 2005 to $740 million in 2011. And a great deal of that went to expats, who became cheaper for Australian employers to hire than actual Australians, which must go some way to explaining how I got a job there. Eventually the Australian government got wise to the rorting, and considerably tightened up the scheme.

—

I'm getting ahead of myself. On my very first night in the country, I started wondering if I'd made a mistake in moving out to Australia. Sasha told me that she was having an evening out with her new colleagues, so wouldn't be able to meet me off the plane.

Instead, I met up with my old friends who had moved over from England a few years earlier. We went to a bar and drank some *bevvies* and everything was perfectly normal until my two friends started having a minor row with each other. Sitting next to our table had been two men, but one of them had got up to go to the bar, or the *dunny*, or wherever, leaving one guy on his own. As my friends were otherwise engaged and this chap was all alone I casually said hello to him. This, in itself, is slightly uncharacteristic behaviour for me. But then he said, "Cool shoes" and I realised that we both had the exact same trainers on. This is not – I should quickly add – the amazing coincidence I alluded to earlier.

We then laughed about what great taste in shoes we both had, and he noticed that I was from England. He asked why I was visiting Australia. I told him I had just got a new job. He asked what the job was. I told him.

And then he called me by my name.

It turned out that I was chatting with the same guy who had asked me about the LAFHA in my job interview, meaning the first Australian I spoke to (outside customs in the airport) was the same Australian who had given me this job in Australia and was to be my boss.

I appreciate that this isn't really an aside about tax, and I'm not saying that I'm especially superstitious or that I really believe that this was Beelzebub taunting me like a scene in *The Devil's Advocate*, but it was pretty freaky.

All right, fine, I do wonder if he was the devil. When Sasha eventually arrived she took quite a shine to him.

—

Most of my new job involved dressing smartly, escorting the finance directors of large companies into our high-end offices, making small talk about cricket and then sitting politely as my boss explained how they could, ahem, restructure their affairs so that they paid less tax. I understood more about the tax than about the cricket, but that's not saying much.[†]

My boss – the one who had asked me about the LAFHA in my job interview, and had the same shoes as me, and may or may not have been

---

[†]   The only time I've been to Lord's I completely lost track of the match, then wondered why no one was cheering the sixes. "Which one is Middlesex?" I asked my friend. He rolled his eyes. "They're on a break. These are schoolkids."

Satan, and Sasha thought was rather *spunky* – was actually a really nice guy, or, dare I say it, a mate. He was called Hal.

Hal had a directness and frankness that was refreshing to me as a Brit, but also educational in terms of how to deal with recalcitrant clients.

One company director in particular seemed to be looking for every reason *not* to sign up to our firm.

"I appreciate this is legal," he said, having had the legality of Hal's suggestions reiterated in every possible form, "but is it *ethical?*"

This was the first time in almost five years of being an accountant that I'd heard a client ask this question. Maybe Hal had been asked this before, as he had a reply up his (short) sleeves.

"Mate, you've got a fiduciary duty to your shareholders to maximise their wealth. It's unethical *not* to take every tax saving you can."

The director looked unconvinced.

"I'm the sole shareholder," he said.

But Hal had a response to that, too.

"You've also got a duty to your employees. If your company goes bust because you've run out of money because you've handed it all to the taxman, then your employees won't be able to feed their kiddos, and that'll be on you."

Ah yes, *think of the children.*

Luckily that director *did* think of the children, and signed up with our firm.

What I most liked about Hal, other than his taste in shoes, was his complete imperviousness to danger. This may have been a typically Australian trait – on the ferry ride over to his part of town the captain of the boat announced, "Lifejackets under your seats, beers at the back of the boat" as if both were of equal utility in the event of a storm.

Though given how frequently drunken sailors needed rescuing from the harbour this may possibly have been official guidance.

We once sat in Hal's garden drinking what I think were "frosties" but may have been "stubbies" (or could have been both) and I asked him if he'd ever seen a funnel-web spider. I asked, because I'd read that one bite could kill a man in 15 minutes.

"Ah mate, just have a dig under the bushes there if you wanna see one." He then proceeded to demonstrate, shifting a few tufts of grass with his fingers to get a good look.

On another occasion we went wake-boarding in an estuary. He told me to ignore the sign that said, "Do not enter the water. Crocodiles. Risk of Death."

"Wrong time of year for croccies," he assured me.[†]

But mostly he felt no sense of danger about whether any of the advice we were giving our clients would be coming back to bite us (like an out-of-season crocodile).

"Things are done differently in Australia, mate."

By way of example he explained that if ever we were late submitting a form to the tax office, while in Britain we would receive an automatic fine, in Australia the tax office accepted the late submission as long as you had a reasonable excuse. But the fun part was that it had to be an *original* excuse – the thinking was that, if your dog ate your homework, then you should leave your next homework out of sight of your dog.

He duly kept a list of all the various excuses he'd made for not submitting legal paperwork on time. He'd been through the obvious ones – fire, flood, theft, crocodiles – leaving me to use my imagination.

[†]   We went on this wake-boarding trip during working hours. Hal seemed relaxed about the risk of us getting in trouble. "I'll get my secretary to say we're at a client meeting," he said. He used this ruse this a lot.

I rather chickened out and scribbled "unforeseen circumstances" as my "excuse". Hal seemed very disappointed with me.

—

I don't know if you noticed, because it seemed so minor, but something rather significant just happened. I'm not sure even I noticed it, at least not the first time round. Increasingly, as I progressed through my career, the amount of responsibility I took on increased. The amount of autonomy given to me increased. The amount of culpability I had for the rorting increased.

Who could say that circumstances weren't really unforeseen? Had I crossed a line?

Tax still felt like a game. No one was downright lying, right? And as long as no one was doing anything the wrong side of legal, what was the problem?

I mentioned this to Hal.

"Everything's more relaxed out here, mate. You ever heard of *Bottom of the Harbour* scams?"

I hadn't.

"They were the biggest tax scandal in history, and you wanna know how many people went to prison over them?"

"Was it zero?"

"Too flamin' right."

Hal had his theories about why the Australian tax system was so similar to the British one, and it was debating the history and philosophy of tax that really formed the basis of our friendship.[†]

My take on it was that every time there has been a major reform of

---

[†]   I assume this is true of most friendships.

tax policy in Australia, the Australians – whether it was the early governors or more recent governments – had to come up with fresh ideas. The easiest place to look for ideas on tax is to examine what other countries are already doing. And the easiest countries to examine are those where their tax rules are written in the same language as the one you speak.

That was my entire theory – that Australia has similar legislation to the UK because we can read each other's rules. [†]

This theory doesn't hold for America (which has a mind-boggling array of deductions, alternative minimum rates and special deals for military veterans), but then America won its independence off the back of its "no taxation without representation" slogan, so their founding fathers had to make a point of being different, tax-wise.

"Nah, mate, that's not how it is," said Hal. He had a different theory. I worry that you'll like his theory more than mine.

"No one ever created a tax rule that makes themselves worse off, and the people in power in Australia have usually been, like the people in power in Britain, the *rich*."

Hal knew his history. Starting right at the beginning, back in 1788, the British gave Governor Arthur Phillip of the First Fleet autonomous tax-raising powers (which makes sense, as it took two years to get a response to a message between Britain and Australia), so being an enlightened man he introduced the world's first tax on governors.

"I'm kidding. He actually taxed booze."

[†]   It might sound like I'm being somewhat frivolous, but in each report into Australian tax reform I've read there is a section on, effectively, how the Brits do it, but not on, say, what the Finnish do.

His justification (other than to reduce drunkenness) was to build a prison – though once the prison was built, true to form, he kept the tax on booze.

Of course, taxes on alcohol are common worldwide, but they tend to affect the poorest far more than the richest, simply because alcohol takes up a greater proportion of a poorer person's expenditure. Hal wasn't saying that poorer people drink more (and certainly not more than *him*), but rather that a poorer person spending the exact same amount on beer as a richer person will be spending a greater proportion of their wealth on beer tax.

Which does, in fairness to Hal, mean that the first ever tax introduced in Australia targeted the poor more than the rich.[†]

"Every Australian schoolchild probably knows the next bit of Australian tax history."

In the 1850s came a tax on gold-digging licences, which were so unpopular (due to their cost – which was paid by poor miners rather than rich landowners – and due to the fact that they were paid for whether gold was found or not (so were not based on "ability to pay") and due to the fact that the miners had no right to vote (the whole "no taxation without representation" saga again)) that the gold miners went so far as to stage a full-on rebellion against the government, taking up arms and throwing up a stockade. It was like the American War of Independence all over again – a group of rebels incensed about taxes imposed by uncaring overlords, revolting against their fellow countrymen, declaring themselves loyal to a new flag, ready to forge a new destiny, ready to fight.

[†]   New Zealand, meanwhile, introduced a tax on dogs, which triggered the largely bloodless Dog Tax War, perhaps most memorable for the observation by Māori leader Hōne Riiwi Tōia that "if dogs are taxed, *people* will be next".

"Only the actual fightin' lasted just ten minutes. The stockade was quickly destroyed by professional soldiers and the ringleaders were either shot or arrested."

In the ensuing trial of the "traitors", popular opinion (and the jury's opinion) led to the ringleaders being released. Indeed the only people in the courtroom who were jailed were two members of the public who were sentenced to prison for cheering when the *not guilty* verdicts were read out.[†]

The legacy of the rebellion was pretty progressive, though, and the Eureka Stockade, as it's known, is usually remembered as a turning point in Australian democracy and liberty. Mark Twain described it as "the finest thing in Australasian history".

"Though he never knew Kylie," said Hal with a wink.

It led not just to a repeal of the gold-digging licences but also to a wider enfranchisement of the Australian electorate.

"In other words the second big tax movement of Australian history was so regressive that it led to a rebellion."

I've since fact-checked a lot of what Hal told me, and I should point out that quite a few commentators claim it was more an attempt by the miners to get out of paying their fair share of taxes.

Anyway, just like with Britain introducing income taxes to fight Napoleon, Australia didn't get their first nation-wide income tax until the First World War. And just like Britain keeping their income tax after the war had finished, so too did Australia. Of course, by this point Australia was a sovereign country, so didn't have to copy Britain, but clearly the same arguments that held sway in the UK were convincing

---

[†]   One of the ringleaders (who managed to escape the stockade) later became Speaker of the House in the legislative assembly of the state of Victoria.

to the Aussies. Specifically, the argument that income taxes raise money, and governments like money.†

But Australia did copy the British system of this time in one respect, in that although they introduced a tax on income, they decided that capital gains – that is, selling something you own for more than you bought it for (which tends to be how richer people make their money) – did not need to be taxed. This little omission not only led to the very rich being able to dodge tax, it led to tax avoidance on an industrial scale, most famously with what became known as "Bottom of the Harbour" schemes, first detected by the Australian Taxation Office in 1973.

Hal just *loved* these schemes.

The idea behind them was that whenever a company was due to pay tax, almost everything it owned would be sold to a new company, which just happened to be owned by the same owner of the original company. In other words, rich people would sell assets to themselves, but *legally* would do so via companies they owned.

As there was no capital gains tax, these transactions would not be subject to any tax at all. The amount paid for the original company's assets would be manipulated in such a way that all that was left was enough cash to pay a fee to the lawyer or accountant who pushed the scheme, but not enough to pay any corporate taxes the companies owed on their profits.

---

† Unlike in America, where Independence Day is a wild celebration, Australian separatists made the disastrous mistake of arranging independence to start on the 1st January (in 1901), thus ensuring that Australians are too hungover to ever celebrate it. That may be why, in 1935, the various states finally agreed to celebrate Australia Day on 26 January, commemorating Captain Arthur Phillip's landing of the First Fleet.

The original company would then be sold on for a dollar or so to someone else (often a dock worker, bizarrely), who would destroy all records of the transactions – sending them metaphorically (and sometimes literally) to the bottom of Sydney Harbour, along with the unpaid tax liability.

These schemes were relatively simple, but highly effective, albeit dodgy to the point of almost certainly being illegal. Lawyers and accountants adored them (especially as they could charge 25 per cent of the taxes avoided).

The Australian Taxation Office estimated that almost 7,000 companies avoided their tax bills in this way, costing the Australian government about a billion (1970s) dollars. Naturally, when the Taxation Office realised what was happening they launched an investigation, conducted by the Deputy Crown Solicitor's office in Perth. This is where things started to get seriously suspect (if they weren't already, that is).

The Taxation Office told the Deputy Crown Solicitor that the tax avoidance discovered had "far-reaching implications". The Deputy Crown Solicitor, however, decided that there was insufficient evidence to support a fraud claim.

Then a senior Queen's Counsel told the Deputy Crown Solicitor that three named people should be charged with "conspiracy to defraud the Commonwealth". The Deputy Crown Solicitor still did nothing.

Then the police recommended that charges be laid against the same three individuals, as did the Commissioner for Taxation. The Deputy Crown Solicitor *still* took no action. The principal legal officer in the Deputy Crown Solicitor's office said that he was too busy due to the "pressures of work", and shortly afterwards he went on long-term sick leave. His successor then spent an entire year deliberately avoiding the investigator from the Taxation Office, before sending a report to Canberra which contained completely false descriptions of complications about the legal case, which helped kibosh the whole investigation.

After five years the Deputy Crown Solicitor in Canberra advised the Taxation Office to drop the case as the evidence was not, after all, sufficient (even though, really, it was).

Theories abound as to what went wrong in the investigation. Most commentators blamed simple incompetence. It remains to be proven whether another factor that played a part in the shambolic and ineffective investigation was the fact that the wife of one of the investigators in the Deputy Solicitor's office was the company secretary of several of the companies being investigated.[†]

—

You may have picked up that little detail about capital gains tax. If you did, you're not alone – so did a senior judge. Australia didn't tax capital gains – i.e. the wealth that the very rich accrue – until 1985. In the 1970s the Australian government commissioned Judge Kenneth Asprey to review their tax system. He observed:

> It is almost universally agreed that capital gains . . . are so closely akin to income in its everyday senses that equity requires that they be taxed as income is.

[†] She was also running an escort agency, for which she used the Deputy Solicitor's office's telephone number as the number to call for enquiries about the escorting, but that seems to have been purely incidental.

I've popped that quote out of the main body of this page because it's this issue which winds me up more than anything else in tax. Hal couldn't see the problem with it, but then he'd be out of a job if he could.

If you make your money selling shares in Apple, surely you should be taxed the same as you are for selling actual apples? But you're not. Judge Asprey thought you should be – indeed he clearly thought *everyone* thought you should be – and eventually (ten years after his report) the Australian government agreed. For a while income and capital gains were placed on an equal tax footing.

A mere 14 years later, however, under John Howard's slightly more right-of-centre government, the capital gains tax rate was effectively halved.[†]

Obviously that halving is bad for *fairness*, but it was great for my job prospects in Australia. It left the field wide open for rorting.[‡]

[†]   The justification for this halving of the tax rate was that some adjustment was needed to offset the effects of inflation, since if all your investments did was increase in value by general inflation then you haven't *really* got any richer. Many countries do indeed adjust taxable gains for inflation, but usually simply by incorporating the *actual* amount of inflation. The Howard government decided it would be better to give anyone who had owned an asset for at least a year 50 per cent off their tax bill. Australian thresholds for *income*, meanwhile, are not automatically adjusted for inflation.

[‡]   New Zealand, somewhat amazingly, still doesn't have a capital gains tax, which historically led to high earners reducing their incomes by buying kiwi-fruit farms (which were an allowable write-off), and then selling those farms for a capital gain. The New Zealand government responded to that particular scheme by specifically legislating against it, rather than just biting the bullet and introducing a capital gains tax.

7

CALL ME MONEY

Something terrible happened.

Sasha met me after work one day, walked me to a nearby park, then told me that she was being sent to audit a coalmine in the Outback, and might be gone for several months.

"Don't worry," I said. "We can still see each other at the weekends."

She told me that she thought it was too far to fly back each weekend.

"I don't mind flying out to see you."

She told me that wasn't a great idea either.

"But then we won't see each other for several months . . ."

She gave me that *pity for the strangled puppy* look again, and ever since then I've used "auditing a coalmine" as a euphemism for breaking up with someone.

Luckily my friends still had their couch to offer me.[†]

[†] The absolute worst part of this is that I saw Sasha three weeks later on a beach with some surf jock. I wanted to say, "Funny-looking coalmine" but we both pretended not to have seen each other. As you can tell from the fact that I'm writing about this *years* later, I shrugged it off pretty easily.

—

Although the Australian branch of my firm was rather small, the legal team occasionally acted for both opposing sides in a dispute. I was rather shocked that this was allowed, but apparently it's common practice at legal firms. To deal with any potential conflicts of interest they would put up a sign on a door that read:

Go no further unless you are working on Project Hades.

And in this way, so the theory went, there would be no leak of confidential data, no accidental helping of the other party. Of course, the whole firm went for drinks on Friday nights, and after a couple of pints of VB invariably someone would ask, "How's Project Hades going?"

At one of these drinks I was introduced to a huge, hairy guy called Bazzo (which I assumed was a nickname, but turned out to be his pronunciation of Bassaux), who was a friend of one of the lawyers at my firm. We were outdoors on a giant terrace, by the sea, and as it was winter time in Australia I was in a light jumper, but Bazzo had his shirt unbuttoned almost all the way to his belly button.

"Are you a lawyer?" I asked, as politely as I could.

He laughed from his gut. "A lawyer? Who'd be a lawyer? I mean, no offence to any of you fukkas." He had two beers in one hand. I don't mean bottles – I mean two pint glasses, one held between his bottom two fingers and his palm, and one resting on top, pinched between his top two fingers and thumb. I tried once to copy this trick, but the attempt didn't end well. I don't recommend it.

None of the lawyers seemed to mind his comment about them in the slightest. Hal thought it was the very height of wit, but then, of course, Hal wasn't a lawyer. He was an accountant.

"So what *do* you do?"

Again his gut did the laughing for him.

"I get wood," he said.

No, "said" is wrong. This was a declaration, a statement of intent, a one-man demonstration of what happens when a certain type of personality is surrounded by people who want his money. I was the only one not laughing. At an opportune moment Hal whispered to me, with a nod to Bazzo, "Potential client." As in, "Start laughing, you tool."

"Who wants to get out of this hole and hit the casino?" Bazzo growled. We all cheered. I cheered too. I'm not proud. And I'm not telling you some of the other things he said.

The comment about Bazzo's "wood" wasn't merely his attempt at crude humour. It was a fairly honest answer (probably one of his *more* honest answers). Despite appearances, he was also an accountant. He worked as a transfer pricing specialist, specifically, and I appreciate this sounds a little specific, in pricing tropical hard woods.

If your Australasian geography is rusty, just to the north of Australia is Papua New Guinea, a country of about 8 million people who are, on average, one twentieth as wealthy as the average Australian. One thing that Papua New Guinea does have, though, is lots of resources, like tropical forests. Other countries are trying to relieve Papua New Guinea of these forests as fast as they can but, environmental disaster aside, that's okay because the lumber companies have to pay tax to the desperately poor Papua New Guinea government when they export the timber.

Or at least they would, if it wasn't for bastards like the transfer pricing specialist I'd just congratulated for winning some cash at the roulette wheel.

Transfer pricing is one of the oldest tricks in the book (though a book that is hidden from the taxman). The idea behind it is to set up two companies, one in the country you operate in and another in a tax haven. You then sell products between the two companies at an artificially high or low price to ensure that your profits arise in the tax haven company, and not where you actually made your sales.

So, for instance, you could make a bicycle for $100, sell it for $100 to another company (which you also own) in a country that doesn't tax corporate profits, then have that company sell the bicycle for $500 to your customer. Your profits (of $400) now arise in a country with no taxes, even if your bicycle was both made and sold to someone in a country that does have taxes.

This trick was to some extent pioneered by the industrialist William Vestey, who was ennobled by Prime Minister David Lloyd George in 1922 despite accusations that Vestey was a tax exile who had fled Britain during the First World War – not for fear of German Zeppelins, but to avoid rocketing income tax rates, which increased almost five-fold between 1914 and 1920.

Together with his brother Edmund, William Vestey (not to be confused with his namesake descendant, the current Baron Vestey) ran a meat-packing business that raised cattle in South America, South Africa and Australia, loaded the processed cows onto refrigerated steamships, then offloaded them into cold stores in Britain, Russia and China, before selling the meat through their own chain of butchers both in Britain and elsewhere.

In other words, this business was almost the prototype for international mega-corporations – innovative, extremely profitable and with some highly questionable (but legal) tax arrangements.

The business was structured with onshore and offshore companies, with assets transferred at prices that manipulated tax liabilities, convoluted inter-company payments and concerted lobbying efforts to get governments to introduce more favourable (to them) tax policies.

Over the century since the Vesteys' innovations, transfer pricing got really out of hand as other international businesses realised how effective it could be. Research by leading American academics Professors Simon Pak and John Zdanowicz uncovered some truly outlandish transfer prices (or as they put it, misprices), including a litre of apple juice purchased by an American company from Israel for $2,052, bulldozers sold to Venezuela for $387 each and – my personal favourite – a single pen bought from Trinidad for $8,500.

Almost all countries have tried to counteract this practice by introducing legislation to insist that transfer prices reflect "fair market prices", as otherwise popping a biro in the post and claiming it was enormously expensive would save any company a small fortune.

And yet, despite this legislation, people like Bazzo were still being paid a decent wage for their transfer pricing expertise, because what does *fair market price* really mean?

Indeed, I once received an email from a recruiter asking me if I wanted to work in the transfer pricing department of a small "bespoke tax solutions" firm. The job offer said:

- Must have five years accounting experience, preferably in transfer pricing.
- Starting salary up to £250,000 plus bonus, plus car allowance.

Which didn't seem too shabby for someone a couple of years out of accountancy school. And to think all they would be doing would be calculating what a "fair" market price should be.

—

Before I met Bazzo, the most famous transfer pricing ruse I'd known about was Starbucks UK's somewhat circuitous purchasing of their coffee beans.

Here's how it worked (and, indeed, still works).

Starbucks needs coffee. A lot of coffee. Where should they buy it from? In fact, where does most coffee come from? Brazil? Ghana? Colombia? Sit tight while I check what's in my cupboards . . .

It's Switzerland. The majority of the world's coffee is bought from Switzerland. Do you not remember hiking though those alpine coffee plantations when you were a kid? Between a half and three quarters of the world's coffee is traded through Switzerland.[†]

So Starbucks in the UK can pay money to Swiss Starbucks for Starbucks coffee. But how much to pay? By law, remember, it has to be a "fair market price". Oh, if only Starbucks knew some coffee experts who could justify a fair market price . . .

Besides, this isn't any old coffee, this is *Starbucks* coffee, and that's worth paying extra for.

The receipt of Starbucks UK's cash in Switzerland is not going to attract much Swiss tax (because that's how things are done in Switzerland), but any payment from the UK is going to reduce taxable profits in the UK.

Of course Global Starbucks would get no richer or poorer out of this transfer price – they're just taking cash out of one pocket and putting

---

[†] You might think I'm cheating by using the word "traded", but Switzerland is also the world leader at exporting actual physical *roasted* coffee. According to the Swiss Broadcasting Corporation, in 2019 Switzerland imported unroasted coffee for an average price of four francs per pound, and re-exported roasted coffee for thirty francs.

it into another – that is, until they add up their tax bill, which someone has just taken a big slurp from.[†]

While I'm talking about Starbucks, you might remember that there were big protests against Starbucks's tax avoidance about ten years ago, but interestingly the main issue wasn't the transfer pricing, but something that looks even more peculiar.

Starbucks pay a royalty fee to themselves for the right to use their own logo (which is as daft as it sounds). In the UK, they pay this royalty from a Starbucks company in Britain to a company in the Netherlands. The company in the Netherlands is also called Starbucks. This royalty payment is tax-deductible in Britain but barely gets taxed in the Netherlands.

This tactic is so common in the business world that it has a name – "the Dutch sandwich". Usually, the royalties are paid from the Netherlands to somewhere else (often in the Caribbean), and it's this payment that allows no tax to be paid in the Netherlands (so the Dutch bit is the filling in the sandwich, not the bread).

Having avoided corporation tax on over a billion pounds of sales, Starbucks UK were called to Parliament to explain themselves. One of the arguments they made in their defence was that trading conditions in the UK were historically very tough (which is presumably why you don't see many Starbucks in the UK) and they had never made an operating margin of more than 6 per cent.[‡]

[†] Starbucks's payments for their Swiss coffee beans have been cleared by HMRC, so while eyebrows may have been raised about a premium being paid for the beans to a Swiss subsidiary, it's at least a premium based in reality (and, I should again make clear, perfectly legal).

[‡] A 6 per cent operating margin means that if their revenue was £100 their routine costs would be £94, leaving them with a profit of £6. And for non-British readers, that aside about not seeing many Starbucks in the UK was a joke. There are more Starbucks in the UK than France, Germany, Spain, Portugal, Italy, Belgium and the Netherlands *combined*.

They added that this margin was *before* royalty payments. In their testimony to Parliament they then explained how they did, indeed, pay a royalty payment to another Starbucks company in Amsterdam, as "is standard business practice for multinationals". Because obviously if it's standard business practice for multinationals it can't be remotely bad. The royalty payment which, they said, "compares quite favourably to other multi-national licensors", was – you guessed it – 6 per cent.

You might remember that there was a bit of a fuss about it at the time – there were protests at a few stores and Starbucks offered to pay a "voluntary" tax payment of £20 million (which merely highlighted quite how optional corporation tax is to big companies).

But then the fuss died down. The news cycle moved on. So what did Starbucks do? They raised their royalty fee to 7 per cent, allowing them to shift more profits to branches of Starbucks in lower-taxed regimes. In fact, in the ten years since their dressing down by MPs, Starbucks UK has managed to make a net loss of an average £10 million per year. You would think that such a failing business would be shut down by its shareholders, seeing how catastrophically it's haemorrhaging money. But in the same time period it has paid out an average £25 million per year in royalty fees (to itself).[†]

Starbucks's consolidated accounts – meaning the financial results of the entirety of Starbucks, and not just individual companies within the Starbucks umbrella – make it plain that international operations are profitable. Even if, in the UK, they're reporting huge losses. Go figure.

The consolidated accounts declare, almost on the first page, that

---

[†] Though as there's more than one Starbucks company registered in the UK, and many of the transactions occurring between these companies and foreign Starbucks companies are hidden from the outside world, even this figure is hard to be sure of. It sounds a bit low, given there are over a thousand Starbucks stores in the UK.

Starbucks is "committed to being a deeply responsible company in the communities where we do business".

Though they've stopped with the voluntary tax payments.

The funny thing is, the UK could stop this shifting of profits via royalty payments any time it wanted to, by using something called a *withholding tax*. A withholding tax is a mechanism that automatically requires a tax payment whenever things like royalties or interest get paid overseas.

For a long time I assumed that the UK didn't have a withholding tax, as despite working in corporate taxes I'd never come across a British company that was paying any. I rather admired those countries, like Australia and the USA, that did have one – if an Australian Starbucks tried to pay a royalty fee to a Dutch Starbucks, the Australian Taxation Office could say, "That's fine, mate, but pay some tax on that fee" and consequently it makes less sense to shift Australian profits offshore as they get taxed when they leave.

But it turns out my assumption about the UK not having a withholding tax was wrong. Actually *wrong* is too strong. My assumption was *almost* right. It's not that the UK doesn't have a withholding tax, it's just that it's comically easy to avoid. *Technically,* British companies that pay royalty fees offshore have to pay a 20 per cent withholding tax. But *effectively,* they don't have to. The reason they don't have to is due to the fine print in some of the UK's double tax treaties. These are agreements with other countries about how cross-border transactions are dealt with, and some of the fine print of these treaties says that, well, you don't have to pay withholding taxes after all, provided that the royalties are paid to a company in places like – yes, the Netherlands (they have their own *slightly different* double tax treaties which allow the royalties to be paid on again to another country without the deduction of any withholding tax).

So a UK company can pay a tax-free royalty to a Netherlands company, and the Netherlands company can pay it on to somewhere else. This is like your friend Bob telling you a secret and saying, "Don't tell Mary", so you phone Cathy and say, "Could you tell Mary this secret for me, please?"

Finding these loopholes in double tax treaties – where two countries treat withholding taxes to a third country differently – is so commonplace that it has a name: "Treaty Shopping".

In Australia there were (and still are) very few Starbucks, and yet no shortage of great places to get a coffee. I hope Australians take that as a source of pride.[†]

Sadly, even in Australia there are sufficient gaps in the withholding tax legislation to create a little wiggle room. In fact, the gaps are so big that one of Australia's most recognisable brands – Rupert Murdoch's News Corp – has been able in some years to pay no Australian corporate tax despite revenues of close to $3 billion.[‡]

The Australian Taxation Office publishes data on the tax affairs of the largest companies in Australia which shows that one in five of Australia's

---

[†] There was also not a single Pret-a-Manger. In fact, not once did I see a shop selling a pre-packed sandwich (as Pret does). At first I thought this was a business opportunity that had just fallen, like a Pret sandwich filling, into my lap. I thought I could open a chain of Pret-a-Manger rip-offs called *Ready to Eat, Mate* and then make my fortune. I mentioned this idea of pre-packed sandwiches to an Australian colleague, who pulled a face, and said, "That sounds disgusting!" I abandoned the idea.

[‡] Though I should highlight that some of this is because print media hasn't had such a great run of it of late. But even before the internet started eroding the advertising revenues of traditional media, *The Economist* was reporting that News Corp had paid no corporate tax in Britain for the entire 1990s, despite making profits there of £1.387 billion.

largest companies pay no corporation tax at all. It was reported that News Corp had paid just $8.5 million in tax on $680 million in profits (and $13 billion in revenue) in the five years since 2015, and that the Australian Tax Office had created a special category for companies at the highest risk of tax avoidance – but only News Corp was in that category.

But this isn't because News Corp and the other companies have been doing anything illegal. For instance, Qantas managed to go ten years without paying corporation tax simply by claiming the depreciation costs of its planes and utilising losses from earlier years (and in fairness, struggling with the competition – who also weren't paying corporate taxes, for similar reasons). In fact, analysis by *The Guardian Australia* in 2021 found that 168 of the largest Australian companies had paid no corporation tax since 2013, despite earning profits of close to $10 billion.

You might wonder how exactly companies weren't paying any taxes. Surely News Corp wasn't just claiming depreciation on printing presses? It took me a while to work out the answer, because it took me a long time to realise that I was asking the wrong question. We need to take a step back – this is really important – and ask ourselves something more basic than, *How do companies avoid tax?*

We can't answer that until we know what a company actually is. I want to do something a bit risky here. I want you to put this book down for a moment and think about this question:

What is a company?

I'm going to give you a moment to chew on it.

—

Annoyingly, Bazzo won quite a lot of cash at the casino. He made sure everyone knew about it, going as far as to introduce himself as "Money" to a young woman we met at a bar, later that night.

"Money?" she said, with a little smile that I think I interpreted very differently from Bazzo. I had a hard time placing her accent – it seemed a little like the Antipodean version of mid-Atlantic. Was mid-Pacific a thing? She had a voice that carried her intelligence in a breezy whisper, and a playful laugh that suggested there were levels to the joke that I was missing.

"Yeah, my real name's Bazzo but all my friends call me 'Money'. Wanna know what sort of car I drive?"

"Not really." She seemed more bemused than annoyed. She and I had been having a pleasant conversation, as much as two people can in that sort of place, at that sort of hour. I doubt we were talking about tax.

"It's an Audi TT."

Recollections vary as to what happened next.

I recall that Bazzo realised that the young woman was more interested in *me*, and after I made a couple of charming but devastatingly witty comments at his expense he decided to back off.

My wife says that the three of us talked for over an hour. She claims that Bazzo monologued about how he could convince the government of Papua New Guinea to accept pretty much any price for timber he told them – that he could export, say, $10 million dollars of wood and then immediately sell it on for $40 million. I honestly have no recollection of him saying that. Though if he did, his under-pricing of timber in Papua New Guinea would also have helped his company avoid (or, perhaps more technically, evade) Papua New Guinean export taxes too.

My wife and I both agree that at some point in the evening Bazzo took his shirt off. It's funny which details you remember.[†]

[†]   I was wrong about the accent. She's from Manchester.

It wasn't Bazzo's naked torso that made me rethink my priorities. It was easy, in the moment, to laugh along with the lawyers who wanted to win Bazzo's business. But somehow what Bazzo was doing seemed worse than anything I'd encountered before. I'd always accepted that the tax system in big Western democracies was stupidly overcomplicated, and that the law allowed people and companies to weave through those laws to arrive at their most beneficial outcome.

There were some things the government asked you to do, like put money into your pension, which saved you tax, and other things you could do, like pay yourself a humongous royalty fee, which some governments had decided not to stop you doing and which also saved you tax. These things didn't seem so bad.

Well, maybe a bit bad, but no worse than, say, getting people hooked on their phones, or selling junk food or being a paparazzo or encouraging gambling or putting flyers under a car's windscreen wipers. I guess I'm saying that I felt society wasn't perfect, but it wasn't awful, either.

But actively depriving one of the poorest countries in the world of tax revenues using bogus transfer prices while stripping their forests bare seemed a step too far. The more I thought about what Bazzo was doing the more furious I became. Looking back on my reaction it seems pretty obvious what was going on – I probably didn't need a psychotherapist to tell me I was externalising, or transferring, or whatever an expensive psychotherapist would call it (okay, maybe I did need one, if just for the right lingo).

It's possible I would have forgotten about him, eventually, but one morning my boss, Hal, slapped me on the back.

"Great news! I've just had an email from Mr Bassaux. He's asked for a formal meeting with us. You must have made a good impression on him."

"That's great," I said. Even though it wasn't great.

"Glad you think so. I've suggested you lead on this."

—

I understand that one of the joys of surfing is its meditative nature. As you wait for the next wave you can sit and stare at the horizon, floating in your own thoughts. I needed a bit of that. What had started as just a job seemed to be going down an increasingly hard-to-justify career path. I felt I needed to meditate a little on life.

As I had done pretty well in my two days of "Surf School", I bought myself my very own surfboard and spent a relaxing afternoon waxing it in my living room, without really knowing why a surfboard needed waxing.

Then I took it out to sea. I bobbed up and down, lying on my board, waiting for a wave. Finally, I caught one, was absolutely too terrified to stand up and careered without any sense of control into a guy with the Southern Cross tattooed on his chest. I apologised, but he still called me a *fucking Pom* (which I'm pretty sure isn't a term of endearment) and threatened to do something to my face that is only usually done to avocados. I never tried to surf again.

Occasionally, I wish something like that had happened on my first ever day as an accountant.

—

Some people view tax avoidance as doing something contrary to the intention of Parliament. I've never been hugely enamoured by this definition, as it requires us all to guess what Parliamentarians *meant* when they laid down the law, rather than just reading the law itself. But sometimes I think this way of looking at things can be helpful. One of the things my firm advised on was import taxes, and Hal told me a trick or too that definitely seemed to be *not what Parliament intended*.

Import duties are an incredibly ancient form of tax. Almost from the moment tribespeople controlled their own borders there have been taxes on anything crossing those borders. Both the Great Wall of China and Hadrian's Wall in northern England were used in much the same way as the Anything to Declare gate is in airports today. In colonial Australia there were even customs duties *between* states, to encourage Australians to trade with the motherland, rather than each other.[†]

And as with sin taxes on alcohol and cigarettes, it tends to be the poor who suffer the most. One dollar on an imported T-shirt is going to be proportionately more of a poorer person's income.

The fact that so-called indirect taxes (that is, taxes on products, rather than, say, incomes) affect poorer people more is well understood by politicians. In the First World War income tax rates were raised significantly (all around the world) but indirect taxes weren't. Indeed the UK Parliament's own analysis was that at the outbreak of the war people earning £50 per year were paying *double* the effective tax rate of people earning £200 per year – and more than anyone earning up to £10,000 per year – not because of the income tax rate, but rather because of the effect of indirect taxes on the products they bought. Politicians were afraid that if they made the poorest people even poorer by raising indirect taxes the cost of living would become intolerable and the masses might turn to communism.[‡]

It wasn't really until the 1990s that the World Trade Organization persuaded most countries to massively lower their import taxes. Up

---

[†] There's no real difference between a "tax" and a "duty" – indeed the name "duty" was originally a bit of clever marketing. If it's your *duty* to pay, then all upstanding citizens will happily pay it, unlike a burdensome *tax*. See also *contribution, community levy, Medicare, social care levy*, etc.

[‡] I totally get that logic. When the beer at my local hit £7 a pint I was ready to wave the Red Banner and start singing "Workers of the World, Unite!" Though I doubt the outrageous prices charged by gastro pubs was quite what Lenin and Marx had in mind.

until then it was common practice for richer nations to put exorbitantly high taxes on the importation of *processed* goods, but let in the raw materials more cheaply. This was one of the (many) reasons why poorer nations stayed poor. Rich countries were happy to buy low-margin cocoa from West Africa, but would not let in high-margin chocolate. I've always thought there's something a little suspicious about the most famous chocolate-producing nations being Belgium and Switzerland, and not Nigeria and Ghana.

The World Trade Organization's argument was that high taxes on traded goods inhibit global trade, which just leads to everyone being poorer. If Australians have to pay more for their cars, then they have less money for their thongs (which I discovered the embarrassing way are not pants (which for American readers are not trousers)).

Not every country has always agreed with the WTO, and import duties have occasionally become a political battleground, in recent times most famously when President Trump imposed tariffs on steel and aluminium imports. The EU responded with tit-for-tat tariffs, but they targeted the tat precisely, with taxes on, among other things, Harley-Davidson motorcycles.[†]

This wasn't a randomly chosen product to put a tax on. Harley-Davidsons are made in Wisconsin, a state Trump won in 2016 with a margin of less than 1 per cent. In other words, if the EU's tariff led to just a handful of motorcycle factory workers losing their jobs, it could have cost Trump re-election. Similarly, China retaliated with taxes on

---

[†] Not that I'm calling Harley-Davidsons 'tat' – they're obviously premium machines. Even the noise they make is higher quality, so much so that you may know that Harley-Davidson once tried to trademark their distinctive sound, described by their lawyer as "a very fast potato potato potato". It must be fun being a trademark attorney.

soybeans, bourbon and oranges, hitting the Trump-voting states of Iowa and Kentucky, and the super-marginal state of Florida.

Perhaps the most famous fallout over import duties was the often misremembered Boston Tea Party, an act of sabotage that was one of the precursors to the American War of Independence. What is rarely remembered is that while this was a protest about the right of the British to impose taxes on the Americans, it was also a protest against tax *cuts*.

In the 18th century, the (British) East India Company had a legal monopoly on selling tea to the American colonies. In return for this monopoly, the company had to pay to the British a 25 per cent import duty on their tea, before selling the tea on to the Americans. This tax made the tea more expensive then it would otherwise have been for American tea drinkers.

Being a resourceful lot, the Americans found a loophole: they simply smuggled in their tea from Holland instead.

So to allow the East India Company to compete with the smugglers, the British scrapped the 25 per cent import duty for any tea the company exported to America, and replaced it with a local (i.e. American) tax rate of just 3 pence per pound of tea (which was equivalent to about an 8 per cent rate).

To put it another way, the British cut the tax on tea consumed in the American colonies from 25 per cent to 8 per cent.

Obviously *ideologically* the Americans had a point, in that they were charged taxes without any say in how they were spent, but the actuality was that due to this tax cut the Americans could buyer cheaper (and, dare I say it, higher quality) tea from the East India Company than they could from the smugglers.

So the Boston Tea Party wasn't led by anti-tax idealogues, but by smugglers who were now being undercut by commercial enterprise.

Perhaps if in the near future the state of Colorado lowers the tax on cannabis it will spur some drug dealers to break into a cannabis shop in protest at being undercut by "legitimate" business and burn all the produce (in one go, I mean) and one day they will be heralded as the instigators of a just revolution?

Anyway, Hal told me how to get around the aluminium tariffs: apparently if you need to export some aluminium tubes, you can stick some cheap netting between the tubes and call them "goals". There are much lower tariffs on sports equipment.

The Ford Motor Company was reported to have avoided $250 million in US import duties by outfitting their Transit vans with seats and windows in Spain and exporting them to the US. They paid the 2.5 per cent import duties on passenger vehicles, then immediately tore out the seats and boarded up the windows, in order to convert the vans into commercial vehicles which would otherwise have suffered a 25 per cent tax.

Even more bizarrely, the 25 per cent import tax on commercial vehicles is known as the "chicken tax", as it was a retaliatory measure after the Europeans taxed American chickens.

—

Our office was small but spacious and filled with light. Everybody was relaxed and friendly. I had a large desk and a comfortable leather chair and worked alongside a tropical pot-plant I'd nicknamed Edward after an old colleague who seemed nice enough but had never once uttered a word in my presence. There wasn't a cubicle in sight. I started to enjoy going to work each morning.

It was so hot that I'd commute part of the way to work without my shirt on, which as most of the commute was next to a beach didn't seem so weird. I discovered too late that some of my colleagues, who took a similar route to work, thought that topless commuting must be a peculiar British tradition.

There were sufficiently few accountants in the team that I found myself working on everything from the rather dry world of "regulatory compliance" (or rather, dry if you were properly complying with regulations) via some pretty niche offshore shenanigans to the opaque world of intra-group payments. I don't just mean opaque to the outside world – it was opaque to me, too. The first diagram of a client's "group structure" that I was shown contained over 150 companies, almost all of them with near-identical names along the lines of "A1A A1A Limited, A1A A1 Limited, 1A A A1 Limited, A A1A A GmbH, A1A1A Limited". And then each company transferred cash to other companies in the group.

I found it hard to concentrate on exactly which company was doing what. I was staring at a page of seemingly identical companies doing almost identical things. I started to feel sleepy (though that may have been the lunchtime schooners, too). This was the first time I'd encountered this particular ruse in the world of international tax mitigation: avoidance by being too mind-numbingly boring to analyse.

Often our firm would hold money in escrow for this sort of client, meaning we'd look after some cash that was due to change hands. As I was one of the few resident accountants (Hal was another), I was the one in charge of the bank accounts.

One of the bank transfers I made got pinged up by our bank's anti-money-laundering checks, and the bank's local branch staff took it quite seriously. I was told that the money wouldn't be released unless I showed my passport and other ID in person along with a letter of authority from my firm's Head of Treasury.

The next day, with the required paperwork, I duly stood in the queue at my local branch waiting for my turn to speak to the teller. The queue was quite long and a bank employee with a clipboard was encouraging people in the line to use the machines instead.

"What have you come here to do today?" she asked me.

"I need to show some ID to authorise a bank payment."

"You don't need ID for that – have you used online banking before?" She had one of those voices where she had to tilt her head to accommodate the changing pitch of it.

"I was told that I *do* need to show my ID."

"Or you can use telephone banking if you don't have an online account."

"I really need to get this amount cleared today."

She could see I wasn't budging.

"How much are you looking to transfer?"

I answered as matter-of-factly as I could.

"Four hundred and ninety million."

—

One of the weirdest issues I had to sort out involved a subsidiary in Guangzhou, in China. They had submitted their tax return to the relevant authorities, but the return had been flagged up, and a government official had come to visit their office.

"You need to submit a return with a higher tax figure."

The manager of the office, who had himself been seconded there from England, had pulled out his file of invoices and begun to remonstrate that the tax figure on the return was correct.

"No, you don't understand," said the official. "I am not asking you to pay more tax. You just need to submit a higher tax figure."

The manager emailed me for advice about what to do. Apparently the government official was keen for all foreign businesses to claim that their tax bills were higher than they actually were, just so that official documents would show how much the city was gaining from foreign investors. They didn't want to deter the foreign investors by actually making them pay such high taxes, however.

I knew that in normal circumstances deliberately putting false information on a tax return was a crime, but I didn't know what the deal was if the local government asked you to do it. I'm still not entirely sure, but I am now more suspicious about any "official" Chinese government statistics.

—

Bazzo spent some time analysing an outsized painting on the wall of our meeting room. He put his nose up close to it, as if considering every brush stroke. Then he turned to us to give his opinion.

"This is really shit."

"It's by one of the schoolkids we sponsor as part of our work with underprivileged –" I began.

"Really shit," said Bazzo.

I mean, it was shit, but that didn't seem like the point. The problem was that he then burst out laughing, and as this was our first formal meeting with him as a prospective client, Hal and I started laughing too. *Ha ha ha, this underprivileged kid is crap at painting.*

"So here's the deal," said Bazzo, when he'd stopped laughing. "I've got a lot of cash parked in the middle of the Indian Ocean and I need to get it somewhere I can spend it . . . So my idea was –"

Hal cut him off. "I need to tell you that this meeting isn't under privileged reporting exemptions."

"What does that mean?"

"It means if you tell us anything illegal we're not obligated to keep it secret."

"Oh," said Bazzo. "Oh . . ."

There was a somewhat awkward pause.

"We could rearrange the meeting to bring a lawyer in?" suggested Hal. Bazzo looked a little blank, so Hal added, "So we could keep it secret."

Bazzo seemed to think that was a good idea.

After he'd left, Hal slapped me on the back.

"Clever of you to remind me about privilege, when you mentioned that painting. I've been caught out before."

I had to wait 'til Friday night to find out what *getting caught out* really meant.

"It happens all the time," explained Hal. "Clients think that you act for them no matter what. So they tell you about some cash they've got stashed in an illegal account and then expect you to advise them on it. But then we'd be breaking the law, and we don't do that."

"But don't most of our clients have cash in illegal accounts?"

"Oh sure, but we don't know that, unless they tell us, which we tell them not to."

"But we *do* know it?"

"Of course." But then he thought about it, and tilted his beer bottle towards me. "But we don't *know* it."

—

I was halfway up a cliff-face on about my fifth date with the young woman I'd met on the night out with Bazzo when I told her that I was thinking of changing careers. I tried to make it sound like an off-the-cuff remark, to show I was so unafraid of the ridiculous drop beneath us that I could strike up a casual conversation.

She leaned back into her harness as if stretching out in an armchair and asked why I felt that way.

I explained that I'd recently met a class of wide-eyed schoolkids on a ferry who'd been astonished by my impromptu lesson in rhyming slang, and it had made me wonder about becoming a schoolteacher.

"Why don't you do some volunteering at a college?" she suggested. "I thought your firm did lots of that sort of stuff?"

She was right, of course. My firm did do that sort of stuff.

The next morning I spoke to Hal about it.

"You want to *teach*?" he said, as if I'd told him I wanted to live in a tent in the Outback.

"Well, we had that email about the firm looking for volunteers to teach a course on tax at one of the local colleges – it clashes with our next meeting with Bazzo, but if you can handle it without me . . . ?"

Reluctantly, Hal agreed. I thought he was being nice. I'd forgotten my earlier assumption about him being the devil.

TRUST ME, I'M AN ACCOUNTANT

In every public-speaking course I've ever been on, the same metaphor inevitably gets brought up.

"You have to imagine yourself as a swan."

I've been on a lot of these courses, it's always a swan.

"Under the water your feet are kicking wildly, but above the surface you look like you're gliding along. No one can see your heart pumping, you are smooth and graceful. Remember that, and you'll be fine."

I looked in the mirror. Did I look like a swan? I looked sweaty. Do swans sweat?

Hal had pulled some strings to ensure I got a place teaching tax, as I'd asked for. But instead of starting me off with a nice low-level course in the basics of tax with an easy-going and not-too-bright class of aspirational teenagers at the local college, he volunteered me to present a three-day intensive course for management consultants, as part of the firm's profitable *professional development* courses for experienced managers and advisors who wanted to know more about tax.

This was clearly his way of teaching *me* a lesson, by throwing me head first into the deep end (which I guess wouldn't have been such a problem if I actually was a swan).

I peered through the narrow strip of glass in the door to the conference room, at the growling bear pit of management consultants. These were people who thrived on competition, on one-upmanship, on showcasing their intelligence. They were all well-dressed and confident, and ready to pounce on weakness.

I needed to look like I was gliding along, a serene swan in the deep end of a bear pit. The class started in five minutes.

I vomited.

Some people say that you should imagine your audience naked. Others that you should stare at the back of the room. Apparently Winston Churchill would write his speeches down, then put them in his pocket so that he would know that if he forgot anything they were there for him, and that gave him sufficient confidence to deliver his speeches from memory.[†]

I find my hands shake. One of my colleagues who had taught on a similar course suggested that I tell the class that I'd just run up the stairs – it would explain the hyperventilating.

"Just tell them you're really unfit – it will get a cheap laugh," she said.

"What do I tell them about the sick on my shirt?"

She thought about it, then offered a solution. "I had such a bad

---

† Churchill was an absolutely shameless tax dodger, incidentally. He enlisted the help of the Chairman of Inland Revenue to personally intercede on his behalf more than once, and claimed that he had repeatedly "retired" from writing in order that his royalties were treated as tax-free capital gains, instead of heavily taxed income, while also using complex schemes to hide his wealth.

hangover once I threw up in a bin in front of a whole conference room. I told them I was pregnant, that seemed to cover it."

"I'll try that," I said.

—

Something I never realised when I was a student was that the person at the front of the class, doing the teaching, can see *everyone*. There's no hiding from their gaze. You can see the couples holding hands, the notes passed between friends, the guys at the back resting their eyes, the people fiddling with their phones. You also get to watch as expressions change.[†]

My first question to the class had been simple. It's the same one I asked you a chapter back.

"What's a company?"

Here was a crowd who wanted to show that they were the smartest guys in the room. They had just been asked what they knew should be an easy question, but they suspected a trap.

"It's the same as a business . . ." ventured one.

"No."

"It's an entity with a limited liability."

"So's a driver of an insured car."

"It's a corporate entity registered at an official corporate listing, governed by the Corporations Act . . ."

"But corporate just means company, so corporate 'listing' or Corporations 'Act' only refers to companies, so what is the actual company?"

[†]   One of my most embarrassing moments that week was saying to an attendee, "If you're going to play with your phone, at least do it above the desk, otherwise it just looks like you're fiddling with yourself." Then we both silently acknowledged that his phone was, in fact, on his desk already.

As you can tell, my lecture was a hoot.

But what *is* a company? I used to think I knew. It was my job to work out the taxes that companies owe, after all. I'd gone most of my career thinking I knew. It was a bit like knowing what a dog is. I mean, look at it, it's a dog.

But I've come to believe that an inability to appreciate what a company is (or worse, an unwillingness to) has led to some of the greatest injustices in the world economy.

That's quite a bold statement, so let's take a step back.

Let's say you've just heard of this great new invention called the steam engine and you think it would be a good idea to lay some railroad track down between your home town and the nearest port. You've written some letters to some moneyed friends and they all think it's a good idea too. What do you do next?

Without any specific rules, you would all have to just hand your cash to one trusted person, who would put it into a bag and hope to goodness that nobody ran away with that bag. And then what? You would probably need your group of investors to buy some land to put the track on, but who would actually own the land? All of you? Would all of you need to sign each and every property deed? Who would be in charge? Who would decide when and how you got your money back?

These problems get even worse if it's not a group of friends, but rather a group of total strangers.

Before the industrial revolution such issues did arise occasionally, but not often enough to cause much of a problem. For instance, the City of London Corporation was recognised in medieval times as a legal body that could enter into contracts in its own name, without every deal that affected London needing to be signed off by every single Londoner.

But with the economic growth of the industrial revolution it became clear that some legal framework was needed to allow strangers to pool their resources – their money – in a streamlined way. Few people could afford to build a railroad or a factory themselves, or send ships to Asia or conduct any other large enterprise, but if people could invest alongside each other then collectively there would be enough money to do so – and a spreading out of the risk of the endeavour.

In the couple of centuries before the first modern Companies Act, passed in Britain in 1844, there had been legally independent bodies created by governments for a specific purpose, most famously the East India Company, granted a monopoly by Queen Elizabeth in 1600, with the specific purpose of plundering India. Unfortunately, some of these early state-approved companies ended up being mired in speculation and fraud, and for a long time the government, and the public, turned away from them.

But it was hard to keep a good idea down. The idea in this instance being to create an artificial person, with the same legal rights as a normal person, owned by a collective of real people, who are legally separate from that artificial person.

The United States followed Britain in recognising companies as *natural persons* in 1866. So the company – the artificial person – can open a bank account and buy up land and own a ship and get sued, all the while existing only in the imagination of the people who own shares in that company, and in a register of companies set up by the government.

It is crucial to understanding what can go wrong with this to recognise that the purpose of the creation of company law was to allow strangers to pool their resources to embark on a common endeavour.

There are other features of *companies*. As the strangers aren't operating the company, they are not held liable for the mistakes made by the directors of the company, most significantly in that they will never have to pay any extra money to cover the debts of the company. This is what is known as *limited liability* – the fact that if an investor buys a share for $100, they can only lose up to that $100, and no more.

So what is a company? Strip it back to its bare bones and it's still that bag that we first collected our cash in when we wanted to build a railway. A bag, a box, a collecting place for investors' cash, a bank account, a means for strangers to aggregate their wealth together.

And from that really sensible starting point everything has gone wrong.

—

At the end of the first day of my course I had talked the consultants through the basics of corporation tax and demonstrated a few numeric examples, though it was clear that what they really wanted to know was not how tax was *meant* to be calculated, but how it *could* be calculated, which is not necessarily the same thing at all.

My teaching was going better than I'd feared, and my nerves had settled as soon as I realised that I may have overestimated what the management consultants knew already. On learning that I was English, one of them asked if it was true that Scottish people don't pay tax.

I later learned that these consultants were earning more than $250,000 a year.

"That's true," I said. "Scottish people are exempt from tax."

—

It's the nebulousness of companies, their conceptualness, their lack of a clear definition, that makes them so hard to tax. Obviously some of their directors cheat, but they really don't need to. The laws don't so much have loopholes; the laws *are* the loopholes.

Because a company is just, well, some sort of abstract entity that only exists on a virtual piece of paper, you have free rein to register your company just about anywhere. In fact, here's a test: where is Apple based? How about Facebook (or "Meta" as it's now called)? Or Alphabet Inc. (Google's parent company)? I'll give you a clue: it's not California.

It turns out that these three companies, as well as McDonald's, Uber, Amazon, Tesla, Morgan Stanley, Starbucks, Coca-Cola, Walmart and the shell companies set up by both Harry and Meghan, and, allegedly, Mexican drug lord El Chapo and about one and a half million other companies are all based in the tiny US state of Delaware. In fact quite a few of these are based at just one address in Delaware, belonging to a rather plain-looking low-rise building. I can't imagine how much post that address gets.[†]

Why Delaware? There are three possible reasons, and I want you to decide which is most likely:

1. Lawyers throughout America are familiar with Delaware's legal system, which is advanced and efficient and allows corporate cases to be heard swiftly in specialist commercial courts.
2. Delaware's rules on incorporating companies allow virtually no information to be handed over to the state, enabling almost total secrecy for the ultimate owners of companies registered in Delaware.
3. Delaware doesn't tax interest payments or royalty payments, meaning that large companies can split themselves into two:

[†] A number of News Corp's papers took great delight in revealing the existence of Harry and Meghan's Delaware companies. Want to guess where News Corp is itself now incorporated? Yup, in Delaware.

a company that operates their normal trade, like selling cups of coffee, and a company that owns the brand image of that coffee. The company selling the coffee can then pay the company owning the brand image a royalty fee. This fee can be deducted from the taxable profits of the company selling the coffee but isn't then taxable in the image-rights owning Delaware company, meaning that companies can effectively wipe out their *taxable* profits without affecting their real-world profits.

There's a well-known tactic in multiple-choice exams – if you're not sure, pick the longest answer.

Though in this case they're all pretty good answers.

My management consultants were taking notes.

—

Almost as soon as companies were treated as *real* people, governments became keen to levy some form of income tax on them, just as they do on *actual* real people. But journalists often get muddled up, perhaps deliberately, when they report on the tax that large companies are paying (or not paying). A BBC report in 2021 declared, "Amazon pays £492m in UK tax as sales surge to £20.6bn." To understand what's going on here we need to unpick how taxes on companies work (or, at least, are meant to work) – and this sort of headline is muddling up two different things.

The first is that "tax" here is a shorthand for *one particular type of tax*. Obviously a headline of "Amazon pays £492m in one particular type of UK tax as sales surge to £20.6bn" doesn't have quite as much impact. Amazon were quick to point out that they pay over £1 billion in another type of tax, and then more taxes on other things too.

The BBC headline was referring to *corporation tax*, also called corporate income tax. Corporation taxes are levied on profits, and profits are definitely not the same as sales.

If you want a bit of a refresher on this (my highly paid management consultants did), when a business sells something they record the sale as their *turnover* or *revenue* or *sales* (which all mean the same thing), and then they deduct from this turnover figure all their corresponding expenses – which for most businesses is normal stuff like staff costs, or rent or utility bills, plus the cost to the business of the thing they've just sold. And what you're left with is *profit*, and it's only on this profit that you have to pay corporation tax.[†]

Simple, right? Well accountants abhor simplicity (because where are the fees in that?). So the profits are actually split up into all sorts of different types of profit – gross profits, net profits, profits before tax or after tax, profits before interest and tax or before interest, tax, depreciation and amortisation (which is just another word for depreciation). And then sometimes profits are referred to as earnings, and some shameless accountants decide to abbreviate the whole shebang, normally when they're dealing with clients, just to bamboozle the clients and makes themselves sound clever. "Oh your EBITDA is down 4 per cent? We can help you with that."[‡]

[†]   For the sake of simplicity I've missed out one enormous step – the "sales" are likely to include a sales tax (like VAT in England, or TVA in France, or GST in Australia), so a sizeable percentage of the sales will be handed over to the government before expenses are even deducted. For some businesses this sales tax can be several multiples of their profit.

[‡]   EBITDA is **E**arnings **B**efore **I**nterest, **T**ax, **D**epreciation and **A**mortisation, which is the same as saying how profitable the business would be if only they didn't need to own anything to make their money, so it's a hypothetical measure that can be used to justify all sorts of dubious reports to shareholders, as in, "Oh sure, we're massively loss making, but our EBITDA is positive." It now seems to have been overtaken in popularity among finance directors by "EBITDAC", or Earnings Before Interest, Tax, Depreciation, Amortisation and **C**oronavirus.

The skill for accountants is making sure that a company has the right *sort* of profits. Ideally, what you want are high *operating* profits, meaning your core business is actually making money, but low *taxable* profits, which is what your company pays tax on. The difference between these two types of profit is mostly due to *financing costs* and, sometimes, *royalty fees*, which if you recall is one of Starbucks's favourite tricks.[†]

—

I met up with the young woman from the night out with Bazzo for what was now about our tenth date (she's called Henrí, and she's agreed that I can refer to her as my *girlfriend* at this point). I can't quite explain why, but we had decided to go on a ghost tour of an old quarantine station on an island out in the bay. Neither of us believe in ghosts, but the old buildings were reasonably interesting, not that I was really concentrating on them.[‡]

Henrí asked how the course was going.

"I feel like I'm on fire," I told her. One of the other people on the tour overheard me, and said that he was feeling like that, too. I think we might have been referring to different things.

[†]   One of my favourite accountancy jokes – which I should warn you in advance isn't actually funny – involves a man interviewing candidates for a new job. The first applicant is a lawyer, who is asked, "What's one plus one?" The lawyer says that in the case of *Numbers* v *Calculations* the judge ruled that the answer was two. Next an engineer is asked, "What's one plus one?" The engineer says that the answer is between 1.995 and 2.005. Then an accountant is asked the same question. He looks shocked. He stands up and goes to close the blinds. Then he leans in close to the interviewer and whispers, "What do you want it to be?"

[‡]   Apparently if ever you do see a ghost the first thing you should do is check for a gas leak, as carbon monoxide poisoning can cause hallucinations. Though I know, I'm ruining the fun, sorry.

There are few things in an accountancy career that you can do on your feet, that pump you with adrenaline, that make you think fast and speak up. I liked it. "Some of my jokes are falling a bit flat, though."

The Australian sense of humour, I was discovering, is very definitely not the same as the British one. On the first morning of my course it had been pouring with rain. "Great tanning weather," I said. My class just looked at me like I was a little awkward. On the second morning I went with "Strewth, it's really raining!" And everyone rolled around laughing. I found it a little hard to work this out, so figured I'd stick to explaining the tax.

—

Starbucks has one real problem when it comes to shifting its profits around: they have to deliver their product – their coffee – in a particular place. That means that it's pretty obvious where they are earning their revenues (if not their profits).

This is not such an issue for some much bigger beasts, who have also found themselves in hot water over their tax affairs, the likes of Google and Facebook. The tech giants don't even need to use royalties to shift their profits around. They can simply negotiate a deal with a customer onshore and then bill for it (and, arguably, provide their services) offshore. This way, the revenue – let alone the profits – is entirely realised offshore.

I've only experienced this particular manoeuvre once, and only indirectly. My friend Kititi had gone to work for another Big Tech company and he phoned me up to see if I could help him get his head around an invoice.

"I spent ages landing this deal [with a household-name UK company], but my accounting team are sending the invoice from our Irish office – are they screwing me over?"

"No." I told him, "they're not screwing *you* over, they're screwing *me* over."

And screwing you, too.

They're all at it. In 2016 it was reported that HMRC had paid Facebook six times more cash for advertising on the social networking site than Facebook had paid HMRC in tax. And that's not because HMRC is spending a fortune on advertising, rather because in one year Facebook paid just £4,327 in tax. That's probably less than you did.[†]

Actually I've just fallen into the same trap as most journalists do when reporting on this kind of story. Of course Facebook paid more than four grand in tax – they paid payroll taxes and business rates and VAT, just not much corporation tax. Indeed in one year Facebook's profits in the UK were hugely reduced because they paid enormous bonuses to all their staff. I *wish* my employer would avoid taxes the same way. And of course those well-paid Facebook staff are paying a lot of taxes themselves.

But the main thing that hugely reduced their tax bill was billing their customers through a company in Ireland, which was itself paying for the right to use the Facebook platform to another company (also called Facebook) which while *based in* Ireland wasn't legally resident there. This tactic is also pretty common.

Companies generally only have to pay tax to a particular country if they're *legally* based in that country (rather than merely *actually* based there) – and many companies (Apple is another one) have taken advantage of different definitions of *based in*. Say one regime says it's

---

[†]   Again, technically, even this amount is only an estimate, as it's the figure that was in their accounts, which means it bears very little resemblance to their actual tax payment. And yes, that's weird, but as the kids on the streets are saying, accounts be like that sometimes.

where you're incorporated but another says it's where your headquarters are, then you can incorporate and establish your headquarters in the opposite regimes and effectively be based nowhere.

Or similarly, the definition of "based in" usually excludes warehouses (as otherwise global shipping would grind to a halt as you couldn't pick up some containers in Lima and drop them off in Barcelona prior to them being shipped on to Oslo), so this means that if your business is, say, delivering things from warehouses, you can legitimately claim that you aren't based in any particular country, even if you are the largest retailer in the entire world and make so much money that your founder can literally take his vacations in space.

Hundreds of millions, if not billions, of pounds, have been shifted to places like the Cayman Islands due to these *perfectly legal* payments.

In short, companies can avoid paying corporation tax because it's a tax that is based on profits, and since royalty payments and interest payments and transfer prices can all be deducted from profits, and revenues from which profits spring can be routed through low-tax regimes, profits can be pretty much whatever you want them to be.

—

One of the management consultants asked me why governments didn't do anything about this. My immediate response – and perhaps I was just trying to sound confident and casual – was that governments don't really care.

My argument was this: companies really are the engines of economic growth – Starbucks employs more than a third of a million people, Facebook employs around 45,000 (interestingly both companies have similar total wage bills). In fact, often governments pay companies to establish themselves within their borders – San Francisco has given tax breaks to Twitter, Washington State has given tax breaks to Boeing, and Tesla has been offered a deal that could be worth over a billion dollars in tax breaks to set up its latest "gigafactory" just outside the appropriately named city of Sparks, Nevada. Even News Corp received a handout from the Australian government to compensate it for losses. And sometimes tax offices just let large companies off – literally telling them not to worry about their corporate tax bills, or the penalties or interest that should have accumulated on them. In the early 2010s, the UK's Public Accounts Committee, chaired by MP Margaret Hodge, found that HMRC had let big business off an almost unbelievable £25 billion in tax liabilities. Apparently HMRC wanted to be more "customer-friendly" (though only if the customer was a multi-billion-pound company).

But maybe the problem is actually that governments do care but can't agree with each other, especially when what's good for one government isn't necessarily good for another – for instance the Australian bank Macquarie was for a long time the main owner of British utility company Thames Water. Thames Water was criticised in Britain for paying no corporation tax (and indeed receiving a tax rebate) despite earning profits of £600 million on a turnover of £1.8 billion (a profit margin most companies would dream of), and then paying dividends of over £1 billion to Macquarie and other shareholders.

If Thames Water had paid more tax, there would have been less cash to transfer to Australia, so the Australian government is hardly likely to heckle the Brits for not being tougher on corporate avoidance.

Not that it was necessarily avoidance. Thames Water were able to escape some of their tax bill by investing some of those profits into a new Super Sewer under London (though they also owned a couple of Cayman Island subsidiaries and paid a hefty amount of tax-deductible interest to Macquarie, which probably helped).

There was a very similar situation with Apple in New Zealand. The *New Zealand Herald* reported that Apple had sold $4.2 billion worth of products in New Zealand, but paid no taxes there. Instead, Apple New Zealand shifted these profits to Apple Australia, where they paid $37 million in *Australian* taxes. The Australian government was hardly likely to complain about that manoeuvre, either.

And then sometimes governments *do* try to do something about it. In 2015 the UK introduced a new tax called the *Diverted Profits Tax* – which was quickly dubbed the "Google Tax", as it only applied to huge, mostly Big Tech, companies that, as the name suggests, divert their profits elsewhere.

As Britain doesn't have any homegrown trillion-dollar tech companies, this was seen on the other side of the Atlantic as a distinctly anti-American tax, leading to the USA announcing that any country that imposed a "Google Tax" would be hit with 25 per cent import tariffs in retaliation.

So what did Britain do, faced with such a threat? Despite its existence on the statute books, Diverted Profits Tax currently raises no revenue.[†]

—

Henrí and I lay on the sun loungers on the roof of her building, casually watching the last of the rain clouds evaporate. I had told her the gist of what I've just told you, though probably – and I hope you're not offended by this – in a slightly more romantic way. She took a few moments to digest it all. I thought perhaps her mind had wandered to other things,

---

[†] Its defenders argue that it's not meant to – it's supposed to scare big multinationals into behaving. Though in 2021 HMRC revealed that they are investigating over a hundred multinationals for non-compliance with the Diverted Profits Tax legislation, so the multinationals are clearly not behaving.

but then she turned to me and said, "Soooo, if *I* set up a company could *I* get out of paying any tax?"

Perhaps you're wondering that, too?

I'll try to make this romantic . . .

The answer is that, yes, you could. Well, maybe. Actually probably not. It depends.

I mean, you could, say, establish a company in the Netherlands to own the copyright of the book about tax you've just written, to which you as an author pay royalties and which then acts as a guarantor to your bank so that you can get a 100 per cent mortgage on a house you couldn't otherwise afford, and you could get the Dutch company to pay just enough dividends to cover the low interest on that mortgage, just hypothetically for instance.[†]

Anyone can set up a company. It's really easy (especially in the UK, where it takes about ten minutes, and will cost about the same as this book). One of the absolute nonsenses of all our tax systems is that the money you earn is taxed differently depending on whether *you* earn it or a company you *own* earns it. This really doesn't make any sense, but it keeps high-street accountants in business – advising on how plumbers and mortgage advisors, carpenters and novelists can most tax-efficiently *structure* their business.

The more you think about this the more surreal it becomes. As companies were invented to allow strangers to pool their resources, it's a bit weird that if you are the only person involved with that company you can still pay less tax. You can sometimes halve your tax bill just by routing your income through a company.

But what's a company? All you've done is make an official notification

---

†   I haven't actually done this. Book advances barely cover the Netherlands incorporation costs. Delaware is much cheaper.

that your business is legally distinct from yourself. So your customers aren't paying *you* (even though you're the one doing the work, sending the invoice and accessing the bank account), they're paying *your company*. You then transfer the money from that company bank account (that only you have access to) to your personal bank account (that also only you have access to, and might even be in the same app on your phone).

But through the magic of legalese, you no longer have a *personal trade*, you only have a *dividend* (which is taxed at lower rates). The company has a trade, but companies pay lower rates of tax than you do. The combination of corporate taxes and dividend rates is often lower than the straight-up income taxes you were paying without the company (and the combination is much lower if you can get the company out of paying any tax).

It gets even more complicated. The company could pay into your pension, which saves your *company* tax and saves *you* tax. They could also pay a little salary – just up to the threshold where you and the company would start paying payroll taxes (like National Insurance contributions). The company could defer paying you until a later year, but lend you a little money in the meantime.

Given that no one else would have any ownership or control of this company you've set up, you would effectively be paying yourself, lending money to yourself and paying your own money into your own pension. But nope, that's not what the law says. You and your company are legally distinct people. And because the two of you (you and your company) pay tax at different rates, a decent bit of planning will save you both some decent (or possibly indecent) tax.

So common is this ruse that when it was revealed that a whole host of BBC stars, from Gary Lineker to Fiona Bruce, were using personal companies to bill the BBC, rather than have simple employment contracts, there was a bit of a collective shrug of shoulders. If the average interior designer or bricklayer is using a company to reduce their tax bill, who are they to point their fingers at Gary and Fiona?[†]

Or at least, no one except the British government seemed to mind. For years, rules known as IR35 have been constantly tightened up, otherwise *anyone* would be able to quit their job, set up a company and then bill their old boss for the services they provided. In other words, but for IR35 we could all operate through a company to save tax.[‡]

So an *employee* can't use a company to save themselves tax, because the government has actively legislated against this, but a self-employed person can – at least, *usually* . . .

The British government tightened the rules on IR35 so much that it inadvertently helped trigger one of the (I'm guessing now forgotten) crises of 2021 – the lack of lorry drivers in Britain.

The rules changed to say that people who previously considered themselves permanently employed "contractors", but operated through their own companies, must now pay tax as if their company wasn't there. i.e. if you were self-employed but primarily worked for the same employer (like a lorry driver, perhaps, choosing your own hours

---

[†] ITV presenter Lorraine Kelly actually won her £1.2 million tax case against HMRC by arguing that far from being a bog standard employee of the *Lorraine* show, she was more akin to a "theatrical artist" playing a role (the role being a chattier, more positive version of herself), so she should be allowed to pay less tax (as self-employed actors do). It so happens that *I* also play a chattier, more positive version of myself at work, but so far my boss hasn't agreed to deduct less tax from my monthly salary.

[‡] The "I" and "R" stand for "Inland Revenue", which has of course long since been renamed (though allegedly the name change happened just *after* the Inland Revenue ordered their stationery in bulk, so the old name stuck around on letter heads and biros for a long time). Other countries have similar rules to IR35.

but mostly working for the same haulage firm), you were now caught by the IR35 rules.

The effect was that truck drivers – or "essential workers", to use the language of the time – were suddenly hammered by massive tax rises.

You may just about remember (if you were here) that in the autumn of 2021 all the petrol stations of Britain ran dry and everyone worried that Christmas would be cancelled for a lack of plastic tat, due to a lack of lorry drivers available to shift it all.

A lot of people blamed Covid (as lorry-driving exams had been cancelled) and other people blamed Brexit (because why not?), but the lorry drivers themselves said that far more significant than Covid were the changes to IR35 rules.

This was wholly predictable. The government raised taxes on lorry drivers, so the lorry drivers quit. (Or, at least, quit Britain).

—

Interestingly, the lorry drivers had something in common with *X Factor* judge and former pop star Cheryl Tweedy, in that she has also failed in her attempt to use a company to reduce her tax bill, though she took it one step further than the truckers.

Cheryl Tweedy owned a company called CC Entertainments (set up when she used her previous married name of Cheryl Cole), of which she was the sole shareholder and sole employee. She then signed an agreement with her company that if her company was successful, she would receive a payment of *capital*, rather than a more straightforward bonus, which would have attracted income tax and National Insurance. Of course, as she was the sole director of the company, she was effectively signing an agreement with herself that she would pay herself in a manner that attracted much less tax.

A partner at the accountancy firm Grant Thornton, which was one of those that marketed this scheme, said of such ploys, "This is not a tax wheeze. It is a share-based incentive arrangement to align employees' interests with those of the company."

That wasn't entirely true, though, and I don't just mean the use of the word "not". If there's only one employee who is also the only shareholder, then in what sense can the interests of the company ever be said to be different from the interests of the employee?

It's almost like it was convenient for all parties to pretend that a company is some *real* person, with its own *interests*, somehow different from those of the person who owns and controls it. Well, as it turned out, it wasn't convenient for HMRC, which recovered £128 million from 56 companies using this "wheeze".

Henrí had a wonderful ability to listen intently while clearly thinking with a great deal of clarity about what I was *not* saying. She paused for a moment to check I'd finished.

"I'm not sure you've answered my question," she said. "Should I set up my own company?"

I was a little torn. A bit of me wanted to show off to her – to create some fantastically complicated corporate device that would show her how skilled I was in all this, because that's the way to a girl's heart, right? A bigger part of me imagined our future life together, and that image was wonderfully wholesome and loving and didn't involve cheating the system.

"I'll write a spreadsheet for you, to work it out," I said. Luckily she knew that was my way of being flirty.

Of course, if *you* want an answer, then yes, if you're genuinely self-employed you probably can use a company to reduce tax. Or if you own a huge multinational coffee chain, then yes, you definitely can.

For everyone else, including truckers, and Cheryl Tweedy, no, you can't. Sorry.[†]

—

I asked Hal how the meeting with Bazzo had gone in my absence.

"Ah, mate, I told him you weren't available and we rearranged it again. You're not getting out of it. But I hoped you enjoyed the management consultants."

After work I met up with Henrí at a whitewashed café by the beach and told her the bad news – that my boss was inflicting Bazzo on me.

"You mean 'Money'?" she asked, with a smile. "Well, I know a way you *can* get out of it."

She'd been in Australia a little longer than I had, and we'd recently had a conversation about how weird it was that as British expats we might only see our parents another half-dozen or so times, what with the distances involved meaning it would only be once every two or three years that we schlepped back to Europe.

She was also more freaked out than I was by the incredible number of Australian creatures that seemed to want to kill us – there were even birds that attacked us when we rode our bicycles, that were themselves eaten by spiders the size of my hand that lived in my apartment block.[‡]

[†]　Or at least, not *legally*. There is a massive amount of so-called "umbrella fraud" in the world in which large companies break themselves up into hundreds of one-person companies in order to stay under the thresholds for employer's payroll taxes and VAT. Indeed, the *Guardian* newspaper estimated that as many as 8,000 companies had been set up in this way to defraud the UK government in the course of that government's "Test and Trace" programme during the Covid pandemic.

[‡]　On one of our first dates Henrí told me that shortly after arriving in Australia she had called Pest Control because of the number of cockroaches in her apartment. "You want Pest Control for *cockroaches*?" they asked, much as if she'd told a British pest controller that she occasionally saw a pigeon in her garden.

I didn't pick up on these cues.

She told me that her career options weren't so good in Australia, she wasn't that fussed about the surfing and she loathed the laborious daily routine of slathering sun cream all over ourselves.

I still didn't see where she was going with this. So she helped me out.

"I want to move back to England," she said, matter-of-factly, while holding my hand.

"Do you want me to come with you?" I asked, feeling a little hollowed out and like I'd been in this situation before.

She twisted away from me a bit, looking out over the sea. Then she turned her face back, looked me in the eyes and sweetly said, "Well, I'm not going back without you."

9

ANTI-TAXERS

I'm one of those people who panics when I have to decide whether I have *anything to declare* in the airport. Part of this is post-traumatic stress, resulting from my deciding to use a loophole to avoid import duties on some suits I had purchased from a tailor in India shortly after I'd become a trainee accountant.

One of my tax tutors at college had told me how Coleen Rooney (wife of Wayne) had been detained by customs officials for not declaring all her holiday shopping. A similar thing happened to Posh Spice (wife of Old) after she brought a diamond ring back into Britain.[†]

I figured it wouldn't be a good look for me in my first year as an accountant to get fingered (possibly literally) by a customs official, and relied on that tutor's advice to *wear* my suits, on the grounds that doing so would constitute personal use and so not be declarable.

Obviously I couldn't simultaneously put on three suits, so I put on

---

[†] The tabloids called it a tax on love. The future Victoria Beckham claimed that she wasn't importing the ring, but merely bringing it into the UK for repairs, before re-exporting it, which exempts it from tax. She is a lady of many talents, tax clearly being one of them.

one, slung another suit jacket over my shoulder and got my (much shorter) girlfriend to wear a third one. We looked ridiculous, but only for the short hop through customs, and I convinced myself that this was evidence of my mastery of tax-avoidance schemes. Then I got a tap on the shoulder.

A gang of customs officials took me to one side. Then one of them made a rather unusual request.

"Could we put these drugs in your bag?" she asked.

She explained that they had a new dog that needed training up, and they had a small stash of narcotics that they wanted to see if the mutt could intercept.

I'm sure you don't need this advice, but please don't allow customs officials to put drugs in your bag. Anywhere else in the world this would be a guaranteed stitch-up. But somehow Gatwick lends itself to trusting officialdom.

I learned two things from this incident:

1. My tax tutor had omitted an important detail. There's an allowance (currently around £400) for non-commercial items you import into the country, so I wasn't avoiding anything by wearing my cheap suits.
2. That trainee sniffer dog was useless. I sold the drugs a week later in Camden Market.[†]

[†] A friend of mine who works for the Border Force told me that every so often the X-ray machines that scan your bags throw up a fake image, showing some form of contraband, to ensure that the people checking the screens are paying attention. Also there is a lot more parrot smuggling than you might readily believe. And the most common place to conceal drugs is inside shampoo bottles. Also I'm kidding about selling the drugs. I've been super careful not to incriminate myself in this book. Obviously I smoked them.

—

Moving halfway back round the world with my new girlfriend was wonderful, but we hardly had the sort of welcome we could have expected if we were *rich*.

For instance, in 2005, to entice David Beckham (husband of Victoria) to remain with their *club de fútbol* Real Madrid, the Spanish government passed "Beckham's Law", which specifically allowed David Beckham to pay a special non-resident tax rate, despite being a Spanish resident by virtue of living and working in Spain.[†]

The first half of the rule was similar to the UK's non-domicile rule, in that it allowed these wealthy foreigners to legally avoid declaring their worldwide income to the Spanish tax authorities. The logic was that David Beckham might not want to pay Spanish taxes on income he'd earned outside of Spain, and if the Spanish made him do so he might decide not to settle in Spain after all.

Now leaving aside whether this would allow David Beckham to park his non-Spanish income in an offshore account and pay no tax on it – and I'm not for a moment suggesting he did this, but he would have been able to under Spanish (and British) law – the iffy part of Beckham's Law was that the Spanish doubled down on the idea that they needed to offer wealthy people a tax incentive to move to Spain, and promptly offered rich foreigners a tax rate of just 24.75 per cent on their Spanish income. This is a lower tax rate than almost any Spanish people would have paid at the time.

This seems to show a remarkable lack of confidence by the Spanish government in the charms that Spain has to offer. I mean, I can

---

[†] Technically, other non-Spaniards benefited from this rule too, but it's Beckham's name that has stuck to the law.

understand why an oppressive dictatorship in a featureless desert might offer tax breaks to rich foreigners, but Spain's quite nice, isn't it?

In other words, the Spanish government's official position was "If you are foreign and rich, you can pay a lower tax rate than everyone else, because we want more rich people to move to Spain."[†]

But after five years of this rather morally dubious law, the Spanish decided that maybe they'd made a mistake, and quietly dropped it. Unfortunately, nobody seems to have told Portuguese national and football superstar Cristiano Ronaldo.

Like Beckham, Ronaldo earns millions from doing things outside of playing football (for instance, both Beckham and Ronaldo frequently get paid to pose in their pants) and, like Beckham, the cash from these other sources of income can be deposited into bank accounts in other countries. Prosecutors alleged that, by not declaring all of this income in Spain, Ronaldo had deliberately breached his Spanish tax obligations.

Ronaldo's lawyers said it was all down to a misunderstanding over what was and was not required under Spanish law.[‡]

But it's easy to be a *little* sympathetic. Ronaldo had done exactly what Beckham had done, in that he hadn't declared his worldwide income to the Spanish authorities. It's just that between Beckham's tenure and Ronaldo's, Beckham's Law had been repealed.

Ronaldo admitted his guilt, and was sentenced to a 23-month jail term and an €18.8 million fine. Though I'm not sure Ronaldo needs *much* sympathy – under Spanish law he didn't actually need to go to

---

[†]   In theory the scheme was open to foreign poor people as well, but the details of the rules made it impractical for poorer people to get any advantage from claiming non-residence.

[‡]   I don't know if Ronaldo had hired some especially cheap lawyers. It seems like a remarkable thing for a lawyer to say. "Your honour, how can this be a crime? I didn't know what the law was . . ."

prison to serve his sentence (as it was a first-time offence) and, if *Forbes'* assessment of his wealth is correct, the fine was equivalent to about two months' worth of his earnings.

In fact, if you're rich it's pretty hard to get sent to prison for tax evasion (at least in Spain).

Lionel Messi (an Argentinian playing for Barcelona) was convicted, also by a Spanish court, of almost the same crime as Ronaldo – hiding income from so-called "image rights" in offshore accounts – and was also given a prison sentence (in his case, a mere 21 months) that he didn't have to serve, after agreeing to pay a fine.

But there really is another way of looking at this. Messi had to pay about half his salary to the Spanish tax office every year, which, according to Spanish newspaper *El Periódico* made him Spain's top taxpayer. Had he moved to, say, Italy, he might have paid just a quarter of his salary in tax (because of lower tax rates in Italy), which would have saved him literally tens of millions of euros a year.

In other words, if Messi had left Spain he would have uncontroversially cost the Spanish government about €70 million per year, but because he underpaid his taxes by just under €15 million the government launched legal action against him. Messi has now, indeed, left Spain.

—

Henrí and I found a small flat to live in together in London, and had a wonderful few months. She was working, but I was trying to find any excuse not to go back to a job in accountancy. I went on a woodworking course, and tried writing a novel. I'd met some old schoolfriends who had set up a business putting on "wacky" races – the kind of runs where you have to swim through mud and get electrocuted or attacked by badgers – and they were making a fortune, so inspired by them I toyed with the idea of running my own, um, running business. Henrí was supportive, or so I thought.

In December we went skiing in France with my friend Kititi and his other half and while on the piste I bumped very literally into an old colleague from my first firm.

My old colleague was there on a "working weekend", as he put it. He explained that he had joined a tiny husband-and-wife operation based in Mayfair that dealt in what he interchangeably described as "private client services" and "wealth management". His role was "client acquisition", which most of the time meant hanging out in the sort of places where people who need their wealth managed privately tend to hang out. This ski resort was one of those places.[†]

"It's the best job going," he explained. "I get flown into all these fab places, make friends with anyone sufficiently rich and drunk, then drop into conversation how I've just used this *fucking clever* firm in Mayfair to help me buy a £30-million pad in Chelsea entirely *under the radar*."

"You don't tell them that you work for the firm?"

"Poetic licence. I normally 'forget' the *name* of the firm, too, so I get their phone number off them so I can WhatsApp the firm's name over when I remember. I get a cut of everyone I bring in."

His voice sounded a little posher than when I'd last met him. He was definitely wearing fancier ski gear than me, too.

He asked me what I was doing.

"I'm thinking about organising a fun run," I said.

[†] Kititi had been to this resort before, when one of his Big Tech employers had hired the entire resort for their staff to attend a "conference" . . . the centrepiece of which was a giant pyramid built out of ice, upon which David Hasselhoff performed his greatest hits. My old firm, by contrast, requested a staff contribution towards the drinks bill at their annual conference, which was at their own office.

There was a long pause. So I clarified, "Maybe a three-legged race."

There was another long pause, as if he was working out whether to pity me or whether I was kidding. He put a comforting hand on my shoulder.

"Well, we're always looking for people to join the team."

I laughed. Henrí didn't.

"He'd love to work with you," she said. "Give me the details."

—

Mayfair is obviously not a cheap place to rent an office, and the husband-and-wife team had set themselves up in what were effectively just two rooms of a grand old Georgian building. There was one room where I was interviewed and where the firm met our clients (on the rare occasions they came to us, rather than us going to them) which had an extremely expensive-looking polished table and framed portraits of long-dead aristocrats on the wall, and another almost entirely bare room where a dozen desks were squeezed in close together, the furthest desk encroaching upon a tired kitchenette. This room, and this desk, were where I would work.

When I first arrived, the wife, who introduced herself as Katerina and I *think* was Russian (though she never once confirmed it), offered me a tour of the office. She opened the one door that separated the two rooms, waved her hand and said, "Here." She seemed to think this was hilarious. Ominously, she added, "We used to rent a room on the ground floor, but there was a flood. It was a good excuse to make some of our employees redundant." She seemed to think that was hilarious, too.

She and her husband, Houghton, seemed not to have conferred before my interview for the job, nor indeed did they acknowledge each other much *during* the interview. I sometimes wonder if they acknowledged each other in their domestic life either. They did, though, make quite a team.

Houghton was what I imagine most people expect of a Mayfair-based wealth-management consultant. He dressed extremely expensively and boringly and drawled in a manner that I think was meant to seem refined, but was more an opportunity for him to search his rather limited mind for the right words with which to finish his sentence. He seemed to have almost no interest in tax as a subject in its own right, but rather viewed it as an annoyance to be dealt with – though dealt with by others. It's barely worth telling you his back story as you can probably guess it all.

Katerina, on the other hand, knew exactly what she was doing. She dressed like a fortune-teller with a Selfridges gift card, and disguised her intellect behind preternaturally red lips and burgundy talons. She mentioned a couple of times about speaking no English when she moved to England, but I never learned whether that was several decades ago or last year.

She was a lesson for me about prejudice, and I think she wanted to be. Too often a client would ask a question to Houghton, whose talents merely extended to agreeing with anything a client said, only for Katerina to answer with a precise understanding of tax law. All of Houghton and Katerina's staff quickly learned not to make the same mistake as the clients.

Houghton claimed that, despite their differences (actually that's not how he put it), they had fallen in love over their mutual admiration for Goethe, the German poet and free thinker, whom Houghton had studied at university and Katerina had simply, well, read a lot of. Having never read a word of Goethe (I mean, he wrote in *German*) I thought I should try and discover what the fuss was about, so bought a layman's guide.

It was entirely unilluminating, except for one quote: "When I fuck up, everyone notices, but no one notices when I lie."[†]

Anyway, that was still ahead of me. I had to get the job first.

In the interview, Katerina skipped the pleasantries and instead drew a picture on a scrap of paper. As this picture explained almost *everything* that this firm did, I'll recreate it for you here. Her question, which accompanied this picture, was, "What are the tax implications of this?"

As you can see, it wasn't a lot to go on.

"Well, hmm, I assume the stickman is your client?"

"Yes."

Houghton interrupted. "Do you know what a goal is called in polo?"

"A chukka? And the box is a company owned by the stickman . . ."

"Yes."

"What's more prestigious, the Kentucky Derby or Royal Ascot?" asked Houghton, perhaps a little thrown himself by the stickman-and-box picture.

"Well, it's not the *Royal* Kentucky Derby. I assume the client is non-resident?"

[†]   Translation is author's own.

"Yes."

"When is it acceptable to wear brown shoes?"

"If the client is looking at my shoes then what I'm saying isn't clever enough. And I assume the company is non-resident?"

"Yes."

"Where is Davos?"

"Switzerland. So you're just asking me about offshoring property?

I clearly passed both their tests.[†]

—

Katerina and Houghton's clients took a little getting used to. At first I thought they were being funny, but it turned out none of it was intentional.

One client announced that his daughter was going to go backpacking for a year after school. "So I need another jet," he said. I laughed. Katerina scowled at me. Obviously his daughter couldn't fly *commercially*.

Another said that he wished there was a large oak tree in his garden. "You should have thought about that 400 years ago," I said. Houghton raised an eyebrow. "We can arrange that for you," he said. And he did.

My favourite was an aristocrat who, when I asked how I should address her, said, "Oh, I'm very informal. Lady d'Estelloire is fine."

But what they all had in common was that, as they saw it, they were being unfairly treated by the government.

"I employ a thousand people – I'm helping the economy already, and now the government wants to take half of everything I own? It's ridiculous."

[†] As you may have realised, Houghton didn't know the answers to his questions, either.

"You're absolutely right," Houghton would reply.

Accountants are taught about something called the *fraud triangle*. The theory is that if someone has the opportunity to commit fraud, and they have some especial need for the money, and they can justify their actions to themselves, then they will commit the fraud. I'm not accusing any of Katerina and Houghton's clients of fraud, but the same trio of reasons could explain why a lot of people see no problem with their own efforts to mitigate their taxes. They can justify it ("I've done my bit"), they need the money ("All my friends have villas on Lake Como, but I don't") and here, in Katerina and Houghton's finely decked-out meeting room, was the opportunity.

Katerina and Houghton used to earn significant fees by acting as the middlemen between the creators of tax-avoidance schemes and the wealthy clients who might be interested in them, but these schemes were now being shut down by the government. HMRC had even gone after some of the film schemes of the types I'd become aware of when I was last in London. They didn't go after the particular schemes I'd worked on, though – those ones were watertight. Indeed they didn't prosecute *any* of the well-known promoters of these schemes, nor their millionaire users – for the simple reason that *none* of those schemes were illegal. Some of them may have been ethically dubious, highly contrived, contrary to the intention of Parliament, outside the spirit of the law perhaps, but not illegal.

Instead, one of the highest-profile prosecutions they brought was against documentary film-maker Chris Atkins, who had produced acclaimed documentaries that, among other things, highlighted Tony Blair's assault on civil liberties.

Chris Atkins didn't save *himself* any taxes from a film scheme, but he was persuaded by an accountant – working with banking partners – to falsify invoices that helped save the accountant's clients £2.2 million in tax. He was persuaded because as part of the scheme he received £85,000 to make a documentary called *Starsuckers*. In other words, he was actually helping a film get made.

Somewhat ironically, the *Starsuckers* documentary exposed the illegal or unethical practices of people in the entertainment industry.

Chris was given five years in prison.[†]

—

Talking of Tony Blair – he once described the tax system as "a haven of scams, perks, City deals and profits", but judging from his recent behaviour he could have added, "Which is great for me!" At the tail end of 2021 the Pandora Papers leak revealed that he avoided £312,000 in taxes by *not* buying a £6.45 million Marylebone townhouse. Instead, he set up a UK company which purchased a British Virgin Island company which was the owner of the £6.45 million Marylebone townhouse.

The effect of the transaction was just the same as when you or I buy a house – you hand over some cash and get given the keys – but by funnelling the money through an offshore entity almost a third of a million in tax was avoided.

Why? Because the £312,000 he avoided was a tax on *houses*, and he hadn't bought a *house*, he'd bought a *company* that had bought another (offshore) *company*. And there's no tax on buying offshore companies.

[†]   Chris Atkins wrote a bestselling book about his time in prison called *A Bit of a Stretch*. It's very good.

Now it just so happened that this offshore company owned the house he wanted, but that's just a happy happenstance.[†]

In Tony Blair's defence, he pointed out that the deal was structured that way because the Bahraini dictatorship-affiliated family who ultimately owned the house preferred to keep everything offshore, and who was he to interfere with the wishes of anyone in the Middle East?

He kept quiet about the offshore purchase at the time, but after it was exposed he stated that he had dissolved the offshore entity, so the house would, from now on, be within the scope of UK taxes. He didn't say he would pay over the £312,000 of avoided taxes, though.

Give yourself a slap on the back if you recognise that what I've just described is pretty much the same situation as the picture that Katerina asked me to explain in my interview with her and Houghton.

Tony Blair was not Katerina's client, but his tax-avoidance ruse is not in even the tiniest way unique. The simple legal fact is that companies – even companies based in tax havens – are allowed to buy houses. That's because companies are recognised as *legal persons*, and just as a normal living person is allowed to buy a house, so too can a company.

It doesn't have to be this way. Companies can't do everything that a normal person can do – they can't vote in elections or enter the Olympics or adopt a child (or even adopt a dog). But they can buy houses, and the fact that they can is the main reason you can't. Or if you *have* bought a house, it's why you can't buy a nicer one.

[†]   Actually it's even worse than this. Technically, the house he bought, despite palpably being a house, is used as an office, which makes it qualify for a lower rate of stamp tax. Had the house been used as a normal house, the stamp duty on it would have been over £800,000 (which also would have been avoided). This distinction is just how the law is written, so using the house as an office isn't dodgy, and is fairly moot as Tony avoided *all* the stamp tax on the house.

—

If you're the kind of person who fancies buying a £20 million pad in Chelsea (or indeed, a £6.45 million one in Marylebone), you don't just pop into a Foxtons or Knight Frank and ask them to show you what they have on the market.

This is because it's not *you* who is going to buy this house, but rather an offshore company. And to set this arrangement up, you may want to visit a little private client services firm in Mayfair.

I want to tell you a tale of two cities. Well, actually a tale of one city, just with two types of purchaser. You, and rich offshore buggers.[†]

It was the best of tax, it was the worst of tax. In 2013, the UK government introduced a *mansion tax*. Apart from some technical specialists in the accountancy and tax world, no one seemed to notice. In fact, during Ed Miliband's dismal attempt to become Prime Minister in 2015 with his signature "mansion tax" policy proposal, almost no one mentioned that we already had a mansion tax, thank you very much.

That's because the already existing mansion tax was targeted at one particular type of mansion – an "enveloped dwelling". Or to use less technical language, a house that is owned by a company.

Accountants, tax advisors and wealth managers like Katerina and Houghton realised that British houses were seen as a wonderful investment opportunity for their international clients. Obviously there were the prestige aspects of owning a swanky London address, but British tax laws are ludicrously generous to offshore investors.

[†] It's been a long time since I read *A Tale of Two Cities*, though I seem to remember that it had a big section on London house prices, right? And I'm definitely not accusing Tony Blair of doing anything illegal, merely tax avoiding. Though that's hardly the worst thing he's been accused of.

A British-born *investor* who wants to buy a flat in, say, Knightsbridge (or anywhere else in the UK) has to pay stamp duties when they buy the flat, capital gains tax when they sell it – and their purchaser has to pay stamp duties too. Then when they die whoever is left owning it pays inheritance tax.

But the British government decided to exempt a foreign investor from all of these, except the first round of stamp tax. Like the Bahraini former owners of Tony Blair's new gaffe, they could buy the house through a company registered in a tax haven, and from then on only have to worry about selling the offshore company, rather than the house itself.

The effect of this on the Exchequer has been truly staggering – so much so that I've wondered at times if anyone in the government understands the implications of what they've allowed. The minority Liberal Democratic Party once tried to put the figure at £750 million, but I can't see how it's not several times as much.

Before we get into the numbers, here's one startling bit of research by investigative journalist and author Nicholas Shaxson that indicates that maybe something fishy is going on: of the first 76 apartments sold in One Hyde Park – the Candy brothers' uber-expensive block of flats opposite Harrods, where the penthouse apartment was listed for sale at an astonishing £175 million – 54 were purchased via offshore companies. That's well over a billion pounds of property in just one block of flats – owned by anonymous companies in tax havens.

To see why the effect of this is so massive, consider how this one block of flats would have been treated for tax purposes had the flats been purchased by British investors.

When each flat was bought there would have been stamp taxes, mostly at rates of around 15 per cent. If the flats went up in value there would be capital gains taxes of 28 per cent on the increase in value *and* the new buyer would pay another 15 per cent stamp tax. If an investor died owning the flat, 40 per cent of it would have gone in inheritance taxes.

In other words, if you bought one of the flats on a lower floor, say for a mere £100 million, and sold it for £120 million to another Brit, who then died, a total of over £80 million would be paid to the taxman.[†]

I'm not saying that I agree that these taxes should be this high, or that I disagree with them (though they are a slight rebuke to people who say we don't tax property enough). Instead, this is the bit that blows my mind.

As the flats were purchased by foreign investors, using offshore companies (or, even better, multiple offshore companies), in reality the total tax payable would be the original stamp tax only – so £15 million, rather than £80 million. This suggests that in just one block of flats in London the government may have lost out on *hundreds of millions* in avoided taxes.

Just one block! There are literally tens of thousands of super-prime homes owned by offshore companies. That's *billions* in taxes that haven't been and aren't being collected. It's madness – and more than a little suspicious. This is a huge tax break for unbelievably rich people. It's not even like they can vote in British elections. I wonder if they donate to political parties? I can't be certain – none of us can – as they're owned anonymously (though Nick Candy, one of the brothers who built the block was at that Christmas party at Conservative HQ during Covid-19 restrictions that led to the resignation of Tory mayoral hopeful Shaun Bailey).

[†] Stamp taxes of roughly £15 million when you bought it and £18 million when you sold it, capital gains tax of £1 million (though less if it was your main residence) and £48 million in inheritance tax.

Slowly, oh so slowly, the government has attempted to deal with the issue, but in rather the manner of a bored nanny asking her charges to play nice. Legislation has been brought in to try and bring these offshore homes into the scope of inheritance tax and capital gains tax – but it's hard to see how this will be effective. For a start, many of these homeowners aren't even paying council tax. And I don't mean due to some clever loophole. I mean they just went, "Fuck it, we're anonymous, why pay £700 a year in council taxes?". I don't see the oligarchs and plutocrats of this world saying, "Oh, we have to declare that when Uncle Oleg died he owned that BVI company that owned that Delaware company that owned that nice house in Belgravia via that Guernsey trust – well, okay then, we wouldn't want to upset the British government."

In fairness to the British government, they did *recognise* the problem of billions of pounds of UK property being owned through offshore companies, but the best they could come up with to tackle it was the world's most ineffective mansion tax – originally levied at an absolute maximum of 0.7 per cent of what your house was worth in 2012, and now still not much higher. And why ineffective? Because if you rent the house to "an unconnected third party" you can exempt yourself from that tax, too. But these houses are owned anonymously, so clearly it's not beyond these owners to claim that they were themselves the unconnected third party.

The anti-corruption organisation Global Witness estimated that as of 2017 there were 87,000 anonymously owned houses in the UK, worth a combined £100 billion. That is billions in lost tax revenues, to benefit people who may be money-launderers or gangsters or worse.

Back in 2016 David Cameron announced his plans to introduce a register of the *real* owners of UK property. A draft bill was put together in 2018. It was then suggested the bill would be implemented in law in early 2021. It wasn't.

It's taken the Russian invasion of Ukraine to put the spotlight on the suspiciously slow progress of legislation to prevent oligarchs buying London property anonymously with dodgy money. Anti-corruption campaigners are already pointing out the flaws in the proposed legislation, such as the fact that a new "Economic Crime Bill" that is supposed to force the real owners of these houses to register their ownership doesn't apply to anyone who owns less than 25 per cent of a house, or to houses owned by certain types of trusts.

Already there are rumours of vast properties not being owned by *one* oligarch, but by the oligarch and four members of their family. If the wording of the Economic Crime Bill stays as it is, those rumours will remain rumours, because no one will be able to confirm the actual ownership percentages.

—

So here's the final kicker – one of the main reasons you can't buy a fancier pad is that almost all the best houses have been bought up by some offshore tax avoider at the top of the chain, aided by our tax and regulatory system.

If we could physically see this happening there would be black holes all over London, and increasingly the rest of the country too. Black holes where houses used to be.

And if you're not British, don't feel so smug, because this is not just a British phenomenon. Offshore buyers "investing" via offshore companies is all the rage in prime real estate spots across the world. By some estimates more than half of American properties that sell for more than $3 million are bought via companies.

For legal reasons I should state that I'm sure there are some perfectly legitimate reasons for buying a house via a company in a secrecy jurisdiction. I just don't know what those reasons are.[†]

—

There have been other attempts to avoid tax on houses. One enterprising chap tried to save almost £900,000 in stamp taxes on his £9 million home by claiming that he wasn't buying just a *home*, he was buying a mixed-use residential and commercial property (which for some inexplicable reason would make it legally subject to much lower rates of tax). His argument was that the communal gardens out the back of his house sometimes had a tea shop in them. As such, the gardens were partly commercial, and so his house was partly commercial too.

He did not win his case.

—

Houghton invited me to join him on a visit to a client whose house in Hampstead had recently been refurbished. Sorry, I made that mistake again – I mean a client whose *company's* house in Hampstead had recently been refurbished. In fact Houghton was at pains to tell me to keep the client's name secret – at first I assumed because he was very famous, but I later realised it was because the client wanted no one (including the tax authorities, and possibly his wife) to know he owned the house.

Also "house" is a bit of an understatement. The rooms above the garage were bigger than the entirety of the flat Henrí and I were living in, and the pool complex was larger than my local public swimming pool.

[†]   Defenders of the status quo claim the answer is self-evident: secrecy. I don't buy that. The rest of us have to put our names on the property register, there are very few reasons why you would genuinely need to keep your ownership secret and, if you really care about secrecy, rent, don't buy.

Houghton even claimed that Mikhail Gorbachev had been invited to stay at one of the neighbouring properties by an estate agent who had offered him free accommodation in a bid to sell that house. I didn't see any sign of him, though, so perhaps Houghton had it wrong. Then again, it didn't seem that any of the homes were occupied.

Our client met us himself, and while Houghton's face was perpetually business-like I was clearly marvelling at the size of the place. It had one of those grand central atriums with two staircases and a ludicrously oversized "modern" chandelier that looked like a whale's ejaculate had been frozen mid-air. The client suggested we follow him to his bathroom, which Houghton didn't seem to think was at all an odd request.

"What do you think of that?" said the client, indicating with two hands quite the most enormous bathtub I'd ever seen. "It's made from a single piece of Italian marble."

"It's a thing of beauty," said Houghton.

"It cost me £600,000."

Which was, I was rather horrified to calculate, more than I could afford to spend on an entire flat. For a bathtub! And then, worse, he added, "Yeah, but I don't know why I bought it. I prefer showers."

I felt like being sick into it. Houghton, though, considered it thoughtfully and said, "I think you were absolutely right to buy it."

On the way back to the office I asked Houghton if we should have remarked on the lack of décor in the client's (or, rather, client's company's) house. Houghton had no idea what I was talking about.

—

The biggest tax break that normal British people will encounter in their lives is the fact that your main home is usually exempt from capital gains tax. This might not, at first glance, sound very exciting, but this really is the biggest tax break *you* are ever likely to get (unless you're not British, in which case your country will probably screw you over when you sell your home). In the UK, when you sell your house you are likely to make a huge capital gain, simply because property prices have gone bananas.[†]

But because there is tax relief on houses, your gain on the sale of your house – provided it's your "main" house – is exempt from tax.

Except . . .

If you haven't always *lived* in your house, say because you've been living in someone else's house, or Secretary Gorbachev has been living in your house instead of you, this tax relief is restricted. But for deeply weird reasons the definition of "lived in" includes what are known as *deemed periods.*[‡]

It's these deemed periods that made me remark on our client's décor choices to Houghton, as they present a gold mine of a tax-planning opportunity, but only if you keep a real eye on the detail and, in some cases, your décor.

[†]   I have an elderly uncle who bought a five-storey house in Chelsea for £14,000 in the 1960s. One of his neighbour's houses was recently on Rightmove listed for £18,000,000. I asked my uncle if £14,000 was a lot of money when he bought it. "Oh, yes," he said, "my salary was only £2,500 at the time." He was a teacher. Somehow I doubt a teacher today will be buying an £18,000,000 house. And yes, I have worked out how many cousins I have to murder to get into his will – it's one or two too many. Maybe.

[‡]   This is a little bit technical, but it is the number one most common thing I get asked about outside the office. So for UK homeowners, if you're interested, these are the rules – you can currently deem your house as having been lived in for: the last nine months of ownership; any time you've spent working overseas; up to four years spent working away from home in the UK; and up to three years for any reason (though you have to actually live in the property before and after most of these reliefs). Though once again, if you want to take advantage of these rules, go and pay for some proper advice.

Normally, if you've barely lived in your house at all, you can still reduce your tax bill to next to nothing provided you *move back into your home again* before you sell it.

And here's the dodgy bit: there's no minimum time period for moving back in.

Now in theory that means you could move back in for five minutes before you sell the place, but HMRC wants proof that you were *genuinely* occupying the property before you handed over the keys to new owners. Normally this "proof" takes the form of some pretty mundane things (like being on the electoral roll). But not always.

One bloke used his Tinder profile as evidence – he argued that he was only looking for dates in *London*, so surely that's where his home was?[†]

And the courts accept photographs of you living in the property and witness statements from your mates, so one good house party might be enough to prove your occupation.

The overriding consideration, though, as always, is the matter of *intention*. If you can prove that you *intended* to live in your home permanently, then if your circumstances happened to change a couple of days after you moved in, well, whoopsie, life is like that sometimes. This has led to some ridiculous court cases where HMRC have had to argue over what someone's *intentions* were.

I studied a lot of these cases during my time at Katerina and Houghton's – cases where someone was trying to "prove" their actual occupation of their property, and what struck me in particular was how just a few small details could swing a case.

In one instance it was shown that a taxpayer hadn't unpacked their

---

[†] Though it's possible that London was where his wife wasn't.

boxes despite claiming to have moved in. In another a witness said there
were no pictures of the taxpayer's loved ones on the walls.

This was the kind of thing I would wake up in the middle of the night
thinking about. When Henrí and I eventually bought our own place I
quickly became conscious that it was soaring in value – but this would
only be a tax-free soaring if we could demonstrate that we really lived
there. There were still boxes that remained unpacked, and our walls
were entirely bare.

Once when my mother came round she remarked on how sweet it
was that I had put a photo of her on our mantelpiece.

"Mum," I said to her, "it's for tax reasons."

—

I spoke to Katerina about the client's bare walls. She laughed.

"Don't worry, if ever it comes to that we'll just Photoshop some
pictures in."

DON'T KILL YOUR GRANDMOTHER

After a year or so working at Katerina and Houghton's, I experienced a number of life events in relatively quick succession. All of them had significant tax effects (though Henrí asked me not to talk about tax efficiencies in my groom's speech). Our wedding was blissful, the flat we bought was just right for the two of us and the baby we were expecting, and my grandmother died.

I hadn't experienced many deaths in my life. Indeed the only recent death I'd had to deal with was back in my old firm, and that had been a rather surreal experience. There was a nice guy called Terry who worked in corporate finance and who would occasionally find himself on our floor; we'd gone out for lunch a few times and we got on pretty well.

Then, one morning, I received an email from HR sadly informing me that Terry had died. This hit me in many different ways – I liked Terry a lot, I didn't know him terribly well (I hadn't known his surname, for instance, until I received the email about his death), as he worked in a different department I only saw him every so often, I still owed him a pizza . . . how was I meant to feel? Sad, obviously, but not devastated. I knew he was married, but I didn't even know who to ask to get his wife's contact details, and she would have no idea who I was, or why I was giving her ten pounds for a pizza.

I half-expected there to be a follow-up email with details about his funeral, but it never came, though a colleague I was vaguely friendly with in HR made a point of coming to see if I was okay. "I know you and Terry were close," she said.

And then life goes on, right? Well, it went on a bit too literally. Two weeks later who should swagger into my office but Terry? He greeted me (and others) fondly, said, "Long time" to me and suggested, with a wink, that we go out for that pizza I owed him.

No one batted an eye. No one said, "How can this be?" or "It's a miracle!" No one, except me, thought anything was out of the ordinary.

I realised that there were two possibilities. One was that I had imperceptibly slipped into a parallel dimension in which Terry had never died (which was my preferred option); the other was that this wasn't Terry. And if it wasn't Terry, then who the fuck had died?

Well, obviously Terry had died – the email about Terry's death made that clear. It was just that this person I thought was Terry *wasn't* Terry. It turned out his name was Reuben.

I never found out who the *real* Terry was – the one my colleague from HR thought I was close to. But I'd mourned his passing. It was a weird emotional state.

—

My grandmother's death had more of an impact on me.

I had been asked to look after my young cousins for the day, so decided to take them to the laser tag centre. I assumed my elderly grandmother would like it, too.

I used to love these games, which involve running around a dark room firing laser guns at other kids, all decked out in plastic armour and helmets that record a "hit". There were strobe lights and dry ice and when you shot someone or got shot your armour would vibrate and say things like "Good shot" or, ominously, "You have one life remaining."

My grandmother didn't enjoy it. In fact, she had a stroke. And shortly after that, she died. It's possible that the timing's a coincidence, but there's a part of me that blames myself.

Death is always shocking, and she was one of those particularly loving, kind grandmothers who I always enjoyed spending time with, so it was especially sad that she'd died.

She lived in Jersey, so I needed some time off to attend her funeral. I asked Houghton if he was okay with me taking a few days' bereavement leave.

"Technically, I don't think it would be *bereavement leave*," he said. Given that he'd suggested *dolphin* as an answer to a question about "types of fish" at our Christmas quiz, this struck me as a little hypocritical.

"Well, the thing is," he said, with words I remember precisely, "the firm's policy is that we can only give you bereavement leave if you really *loved* your grandmother."

I had never heard anything quite so amotional (which possibly isn't a real word, but I can't think of a better way to combine amoral and unemotional). I stared at him blankly, not quite sure I'd understood correctly, and he clearly felt the need to justify this further.

"Katerina and I have discussed this point at some length, and what we're concerned about is staff taking bereavement leave just because someone they're not especially close to has died. So hence the requirement that it has to be someone you *really* loved."

"Are you asking me how much I loved my grandmother?" Given I was dealing with an accountant, maybe he wanted it expressed as a percentage.

"Just have a think about what I've said."

I did think about it.

I thought he could have said, "I'm sorry for your loss, take as long as you need." Or even, "I'm afraid bereavement leave is more for when you're so distraught you can't work, so take annual leave instead." I probably would have had a fair amount of respect for him if he'd said, "Look here, you entitled prick, you're always slacking off in one way or another, the best I'll offer you is unpaid leave."

But he didn't say those things. He may have *implied* one of them, but I still figured that maybe this wasn't the firm where I wanted to spend the rest of my working life.

—

Inheritance tax is always a tricky one to discuss, because on the one hand it involves talking about people dying, which is always sad, but on the other hand we're going to talk about how to get richer out of them dying, which is a bit of a silver lining.

A lot of countries don't have any inheritance tax, such as India, Australia, Sweden and Canada. Actually there are some tax implications of dying in Australia, referred to, officially, with true Australian directness, as the Super Death Benefit, and Canada sneaks it in another way by making the dead person pretend to sell everything they own.[†]

[†] You may remember from earlier that Australia also does something really clever that most other countries don't do – when you inherit something in Oz, you inherit it with the same officially recognised cost as the person who left it to you paid for it. This is a bit of a technical point, but it stops people avoiding capital gains taxes by, well, dying, as it simply makes your next of kin responsible for your own capital gains tax liability. In most of the rest of the world any gains you accrue in your lifetime are written off at your death, but I guess because Australians live in a country where even the plants can kill them, the Australian government needs to stop people dodging taxes via an untimely poisonous death.

In America, officially you have to be a proper "0.1 percenter" to suffer inheritance tax on your estate, though unofficially there is another take on this – according to Donald Trump's Chief Economic Advisor, former Goldman Sachs banker Gary Cohn, "Only morons pay the estate tax." He later clarified that by "morons" he meant "rich people with really bad tax planning", which is one of those clarifications that perhaps revealed a little too much about his opinion on whether rich people should pay tax.

But in the UK, the tax is more straightforward. If you're poor (when you die) you don't pay any inheritance tax. If you die rich, you also don't pay any (we'll see why in a second). But if you're somewhere between the two, things can get ugly.

It's a famously political tax, with the traditional right-wing argument being, *What could be a more fundamental human right than providing for your children?*, and the traditional left-wing argument being, *What could be more unfair than being born with a silver spoon in your mouth?* They both seem like pretty good arguments to me, though I've always thought that the silver spoon argument is undermined by the entire Western world being born with a silver spoon in its mouth. Most people think the top 1 per cent of earners should pay more tax. I suspect you do, too. But if you have *any* job your salary probably puts you in the top 1 per cent of earners *globally*. Does that change your opinion? Should more of your income be given to the poorest people in the world? Usually the answer's "no". Of course rich people should pay more tax, but often what is meant by "rich people" is "people richer than me".

And then of course the *looking after your kids* argument is slightly undermined when you're a billionaire and you intend your kids to stay that way too – how much "looking after" can one kid need? But then I guess we all like to remain in the lifestyle to which we're accustomed (which is part of the argument to justify large divorce payouts).

Inheritance taxes are often thought to be one of the main causes of the destruction of the British aristocracy – if you ever watched *Downton Abbey* you might remember how preoccupied the Granthams were with death duties. But these taxes have existed in some form or other for hundreds of years. In the 17th century there was Probate Duty (introduced to help fund another war with France); then in the 18th century that became Legacy Duty (to help Britain fight America),[†] which in turn became a succession of near-identical duties until finally in 1894 Chancellor William Harcourt introduced an Estate Duty, on the grounds that:

> The whole system is difficult and complicated . . . here a patch, there a patch, but each successive modification has only left confusion.

And yes, he was right, though he could have been talking about any tax, at any time. And it's not like he sorted it out once and for all. In 1949 the Labour government introduced a whole host of reforms to deal with the complexities and lack of fairness of the Estate Duty, though it was still sufficiently unfair that another Labour government replaced the tax with an entirely new one, which was *still* sufficiently unfair that the Conservatives introduced inheritance tax in 1986. Whether it's still unfair in its current form I'd like you to decide . . .

—

The basics of inheritance tax are that if you die – sorry, *when* you die – you add up the value of everything you own. The first chunk of it is tax free and then you have to hand over 40 per cent of the rest of it to the

---

[†] Which, had the tax raised sufficient money, might today be called West Britain.

taxman. Or at least, someone has to hand it over to the taxman . . . you don't do it, because you're dead.

Inheritance tax should be one of the simplest taxes to get your head around, but it's so simple that historically it was also super simple to avoid. When you found yourself on your deathbed, with mere hours to live, you could summon your loved ones to your side, say a few kindly words, then do the sensible thing and turn your attention to your accountant. You could ask your accountant to arrange the transfer of all your worldly goods to your next of kin (or your lover, or whoever, it didn't really matter). And then you would die – but crucially, you would die penniless.

So following the rule for inheritance tax as I've just described it, you would add up the value of everything you owned, but it would add up to nothing, because you'd given it all away (minutes earlier). Consequently there would be no tax to pay.

Obviously this is too easy a ruse. You could even go one dishonest step further by writing up the contract that transfers all your worldly goods, signing it, then leaving the date blank. Your accountant could fill it in after you died – but fudge the date to be one day before you popped it.[†]

So to prevent rich, dishonest people doing this there is a further rule. When you die, you also add up the value of all gifts you've made in the seven years before your death. The first chunk of those gifts is tax free, but 40 per cent of the rest has to be paid to the taxman – by the people who received the gifts (regardless of how rich the people who receive the gifts are).

But there's a problem with that, too. If it really applied to *all* gifts you

---

[†]   Just to be clear, I am not for one moment advocating that you actually do this. Fudging dates on official documents is 100 per cent illegal. If you're really desperate to cheat the taxman there are much better ways to do it.

had made in the last seven years, then the poor executors of your estate would have to track down every last Tinder date you'd been on and say, "Remember that guy who paid for your slightly disappointing meal in 2017 who you never saw again? Well, he's been hit by a bus, so now you owe the taxman £20."

To deal with this problem the Inheritance Tax Act contains some exemptions, most of which (though in fairness not all) seem to have been written with wealthy people in mind.

To start with, you can ignore the normal stuff you might give your family members – otherwise every bowl of Coco Pops I lay out for my children would potentially be taxable. You can also ignore small gifts. If you've got your tax-planning hat on you might want to know what counts as small. *Small*, it turns out, depends on how rich you are. For most of us, it's £250, but for the rich, it's pretty much anything they want it to be.

Hidden away in the exemptions is a rule than you can pay pocket money to your kids (or anyone else), provided that you do so regularly, you have sufficient income to do so and paying it doesn't reduce your standard of living. In other words, if you're a billionaire you could quite comfortably squirrel a million a week to your offspring and legally avoid £20 million a year in potential inheritance tax.

Not that you need to. This sort of tax-avoidance plan is decidedly middle-class – and more typically used by elderly relatives paying for their grandkids' school fees rather than billionaires worried about their succession.[†]

You see, two of the biggest exemptions from inheritance tax are for the two types of people who tend to have the most money: landowners and business owners. And the exemptions afforded them

---

[†] Whenever I dine out with my parents I like to suggest that they pay for the meal, because it'll make the meal 40 per cent cheaper (in the long run).

mean that those types of people barely have to pay a penny to the taxman when they die.[†]

More specifically, if you own agricultural land, the entire value of that land is exempt from inheritance tax. You don't even have to farm the land – either you can get someone else to do it for you, or just leave it fallow and claim you're helping butterflies find their soulmates. Some landlords have even put a box of snails in their otherwise empty shops to claim that they're snail farms – which also makes them exempt from business rates.

Non-agricultural land doesn't cut it, by the way. If you have a house with a garden, that garden is taxable (no matter how infested with snails). But if that garden is a 1,000-acre estate, then it's not (because it has agricultural value).

Although if you have a house with a garden and a good accountant, there's another option available – more on that in a mo.

So say you're the Duke of Buccleuch and, largely thanks to the battlefield heroics of your great-great-great-great-great-great-great-great-great-grandfather, you find yourself owning about 1.5 per cent of Scotland, you can be assured that you can pass this colossal estate on to your children or, presumably, great-great-great-great-great-great-great-great-great-grandchildren, without paying tax, provided the land has an agricultural value, which it does.

But my granny's old cottage in Sussex, that was taxable.

Looking for other examples of big estates, you might notice that the Duke of Buccleuch's estates are not a patch on the Duke of Westminster's.

[†] The rules in the US are pretty similar – most businesses and farms are exempt. This rule exists partly thanks to lobbying efforts to highlight the supposed mass unemployment that would result if rich estates were taxable. No, really.

Sure, they're twice the size, but the Duke of Westminster owns something that Buccleuch doesn't: Mayfair.[†]

The current Duke of Westminster, Hugh Grosvenor, inherited his estate when he was 25 years old, and was widely reported to have become the richest person under 30 in the entire world. These reports weren't, however, true. In fact the bit about him owning Mayfair isn't quite true either.

Here's why.

The Grosvenor family has form when it comes to tax avoidance – it was a ruling in a tax case in 1936 involving the 2nd Duke of Westminster that provided the legal justification for almost the entire tax-avoidance industry. The 2nd Duke was a bit miffed that the wages he paid his gardener weren't deductible business expenses, so he drew up a contract that agreed to pay the gardener a certain amount at certain agreed times – which while sounding like a normal employment contract was worded in a way that circumvented the law of the time. The Duke was taken to court for tax evasion, but fellow peer Judge Lord Tomlin ruled that:

> Every man is entitled, if he can, to order his affairs so that the tax attaching under the appropriate Acts is less than it otherwise would be.

In other words, there's nothing in the law that says you can't avoid tax by using a little ingenuity. The judge did acknowledge that fellow taxpayers may be "unappreciative" of this ingenuity.

[†]   The Duke of Westminster owns even more land than the Crown. Historically, though, the Queen was always able to use her own special loophole: it was *Her Majesty's* Revenue & Customs. (Though just to be on the safe side she set up some holdings in the Cayman Islands.)

The Dukes, now with the law firmly on their side, subsequently really got into the swing of things. After getting stung in the 1950s with the largest inheritance-tax bill ever paid in the UK when the *3rd* Duke of Westminster died, the *5th* Duke launched a 12-year legal fight to prove that his uncle, the *4th* Duke, had died as a result of injuries he sustained fighting during the Second World War. His case was challenging, as it was widely accepted that the 4th Duke had died of cancer 22 years after the war had ended. Still, anyone who died in the service of their country was exempt from inheritance tax, so it was worth a shot.

He won the case.

But the really big tax wheeze, and the reason the 25-year-old Hugh Grosvenor could avoid an estimated £4 *billion* tax bill, was that most of the Grosvenor family's wealth had been transferred into *trusts*.

If you're not quite sure what a trust is, I'll tell you: a trust is . . . well, I don't want to get too technical, but it isn't really anything. There's no object or entity, real or imagined, that you can point at and say, "That's a trust." It's more a *relationship*. Well, maybe a relationship and a bank account. Though as a financial and legal concept, trusts date back to at least the Roman times (which probably means they pre-date bank accounts).

In a typical scenario, some crusty old aristo might marry a much younger wife, but be worried that she's only after him for his money. So he wants her to have *access* to his wealth, but not actually own it – lest she just flog it all once she gets her hands on it, rather than look after the aristo's children from his first marriage when the old chap dies.

So the rich old fella might ask an accountant to manage his wealth *on behalf of* the trophy wife and the kids. The estate gets put into a *trust*, of which the accountant is a *trustee* and the kids and wife are *beneficiaries*.

You can invent complex rules about how and when they all get their share. I had an old schoolfriend, for instance, who said that he had a family trust that would only release funds to him once he got married. He had to wait for one of David Cameron's more progressive policies to become law before that was a realistic possibility.

Going back to our example, cleverly, or unscrupulously (depending on how you see this), the wealth that's in the trust doesn't now belong to anyone. It can't belong to the rich old dude because he's gifted it away. It doesn't belong to the wife or kids because they can't do what they want with it. It doesn't belong to the accountant because he or she is just managing the money. The money – the wealth in the trust – belongs to the trust (which doesn't exist). And the trust, because it is nothing more than an abstract legal relationship, a *concept* if you will, cannot die. And if you cannot die, then inheritance tax cannot come into play.[†]

So when the current Duke of Westminster's father died, young Hugh didn't inherit Mayfair. He didn't inherit the £10 billion that the papers reported he did. Because the family trust owned these things. And it wasn't the trust that had died. The new Duke was merely a beneficiary of the trust, just as he had always been.

In fairness, not every last penny in the Grosvenor Estate is held in a trust. But even the bits not held in trust can be exempted from inheritance tax. If ever you've had the pleasure of wandering around Mayfair you may have noticed that it's hardly the swamp it was when one of Hugh Grosvenor's ancestors married a 12-year-old to get his hands on it (not that that was unusual at the time), but nor is it farmland.

[†] Well, kind of. There are some things in tax that you can figure out for yourself rather than pay an accountant to do it for you, but trust law is not one of them. There are all manner of peculiar *ten-year rules* and *chargeable lifetime transfers* that could catch you out, if you do it wrong. If you want to use a trust, get a tax advisor who specialises in trusts.

No matter, your wealth doesn't have to be in agricultural property to avoid inheritance tax, because – good news! – "business" property will do, too. The Grosvenor Property business doesn't just rent out big posh mansions, it also actively develops property. This makes it a qualifying business, so exempts it from inheritance tax.

In fact, many seriously wealthy families put their wealth into "family investment companies", with each family member owning shares in the company. Structured right, these "investment" companies can be treated as actively trading businesses, allowing the family's wealth to be shielded from inheritance tax.

I'm not saying that this is some obscure loophole, by the way. This is the very intention of the legislation. If you own land or a business, or if your £10 billion fortune is held in a trust, then you don't have to worry about inheritance tax. Inheritance tax is simply not a tax for billionaires.

—

Perhaps surprisingly, Katerina and Houghton didn't deal much with inheritance tax (or at least they brushed off my attempts to get some free advice about my grandmother's estate), but one of my colleagues took pity on me and arranged for me to have a chat with a relative of his who worked in "trusts and estates". This is the normal description for this field of tax, since it sounds better than "death taxes".

The trusts and estates advisor was called Arthur, though Merlin may have been more appropriate. The first thing that struck me about him (apart from his beard, which looked older than he did) was his lack of shoes. The second was the dreamcatcher on his wall.

Arthur indicated that I should sit down opposite him, and he seemed to rather relish the opportunity to show off his talents.

I explained that I was there to talk about any planning opportunities in relation to my grandmother's estate.

"Here's what you do. Grandfather still alive?"

"No."

"Shame. Could do with his nil band."

Empathy is not a prerequisite to being an accountant.

The gist of the advice (which is still generally the advice given) is to shift as much money into a trust as possible without triggering a tax charge. Nowadays you can transfer about fifty grand a year. So if you started in your forties and died in your eighties you could swing about £2 million into a trust. That's £4 million for a married couple, who could also get about another £1 million from general, normal thresholds.

In other words, the poorest estates don't suffer inheritance tax because they're below the thresholds. The richest estates don't pay tax because farmland and businesses and a lot of what "non-domiciles" own are exempt. And the well-advised really-rather-considerably-but-not-spectacularly well off don't suffer inheritance tax because they can shift their wealth into trusts (this used to be a much, much easier thing to do, which is why a lot of super-rich Brits live off their trust income, but *you* can now only put away fifty grand per year, you know, just in case you happen to have that kind of moolah lying around).

So if all these people can sidestep inheritance tax, who actually pays it? I had a bad feeling I knew the answer already.

When Arthur had finished explaining how my grandmother should be transferring her supposed vast wealth into a trust, he asked if I had any questions.

"Does it make a difference that she's already died?"

"Oh . . . Not much we can do, then. You should have come to me years ago."

"Oh bugger. I don't suppose her having lived in Jersey makes any difference?"

His dreamcatcher let out a puff of smoke. It turns out I'd said the magic words.

—

Jersey is a bit of a funny place. It's said to have more sports cars per head of population than anywhere else in the world but an island-wide 30mph speed limit – though most of the owners of those cars probably view 30mph as a bit racy.

It's so safe that front-page newspaper headlines warn of things like "Handbag Stolen" and "Car Window Broken", yet there's an average of one gun owned for every ten people. I guess the residents are thinking, *Just in case someone comes for* my *handbag*.

It's also a great place to visit, with enormous beaches, two historic and well-preserved castles, lax tax laws, delicious fudge, little corporate oversight and an amazing underground hospital built by the Germans during the war.

Jersey has a population of just over 100,000, but, as of 2017, 45,000 registered companies. That's about ten times more companies per head than are found in England, which has itself seen an explosion in the number of companies since our own corporate oversight rules were for no obviously good reason relaxed by the coalition government in the early 2010s.

I'd love to tell you what all these companies are doing there, but in truth I don't know. No one does. Jersey simply doesn't ask them what they're doing. Or, more specifically, it doesn't ask for any information on foreign-owned companies (which is most of them – at least, I think it is: it's surprisingly hard to find out, which is kind of the point).

The veteran tax campaigner Richard Murphy has estimated that a maximum 2.8 per cent of all the companies linked to Jersey pay tax, and that the true figure may be much lower than that.[†]

Jersey has no capital gains tax, no inheritance tax, normally no corporation tax, a 5 per cent VAT rate and a maximum 20 per cent income tax rate (which the Nazis imposed on them, but they haven't repealed since). It is also – crucially, you would think, for my grandmother – not part of the United Kingdom.[‡]

This combination of low local taxes and relaxed bureaucratic interest in offshore wealth stashed on the island are the typical hallmarks of what are commonly called tax havens.

Of course every tax haven, including Jersey, says that it's not really a tax haven – though obviously they don't want to lose good business opportunities by *convincing* anyone that they're not tax havens – that would be disastrous. It's a very fine balancing act i.e. "We're not a tax haven, unless you need a tax haven . . . ?"

The advocacy group the Tax Justice Network creates a global ranking of tax havens each year, and in 2021 named Jersey as the eighth most significant tax haven in the world, with a Haven Score – a term created by the Tax Justice Network to measure how much scope for corporate tax abuse each jurisdiction allows – of 100 out of a possible 100, indicating "unrestrained scope".

Four of the top ten tax havens named by the Tax Justice Network are

---

[†] Richard Murphy is the envy of anyone who writes about tax for coming up with the best book title: *The Joy of Tax*.

[‡] Well . . . it's part of the British Isles, has King Charles as head of state and is defended and represented overseas by the UK government, but that doesn't mean it's part of the UK. At least not for tax purposes. Or, indeed, for NHS purposes (which is probably a good thing for their economy, given the number of old people needing health care in Jersey).

British Crown Dependencies or British Overseas Territories, with the British Virgin Islands taking the top spot. The BVI are a cluster of islands populated by around 35,000 people (including billionaire Richard Branson, who has a whole island to himself); they have six commercial banks and are estimated to be home to almost half the world's offshore companies.

The British Virgin Islands prefer to refer to themselves as an offshore financial centre rather than a tax haven, though I'm not sure the absence of corporation taxes, sales taxes, capital gains taxes or inheritance taxes is entirely coincidental. They do have an income tax, but the official rate is 0 per cent.

You might wonder why Britain doesn't deal with these havens – after all, the British Virgin Islands' residents are British citizens and we share the same head of state (and army). There are a few answers to that. The first is that Britain is a tax haven too. That's not just my opinion – we're number 13 on the Tax Justice Network's list.

Another reason is that Britain has given autonomy to these islands and any attempt to take it back is always met by howls of "neo-colonialism".[†]

From these islands' perspective it is easy to see the advantage of being a tax haven – you get millions in fees from all around the world just for hosting a few abstract legal entities. Indeed Ireland was taken to court by the EU after Ireland refused to charge Apple more in taxes – i.e. a country argued that it should have the right *not* to charge tax. On the surface that looks weird. After all, if Ireland lost its case Apple would owe it more tax. But then, what was Apple doing in

---

[†] Since I wrote this the former Premier of the British Virgin Islands, Andrew Fahie, has been arrested in the USA for alleged drug-smuggling and money-laundering, and the British government is conducting an enquiry into the islands' governance structure. So it could change (though I'm not betting on it).

Ireland in the first place? It wasn't the sunny climate that attracted
Apple to Ireland. Maybe it was the Guinness?

Ireland is number 11 on the list.

Then there's the fact that the British government has refused to
acknowledge the British Virgin Islands as a tax haven. In 2013, perhaps
stung by the French government adding Jersey, Bermuda and the BVI
to a list of "uncooperative tax jurisdictions", David Cameron said, "I do
not think it is fair any longer to refer to any of the Overseas Territories
or Crown Dependencies as tax havens."

In 2016 the Panama Papers data leak showed that the British Virgin
Islands were still the most popular jurisdiction used by (now closed) law
firm Mossack Fonseca, which incorporated over 100,000 companies
on the island.[†]

—

Anyway, I'm getting ahead of myself. None of this data had leaked back
when I attended my grandmother's funeral.

Also I should reiterate that all these places deny being tax havens.

Jersey's neighbour Guernsey (number 17) has claimed that it is "part
of the solution in the fight against financial crime".

My old man once tried to open a bank account in Guernsey, and told
the teller that he wanted to deposit some cash. The teller looked a little
shiftily at him, then invited him into a private meeting room, to meet
the bank manager.

[†]   There have been three big data leaks that all begin with "P", and it's easy to get
      them muddled up. "Panama" was a leak of Mossack Fonseca's data in 2016,
      "Paradise" was a leak of a different offshore law firm's data in 2017 and
      "Pandora" was a leak of data from 14 financial service providers in 2021.

"How much do you want to deposit?" the manager whispered.

"Erm, about £100?"

The two men stared at each other for a few moments.

Then the manager laughed. "I don't think we need a private meeting for that. I thought you were going to say a lot more."

I'm sure the manager was part of the solution in the fight against financial crime.

—

The issue with my grandmother's estate was that she wasn't an international tax avoider and had spent more time solving crosswords than conspiring with accountants.

Yes, she lived in Jersey, but she still owned the little cottage she'd grown up in. It wasn't spectacular, and had it been in Jersey would have been exempt from taxes, but it was in the south east of England, making it pretty much automatically worth more than the threshold for UK inheritance tax.[†]

So, unlike the Duke of Westminster's £10 billion estate, or Richard Branson's business empire, her estate was taxable.

—

That's not to say that other members of my family didn't fancy themselves as international tax avoiders. Well, of sorts.

[†]   At the time of writing, the threshold above which you have to pay inheritance tax in Britain is £325,000. I say "time of writing", but really it's been £325,000 for over ten years (meaning inflation – especially house price inflation – has dragged a lot more people above the threshold).

Another one of my many uncles had got divorced when I was still a child and had lived with his girlfriend in his house in South London ever since. Given that he'd bought the house back in the Seventies and, you know, London house prices, this house was probably worth at least £5 million by the time that he was diagnosed with a cancerous tumour.

This was very sad (the tumour, not the house price), and devastating for his family, but obviously massively tax-inefficient too. He had never married his girlfriend, so on his death she would be unable to inherit the house – as the inheritance tax bill would be around £2 million. So quietly, unceremoniously, having never felt inclined to do so before, they got married in the hospital chapel. He died shortly afterwards. The wedding had saved his widow £2 million.

A similar thing happened to another friend of mine. She was also diagnosed with a tumour, and also shared a house with her boyfriend. Her boyfriend is rather religious and apparently had long wished that they should get married. She'd resisted the ideological arguments, but surrendered to the tax argument. So similarly they got married in a small ceremony, prior to her last-chance operation.

Against the odds, she awoke from the surgery with the news that the tumour had been completely removed. Apparently her first words were, "Oh my God, I'm bloody married." She still wonders whether her boyfriend and her doctor were conspiring.

—

The house in Sussex had been used as an occasional holiday let and was left to all my grandmother's surviving grandchildren in her will. Annoyingly, there were ten of us. My dad suggested that we visit the house "to see if there was any furniture we might want".

It seems that some of my cousins had the same idea. There were suspicious rectangles of dust on the walls where pictures had been removed, and a noticeable lack of a telly. To this day I don't know if the official valuer had been called round before or after these items had been removed.

My dad moped around the house feeling mournful, as you might imagine. But when he got to the kitchen he smiled, and then started laughing.

"Did I ever tell you about what happened when *my* grandmother died?" he asked. He probably had, but I said, "No."

"My mum went in and tidied up her old house – she hoovered and dusted and threw out all the old food in the kitchen . . . well a few days later her sister phoned up frantically asking where all the food was. My mum explained that she had binned it all. Her sister was beside herself – apparently my grandmother hid her diamonds in the sugar bowl."

He lifted the lid of the sugar bowl and peered inside.

—

You might have noticed one of the big problems with anything written about tax.

My grandmother's cottage was worth about £400,000 when she died. To me, sitting in my flat in London, that's not a preposterous amount of money. I don't live in an especially posh bit of town, but £400,000 round these parts will just about stretch to a one-bedroom flat, maybe with a little balcony if you're lucky. It doesn't seem fair to me that someone in a small one-bedroom flat, perhaps sharing it with their boyfriend, is deemed so rich that if they pop off their next of kin will have to pay a tax bill in the tens of thousands to keep ownership of the flat.

And yet of course to someone else £400,000 will seem like dream-come-true money. Someone earning minimum wage and saving every penny they earn would have to work for 21 years to save up £400,000 – and that's with someone else housing and feeding them.

Inevitably this means that it's difficult to look at the fairness of tax rules without being biased by our own perspectives. Some of you will think I'm an ass for dismissing the owner of a £400,000 flat as "not wealthy", others may have spent that much on a car (though probably more of you are in the ass camp rather than own a Bentley, at least statistically).

But I think we may be able to agree on one thing – if we're going to have a threshold above which we have to pay inheritance tax, then *everyone* above that threshold should pay the tax.

Though for legal reasons, I'm not going to tell you what was inside the sugar bowl.

I will give you some free advice, though. If your parents are British and still alive and have more than £325,000 each, give them a call and tell them that you love them. Then explain how giving you their money *now* could save a fortune in tax.

Good luck.

HER MAJESTY STRIKES BACK

In 1999 Lucasfilm released *Star Wars: Episode 1: The Phantom Menace*, widely considered to be the greatest of all the *Star Wars* films.[†]

I was wildly excited to go and see this movie, but turned up late to the cinema and had to sit so far off to one side that when the famous scrolling text that explains the context of each film appeared it seemed to slant off to the top right of the screen. Here's your starter for ten: what *was* the context of that film? As in, after it said, "A long time ago, in a galaxy etc., etc.", what did the next writing on the screen say? I guess I'm asking, how does the entire *Star Wars* saga begin? What was the single event that kick-started an intra-galactic war (and, retrospectively, a multi-billion-dollar film franchise)?

It passed me by the first time, partly because of the angle I was reading it at, but by 2017 my son was old enough to want to watch the film, so I sat through the saga again. I read the scrolling text out loud for my boy, just in case he missed any important detail. Well okay, just

---

[†] Just a reminder that for the purposes of anonymity (and not getting sued) I need to change a few details every so often.

so *I* didn't miss any important detail. And there, on screen, was the answer.

Two Jedi knights had been despatched to the small planet of Naboo to help resolve – wait for it – a tax dispute! A fucking tax dispute! The whole *Star Wars* saga kicks off because the Nabooians can't agree how much tax to pay. I had to apologise to my son for swearing, but seriously, a tax dispute?

But then I started to see tax disputes everywhere in children's literature. Remember *The Little Red Hen*? It's often one of the first books that children learn to read. In case you've forgotten it, the little red hen asks for help from some other animals to plant some seeds, but they all refuse. Then the hen asks for help watering the seeds, and still they refuse. Then she asks for help in harvesting some seeds, and taking them to the miller, then the baker, and all these times the other animals refuse to help. It's riveting stuff. But right at the end the hen asks if any of the other animals would like to share the finished product – a loaf of freshly baked bread. Suddenly the pig and the rat and the rest of them are all saying, "I will" and licking their lips.

This, clearly, is about tax. Should the hen, having put all the effort into generating this little ball of edible wealth, share her spoils with the rest of the animals? I mean, clearly she relied on the common resources of society to get to the point where she had any bread to share, but did she owe anything to the lazy animals who hadn't directly helped her get it?

Interestingly, the story tends to end in one of two ways. Most commonly the hen agrees to share the bread. She's a good egg, so to speak, and knows that just because someone else had been a bit of a dick doesn't mean you shouldn't share what you have in times of need.

In another version (and the first version I read my kids), the hen pulls out a switchblade and says a slightly more kid-friendly version of "Stay back, motherfuckers, the bread's mine!"

Kids' books are riddled with messages about tax. Whether it was *Peppa Pig* or *PAW Patrol*, there always seemed to be some tax parable lurking in there somewhere. But after a while I realised what the issue was. Half the time the moral of these stories was about sharing. It doesn't matter if you made the bread yourself (or in the hen's case, got the baker to make it – and it's never clear whether he got paid or not), it's just that the decent thing to do is share.

This caused me a little twinge of guilt. What if, just hypothetically speaking, my entire career had been about helping people, you know, *not* share?

I fondled the switchblade in my pocket and decided not to think about it.

—

Small tax advisory firms like Katerina and Houghton's were having a tough time. The golden era of tax-avoidance schemes was coming to an end, so it was becoming harder and harder for Katerina and Houghton to justify their really rather punchy fees to their clients. And it was harder to find new clients, too, as the golden era of golden visa schemes – which gave wealthy foreigners an easy pathway to British residency and citizenship – had just been made less gilded. A golden visa applicant has to invest at least £2 million (and up to £10 million) in a British company and prove that they aren't corrupt or a criminal. But prior to 2015 they only had to prove their lack of criminality to their own professional advisors – people like Katerina and Houghton – who would earn significantly more fees if they could manage that £2–10 million investment.

In other words, prior to the rule changes, Katerina had a lot of conversations that went like this:

"Привет, are you a money-launderer?"

"*Nyet.*"

"Then welcome to our firm."

But after 2015 the right to do these checks was taken away from the professional advisors, so another flow of easy fees was disappearing. Katerina and Houghton were becoming ever more concerned with how to keep their income, well, incoming.

Houghton liked to remind me that the trick to retaining clients was to say "yes" to every request.

"We can work out the technicalities later."

By "technicalities", he meant "legalities".

And what the clients requested most often was to *mitigate* their tax liabilities (all the way to zero, usually), and Katerina and Houghton and the team spent a lot of time thinking about how to do this.

Unfortunately for them, HMRC had been thinking quite hard about the whole tax-avoidance thing too, and the government had finally passed a piece of legislation that was to be to the tax avoiders what *The Phantom Menace* had been to my love of *Star Wars* films.

This was the legislation that was to end the golden era. And by 2015, when Katerina and Houghton invited me to join their small firm, this new piece of law was in full force.

The legislation was called the GAAR, which sounds a bit like something Chewbacca might say but actually stands for General Anti-Abuse Rule.

It was a fantastically powerful piece of legislation. The gist of it was that if you set up a tax-avoidance scheme, then the scheme doesn't work. That's it. HMRC didn't have to explain why a scheme didn't work, or which particular parts of the scheme were faulty, it was just "if it's a scheme, it won't save you tax".

Or more technically, if there were *arrangements* to avoid tax, and those arrangements were *abusive*, then HMRC could ignore whatever had been arranged and ask for the full tax to be paid now. A tax dodger could still take HMRC to court to argue that their arrangements were not dodgy, but the onus of proof was now on the taxpayer, rather than the other way round, and HMRC got their tax upfront.

In theory almost any arrangements could be caught by the legislation, but that is rather the point. Don't want to work late tonight even though you'll get paid overtime? Well, that's an arrangement that will mean you pay less tax . . . but is it abusive? To debate that point there is an independent advisory panel. Though it's "independent" in the sense of being appointed by HMRC.

Katerina felt there was a real injustice to this new *equivocal* law. Her position was essentially, "Uncertainties in the law used to be taken advantage of by tax advisors, now they're being taken advantage of by the taxman. Honestly, the taxman's behaving like we used to, it's outrageous."

To survive the GAAR, the tax avoiders had to adapt, which meant either relying on the inherent distortions and injustices in the tax code as it was written, or just ignoring the GAAR, the taxman and any other authority, and hiding their cash. Or by not being British, so not subject to the GAAR. Or by denying their "schemes" were "schemes" at all. In other words, the *golden* era may have ended, but that didn't mean the party had to stop.

I asked Houghton what he thought of the GAAR.

"Oh, I don't think anyone's paying much attention to that," he said (though by "anyone", I think he meant *himself*).

—

There were a few things about Katerina and Houghton's firm that didn't add up. For one thing, no one gave me a straight answer about what had happened to my predecessor – the person who had my role before me.

More suspiciously, some of their clients' wealth profiles on our internal systems were *incomplete*, or unnecessarily password protected. One of the clients owned a restaurant that I happened to know, as it was not far from where I lived. When I looked at the accounts of the restaurant I couldn't believe how much money it was making. I mean I *actually* couldn't believe it, as in, there was no way the revenue figure was true.

Unlikely turnover figures are a well-known red flag, as they indicate possible money-laundering. A drug dealer who wants to make their income look legitimate can put their cash through the tills of a *normal* business – like a restaurant – to hide the fact that the true source of their wealth is illicit. The funny thing about this is that, having created seemingly legitimate income, they now owe taxes on that income. So while there may be no VAT on drugs, there may be VAT on the fake pizzas that the restaurant claims were sold in order to launder the cash made by selling drugs.

I asked Houghton about this. He tried to imply that I'd misunderstood the accounts.

"These are consolidated accounts," he said, "so that's the income of the whole *chain* you're looking at."

I had opened my mouth to ask a follow-up question – like why didn't the accounts say that they were consolidated, like they're supposed to – when he added:

"In fact I've been meaning to lighten your workload. Let me take that client off you."

—

While some money-launderers end up paying taxes on their criminal enterprises as part of their laundering efforts, this hasn't stopped money-laundering from being a seriously big business. Though like other big businesses, the money-launderers do usually try to minimise their tax bills.[†]

So even money-launderers need good tax advice. But giving them that advice is very illegal.

There's a misconception that money-laundering is something that only seriously hardcore gangsters get involved with, but this isn't quite true. You might have done some laundering yourself. Any time the proceeds of a crime are made to appear legitimate, a money-laundering offence has been committed. But because tax evasion is a crime, and the proceeds of that crime are the taxes you've not paid, and spending those unpaid taxes on normal stuff conceals the illicit origins of the money, then any time someone commits tax evasion they also become a money-launderer.

So if you've ever downloaded a song illegally, or underpaid a tab at a bar, or not put money in a parking meter because *you'll only pop into the shops for a minute*, then you've not just evaded taxes, you've laundered money too.

One of the biggest fines for failing to prevent money-laundering was recently handed to NatWest bank, who were fined £264 million in 2021 for failing to spot that one of their customers was laundering money, despite the customer, supposedly a gold dealer with an annual turnover of £15 million, depositing £365 million with the bank over five years, including £264 million in cash. Hundreds of thousands of pounds

---

[†] Probably the most famous money-launderer of all time was Al Capone, and some people believe that the term "money-laundering" comes from the fact that Capone disguised his bootlegging profits as the legitimate income of his chain of launderettes. In truth, I can't find much evidence that supports this – and in the end he wasn't convicted of money-laundering (or murder or extortion or selling illegal booze); rather he got sent down for 11 years for tax evasion.

would be deposited in a single go, often in black bin liners (which split open due to the quantity of cash). My favourite part of this report was that staff disregarded automated systems that were pinging like mad at the suspiciousness of these deposits. I can imagine the alarm going and a bank clerk saying, "Just ignore that, it's always going off."

No staff members at NatWest were prosecuted, but NatWest itself now has a criminal record, which presumably it has to declare when it applies for a loan.

If an accountant suspects money-laundering, they're supposed to report it to their firm's money-laundering reporting officer. My firm's money-laundering reporting officer was Houghton.

—

The Pope has denounced those who avoid paying their dues as committing *un peccato gravissimo* – a grave sin.

The Pope doesn't pay taxes, incidentally, but in fairness he doesn't have a salary. I believe the saying about church careers is that the pay is lousy but the perks are *out of this world*.

Though if he did have a salary, he still wouldn't have to pay taxes, because there aren't any taxes in the Vatican.

Italy does levy taxes, and a lot of the Vatican's money-making enterprises are, unsurprisingly, in Italy, but the Vatican is largely exempt from Italian taxes, too. Indeed, in 2016 the Court of Justice of the European Union ordered Italy to recover unpaid property taxes from the Vatican, which Italy's tax inspectors had been reluctant to ask for. You know, in case they went to hell for it.

This does make me wonder, just a bit, whether what the Pope meant was that not paying your taxes is a very grave sin, when it's someone else not paying them. Or at the very least it's open to interpretation, which I don't think is too controversial a thing to say about papal declarations.

I don't want to suggest that the Vatican is in any way worse than other organised religions, by the way. In researching this book I've tried to find an example of *any* religious organisation that pays tax. I've only found one: the Church of Satan. Read into that what you will.[†]

—

One Monday morning I received a text message from an unknown number. It read:

> Don't come in today, inspectors here

Now I don't normally need much encouragement to not go to the office, but I felt the need to check that this was a genuine message. That, and I was naturally a little intrigued.

No one at the office answered my calls. Eventually I got a WhatsApp from one of my colleagues, who confirmed that tax inspectors had turned up unannounced.

"Any idea why?" I asked.

I could see the little typing dots of his reply come and go. He was clearly thinking carefully about how best to phrase his response. Then it came:

"Are you joking?"

Still, I assumed that it was no big deal. Apart from when I worked for Wilhelm, the only time I'd dealt with "inspectors" from HMRC was when my friend's church got raided after he, in his role as treasurer, overclaimed his gift-aid rebates. Actually "raided" is probably too

---

[†]   Apparently the Church of Satan doesn't believe in a literal Satan. When they were asked, via Twitter, "If you don't believe in a literal Satan, who does?", the Church of Satan replied, "Christians."

strong a word – when I arrived to help out I found the treasurer, the tax inspector and the vicar all sharing a pot of tea.

Gift-aid rebates had become a touchy topic for the tax office. The idea behind these rebates is that both charities and donors to those charities can receive sizeable tax refunds. However, the notorious advisory firm NT Advisors (remember them?) had set up a charity called the Cup Trust that had requested over £50 million of tax refunds on over £175 million in donations. The controversy was that only 0.1 per cent of these donations was given to actual needy causes, so HMRC was now on trigger alert for similar manipulation of the rules.

Not that my friend at the church was doing anything naughty – his church's situation was resolved amicably. Apparently the tax inspector recognised the vicar from his former diocese near the tax inspector's old office and decided that instead of accusing anyone of criminal negligence (or worse), he would help correct what he was sure was an innocent error.

After the tax inspector left, the vicar shared a little secret with me:

"The local tax office used to put on their Christmas panto in my old church. The funny thing is, they always paid for the venue hire by bank transfer but gave the organist an envelope of cash."[†]

HMRC have more powers than the police do when it comes to turning up unannounced and demanding access to your files. Murder someone and the police need a warrant, but mess with the government's money and boy, you're in trouble.

When I finally got back to the office, Katerina and Houghton and one

---

[†] It's not illegal to pay someone in cash, just as it's not illegal to move 9,000 staff to a Newcastle office owned by a British Virgin Islands company itself owned by Tory party donors, as HMRC are. But it's not a great example to set.

of my senior colleagues called Niall were nowhere to be found and were not answering their phones. We were also all locked out of our intranet and emails, which meant we didn't have much to do except speculate on what had happened (and go to the pub).[†]

One of my colleagues who had been in the office when the inspectors had arrived filled me in a little about what had happened.

"It wasn't just the HMRC inspectors. The police were here too."

"That sounds bad."

"Yah. Did you know it's illegal not to hand over your passwords?"

"To your laptops?"

"And our phones. Did any of your clients ever claim Research and Development Tax Credits on bitcoin mining?"

I laughed. I probably shouldn't have.

"No. Never."

"Sensible."

The theories we formed of where Katerina and Houghton were grew more and more unlikely as the day, and the beers, wore on. By mid-afternoon the leading contender was that Katerina had fled the country in an elaborate disguise and Houghton had been murdered by Spetsnaz. I was convinced it was more likely to be the other way round.

"I tell you, *Katerina's* been murdered!" I banged my fist on the table, in a moment when my lack of sobriety hit me rather hard. It was barely 3pm, I was pretty sure I was shouting and Katerina had just arrived at the pub, neither in disguise nor murdered.

—

"We're just paying a little fine," Katerina explained. "It's no big deal."

[†]   My favourite coffee mug was also missing. I still wonder if HMRC took it as evidence, as it said, "It's not tax evasion if it's signed off."

Houghton had also joined us in the pub and seemed equally relaxed. "You know what they say," he said, "punishable by a fine means legal for a price." But he then added, "Though Niall won't be working for us any more."

It all seemed to be nothing but a misunderstanding about some overclaimed Research and Development Tax Credits. These credits are similar to the Film Tax Relief that I'd worked with before. Essentially, any company that spends money on scientific endeavours can receive either a tax break or straightforward cash from the government, in proportion to the amount of research the company has done.

This seems a pretty sensible idea, though while I don't want to knock a scheme that involves funding science, the mechanics of the scheme have left it vulnerable to abuse.

In 2017 two big cases had hit the headlines. In one, five defendants were jailed for their part in luring 730 investors to invest in a supposed research project to help reforest the Amazon and, as a nice side effect, save the investors £107 million in tax. But very little research was ever conducted, which made the whole enterprise fraudulent.

In the other, three men were convicted for a similar "research" scheme, which also claimed to both save tax and rainforests. Though this scheme went even further – not only would trees be planted, but a cure for HIV would be found, too. I mean, wow.

Both cases involved circular transactions, secret offshore accounts and fraudulent claims . . . And very little actual research.

In one of the cases the defendants went to huge lengths to keep everything anonymous – they instructed their Swiss bankers to forward no mail or message to the UK under any circumstances, so that nothing would be discoverable in the UK. What caught them out was something I'm sure we all do – it's almost impossible for anyone to remember all their passwords and bank account numbers, and even harder if there are dozens of them strewn across multiple secretive tax havens, so one of the defendants *wrote down* the crucial info on a couple of scraps of paper, which he hid in his house, in England. The scraps were found when his home was raided by HMRC.

The five defendants in that case received between five and eleven years each in prison.[†]

At the heart of the other case was a company called Ethical Trading and Marketing Limited (how could that be bad?) and – just in case you doubted the veracity of Ethical Trading's claims about curing HIV while saving the rainforests – world-renowned conservationist Professor Ian Swingland OBE, founder of the Durrell Institute of Conservation and Ecology at the University of Kent, had provided the scientific assurance that the scheme was legit.

The only problem was that Professor Ian Swingland was lying. The reassuring documents were faked. In doing so, he committed pretty much the same crime as documentary maker Chris Atkins who, if you remember, got five years. But rather than seeing the inside of a prison cell, the professor was stripped of his OBE. That'll learn him.

Of course, you don't have to create an elaborate web of offshore trusts and partnerships and Isle of Man companies (as the R&D fraudsters did) to defraud the Exchequer.

Three men in Birmingham simply applied for a £29.5 million tax rebate after claiming to have spent £137 million developing an IT healthcare system for Middle Eastern clients. They literally just submitted a tax return and in the box that says, "Are you due a rebate?"

[†] Arguably the jury did time, too. Due to its complexity, the case took so long that one juror conceived and gave birth during the trial (I assume not in the actual courtroom, though reports are unclear).

they wrote, "Yes, £29.5 million, please" (or words to that effect). I assume they thought HMRC would just say, "Sure, here you go, here's almost £30 million", but instead HMRC asked for some evidence. The three men sent a falsified bank statement.

The bank statement didn't work. The trio were jailed for a total of 21 years.

—

I never got to the bottom of *exactly* what Niall, my senior colleague, had done, other than that it was something to do with cryptocurrencies, which was definitely not something I'd been involved with.

In fact the closest I'd ever got to cryptocurrencies was when one morning in the office about a year earlier I logged onto my computer and discovered that I had received an email with the subject: Advice Without Borders. Immediately I thought of Wilhelm. It had been a few years since I'd last spoken to him, but this had his manicured fingerprints all over it. Actually, do you manicure your fingerprints? It was the sort of thing I could imagine Wilhelm doing.

Anyway, I was right. Wilhelm had discovered bitcoin.

My friend Kititi described it to me like this: cryptocurrencies are valuable because they have a utility, and that utility is helping you buy drugs on the internet.

I've since been told it's more complex than that.

For a start, few cryptocurrencies are truly *anonymous*, as the whole point of the "blockchain" technology that underpins them is to create a decentralised ledger of transactions (i.e. a record of what has been purchased). But they are often called *pseudonymous* as, while the transactions might be publicly available, the real person behind the transactions isn't, not least because of software known as "tumblers" that allows the mixing of cryptocurrencies from different sources in exchange for fresh or, if you prefer another term, "laundered" coins.[†]

I read Wilhelm's email several times, trying to make sense of it. I didn't really understand any of this crypto craze. I wanted to, don't get me wrong. But getting my head around cryptowallets and tumblers and Ethereum and dogecoin felt like a challenge too far when it had taken me six months at the start of my career to realise that I didn't need to use a calculator to add up a column of numbers in Excel.

Wilhelm's email was filled with superlatives about the wonderful opportunities that this transnational new currency had, how it was ideal for the international jet set, how it allowed accounts to be calculated without reference to national borders. All taxes are at least to some extent based on where the wealth is generated, and here was wealth to be made in the lawless frontier of cyberspace. Not that anyone says cyberspace any more.

It wasn't immediately clear whether his email was a marketing effort, or whether he was trying to recruit me. Bitcoin was in the news back then, but nothing like it is now. One bitcoin at the time was worth less than £1,000.

As far as I could make out, Wilhelm's idea was that it wasn't just currencies that could be decentralised – whole businesses could, too. If a business was offshore, with international customers and international staff, then everything they did could be conducted with stateless and potentially anonymous currencies. He seemed convinced that he'd found a means to leave any country's jurisdiction. And that meant he'd found a means to avoid any country's tax.

[†] Laundering cryptocurrency is just as illegal as laundering normal money. It's also a big industry. A Russian national was recently arrested in a small Greek village and indicted in the USA as the operator of a digital exchange that had laundered $4 *billion* worth of cryptocurrencies.

I spent some time thinking about this. A couple of years earlier I would have thought, *Gosh, how clever*, but increasingly I wasn't sure which Little Red Hen I wanted to be.

I told Henrí about Advice Without Borders. She was unimpressed, but not for the reason I expected.

"Everything's 'without borders' these days – doctors, reporters, libraries. I read about 'Clowns Without Borders' the other day. Can't he think of something more original?"

I decided to forget about the opportunity to get into Wilhelm's bitcoin "solutions" (what that really meant, I didn't want to know), and instead wondered what the headline would be when one of the clowns without borders trod on a landmine.

At the time of writing this, one bitcoin's worth more than £35,000.

Anyway, HMRC didn't think any of this was *Gosh, how clever*. Just because bitcoin made tax evasion and money-laundering a little bit easier, it didn't mean it made those things a little bit more legal. Indeed British law states that no matter where the bitcoin is, if you're in Britain you have to pay tax on your bitcoin gains. Not everyone *is* declaring their crypto gains – in just two seizures in June and July 2021 the Metropolitan Police seized over £300 million of cryptocurrencies.[†]

—

A week or so after our office got raided, Katerina and Houghton invited me to lunch. Katerina told me that she was very impressed with my tax

---

[†]   Though I don't know how you actually "seize" a cryptocurrency. Does some copper just put a £300 million USB stick in their pocket? Heist movies in the future are going to be *rubbish*.

knowledge and Houghton said he thought I had a real rapport with clients. He said he was sure I would "go far".

"You're absolutely right," I said. Katerina laughed, but I'm not sure Houghton had the first clue why.

But I was on edge. Something ominous was in the air. You may have noticed something different was now happening. Previously, whenever some famous, rich person got involved in a tax scheme they either got away with it, or the scheme failed and they paid over their tax.

Now people were being jailed. On the surface it can be hard to see what's so different between this thoroughly illegal *evasion* that lands people in prison and the *avoidance* we've mostly been dealing with. They both involve a manipulation of the truth, they both seem at least a little dishonest, they both save you from paying tax.

If it helps, consider a jellyfish. Is it a fish? Instinctively you'd probably say "no". A fish has a backbone and gills and scales and a jellyfish is consequently definitely not a fish. But then why is it called a fish? Surely someone thought it *was* a fish? Isn't *fish* sometimes used as a shorthand for *creature that lives in the sea?* Didn't we say as much a little while ago? A jelly*fish* must belong to a category of *things called fish*. And aren't the boundaries between species fairly blurred? What if I could show you a reasoned argument from a Professor of Piscine Studies that jellyfish have many fish-like characteristics? How sure are you *now* about that jellyfish not being a fish, in at least some sense of the word?

But is a jellyfish a volcano? No, it's not. There's no ambiguity there. There's no possible truth. Any professor who said otherwise would be stripped of his OBE.

So really, the difference is about ambiguity. If something is debatable, it's avoidance. But if something is an out-and-out lie, then it's evasion. If your tax return asks what your income is and you know you

earned X but you say Y, that's evasion. If you know you should have paid
sales tax and you didn't, that's evasion. If you hide or cheat or steal,
that's evasion. And if it's evasion, you go to prison.[†]

Which does mean that there's an easy way out of being a tax evader:
get your accountant to do the evading for you. That way *you* are not the
one who is lying.

Katerina seemed unsure how to discuss this delicate matter
with me.

"You know some of our clients . . . they have certain *special*
requirements . . ."

I tried to look as expressionless as possible.

". . .and they pay *extra* if we can totally remove them from tax, all
very low profile, of course."

All I managed was a rather non-committal "Um, hmm?"

Katerina explained that they were looking for someone to take over
the work that Niall used to do, before his unexplained departure from
the firm. She asked if I wanted to take over his role, which would mean
getting a pay rise, taking over his clients and, I now suspected, almost
certainly eventually going to prison.

I politely declined.

—

I'd love to tell you what happened next, but I can't, not precisely.
I understand that this is a common phenomenon with accidents – that
everything *after* getting hit by a car can be described with absolute

---

[†]   Well, sometimes. Country singer Willie Nelson managed to underpay his taxes
      by an astonishing $32 million, but rather than go to prison he sued his
      accountants and agreed to release an album called *The IRS Tapes: Who'll Buy
      My Memories?* from which all profits were given to the taxman.

clarity, but the events leading up to it have simply not been laid down in our memories to be recalled.

I was on my bicycle, the light was green, a police car ran a red light and I had time to lift my left leg so that the bumper of the police car didn't crush it. I fell onto the bonnet and within half a second the police car hit a minibus, which I was then thrown against.[†]

I don't remember any of it hurting, weirdly, but I do remember a chap who looked a bit like Russell Crowe coming over to help and saying, "Wow, your foot is totally fucked." I don't think he was a trained medical professional.

It made the news, but sadly only the traffic news, because we blocked quite a busy crossroad. Apologies if you were stuck in traffic that day. Looking on the bright side, it got me out of going to work for a few weeks.

Staying in hospital gave me time to reflect on what had happened to my career, mostly because the phone signal was *rubbish* and you had to pay to watch TV, so there wasn't much else to do except look at the missing tiles on the ceiling and *reflect*.

I discovered that the curtains between beds were designed to be disposable, but budget constraints meant that they were left hanging permanently. The food was really bad. The doctors all looked tired. I wondered whether any of this was partly my fault.[‡]

[†]   The driver of the police car told me that police cars were very rarely in traffic accidents, because of all the training the police have. I asked a friend of mine who is also a policeman whether this was true. He laughed. "They're called 'Pol-Cols' – police collisions, they happen *all* the time." It also transpired that the police only accept a maximum 50 per cent of the liability, so it's not like I even got a new bike out of it.

[‡]   Actually for the first few days I didn't have a single negative thought, as I was high on morphine.

But at the same time, whenever the doctors or nurses or physios or radiographers or other patients learned that I was an expert in tax, they all asked me the same question:

"So can you tell me some trick to lower my tax bill?"

And yet the consequences of this question were all around them, plain to see.

I realised the Wilhelms and Katerinas and Hals of this world were just serving a basic human need. People want to keep more of what they have. I started to wonder if the core problem wasn't that there were a few bad apples abusing the system, it was that we had a tax system that wasn't fit for purpose. It should be fair and simple and unarguable. Unmanipulable. If you see other people cheating the system, then immediately that system no longer seems fair. Indeed it no longer *is* fair. I knew what I needed to do. I had to fight the system.

Though maybe that was the morphine talking.[†]

[†]   And big thanks to the medical team. Two pins in my ankle, a short while in a cast and some state-sponsored leg massage and I was back on a bicycle before long. Sadly my replacement bike got nicked from outside a different hospital a few months later (the police declined to investigate).

And I realise it could have been a lot worse. Crypto pioneer John McAfee (of McAfee virus-protection fame) made pretty similar claims to the ones Wilhelm was making – that cryptocurrencies were the future. Though the US government alleged that John McAfee had failed to pay his income taxes (and been part of a $23 million fraud). McAfee claimed that a war was on between governments and crypto, and that he was a "major target". He tattooed "$WHACKD" on his arm and claimed, "If I suicide myself, I didn't." While awaiting extradition to the US from a Spanish prison, in order to stand trial for tax evasion, John McAfee killed himself. Conspiracy theorists went nuts.

I WOULDN'T START FROM HERE

Of the 535 members of the US Senate and House of Representatives, there are more qualified pilots (12) than qualified accountants (11). Yet Congress oversees a tax system that collects over $3 trillion in taxes (and doesn't have to land any planes). There's a similar lack of accountants in parliaments all around the world. Tax systems are so complicated that even qualified accountants can't understand the consequences of all the rules, let alone politicians, let alone laypeople.

So we have a situation where people who don't understand tax rules vote for politicians who don't understand tax rules who then come up with more tax rules. No wonder it's a mess.

Politicians can't write the rules themselves, so they get accountants to help. But it's in the interest of both the accountants and the government to keep everything complicated. The accountants keep their fees (and their loopholes) and the politicians get to keep their donations from special-interest groups and to keep raising taxes without the electorate understanding what they're doing.

And politicians inevitably write their laws in response to short-term issues and media stories, often with a patch or a tweak, but never stepping back and saying, *What should the big picture look like?*

There are almost too many examples of this to know where to start, but here's one that really riles me.

Former UK (Tory) Chancellors George Osborne and Philip Hammond both announced during their chancellorships that they were going to scrap a tiny little tax called Class 2 NIC, which was one of seven different types of National Insurance contributions that British workers are exposed to. This would have saved about three million self-employed people £150 per year. Hammond called the tax "regressive and outdated" and said that it was "right that it should go". But he then changed his mind. Here's a quiz. Did he do so because:

a) the tax brought in close to half a billion pounds in tax?

b) abolishing the tax would make some poor people poorer?

He didn't even have the balls to announce the U-turn himself, but instead got his colleague Robert Jenrick to do it for him. Jenrick claimed, ludicrously, that some people on very low incomes would somehow be *poorer* if they paid *less* tax.

I might try this line of reasoning on my kids. "No, you can't have any pocket money, you'll get poorer if I give you more money." Only, I don't think my kids are that stupid.

And yet most newspapers just reported this claim as fact. Journalists aren't tax experts, either.

Jenrick's argument was that to get a state pension you have to demonstrate that you've paid sufficient National Insurance contributions during your life, and as the threshold for paying Class 2 NICs is lower than for other types of NIC there could hypothetically be people on a certain narrow band of income for their whole lives who wouldn't now qualify for a pension, unless they paid a different type of NIC that was a bit pricier than the one that was not now being abolished.

Got that?

If it sounded like a paragraph of garbage, that's because it was.

Personally, if I was in charge of both tax rules and pension rules, and a tax-related pension issue came across my desk I'd say, "Well, let's change this daft pension rule, then." But no, Jenrick went with a slightly cleaner version of "Fuck you all, we're keeping the regressive and outdated tax."

The good news is that this means that, whichever answer you gave for the little quiz just now, you got it right. Well done.

And just in case you have any sympathy for Robert Jenrick, remember that he became the housing minister who personally intervened on behalf of billionaire Tory (and Labour) donor Richard Desmond (former publisher of top-shelf magazines *Barely Legal* and *Readers Wives*) in a planning application in the impoverished London Borough of Tower Hamlets. Jenrick decided to push through planning approval *one day* before a new community levy would have come into force – a levy that would have provided the borough with over £40 million.

In other words, a Conservative minister decided to use his political powers to save a billionaire about £40 million in tax, at the expense of the poorest borough in London. The decision was later overruled by the courts.

There's so much to get annoyed about in this.

Here we have a politician deliberately keeping an "outdated and regressive tax" because it raises, well, tax. By his own assessment it does so regressively – i.e. the poor pay more of their income towards it – yet he kept it. Just imagine: the alternative would have been to raise taxes on richer people, and we can't possibly have *that*.

But then worse, he blamed his U-turn on an extremely obscure technicality about the interplay of pensions and National Insurance – an interplay that was entirely within his party's remit to fix.

—

I wanted to be one of the good guys, but I was struggling to see who the good guys were. I wasn't naive enough to think Katerina and Houghton were the good guys, but the lawmakers clearly weren't acting entirely morally half the time, either. Nor were the tax inspectors above reproach . . .

One of Katerina and Houghton's clients was called Pierre. He had settled in the UK some years before and established a business procuring IT specialists for obscure corners of high finance. On a work jolly to the Henley Regatta he'd met a posh fellow who raved about a boutique firm of tax advisors based in a tiny office in Mayfair. Sadly the posh fellow couldn't immediately remember the name of the firm, so had taken Pierre's phone number in case he later recalled it – which he later did. And subsequently Pierre found himself being charmed by Houghton in our grand meeting room while being looked down on by a triptych of painted aristocrats.

Pierre's problem was that the British government hadn't been content to just pass legislation, like the GAAR, to stop *new* tax-avoidance schemes. It had passed some legislation to go after some *old* tax-avoidance schemes, too.

You might think the most sensible thing for the government to do would be to try and recover some of the lost billions from offshore trusts and dodgy capital gains and non-domicile claims – to generally go after the really rich buggers who pay lower rates of tax than their cleaners – but no, the government decided that the real villains of this story were the nurses, IT consultants and general contractors whose employers had asked them to use a tax-avoidance scheme that depended on *disguised remuneration*. Specifically, these employees weren't going to be paid a salary, but rather would be *loaned* money instead.

There is one person in particular I should mention here, because he's the one celebrity whose name *always* gets brought up whenever I find myself in a conversation about tax dodging. It's the comedian Jimmy Carr, and what he did was very similar to what this new legislation was targeting.

Though while Jimmy is famous for dabbling with tax avoidance, what is less well known is what he actually did, or how many other people did it too. Or, for that matter, how eloquently he dealt with the fallout.

Jimmy Carr is hardly the first comedian to have had a run-in with the tax office. His predecessor Ken Dodd was once acquitted of 27 charges of tax evasion, with his barrister quipping that "Some accountants are comedians, but no comedians are accountants."[†]

But Jimmy bore the brunt of it more than almost anyone else. It probably didn't help that not long before he was revealed to be involved in a dodgy tax-avoidance scheme, he had performed a sketch lampooning Barclays Bank's "1 per cent tax scam", after Barclays had been reported to have made as much as £1 billion per year promoting what former chancellor Lord Lawson described as "industrial-scale" tax avoidance.

But Barclays' actions have been largely forgotten. It may have helped them that they took out a midnight super-injunction to stop anyone

---

[†]   Ken was another person who married his long-term partner just two days before he died to save her a huge inheritance-tax bill.

reporting on their schemes, or simply that most people expect that sort of behaviour from banks (they were hardly alone in the banking world in promoting tax avoidance). Jimmy, on the other hand . . .

Jimmy Carr's scheme was called K2. As a little heads-up, if ever you're invited to save tax by using a scheme that has a *name*, don't do it. Jimmy was one of 1,100 customers who collectively paid a Scottish accountancy practice called Peak Performance an estimated £24 million in order to save themselves around £168 million in tax.

The scheme, like many of these schemes, was remarkably simple. Peak Performance would set up a legal entity called an Employee Benefit Trust in Jersey to receive any payments that their clients, like Jimmy, were entitled to (i.e. instead of Jimmy being paid directly by a theatre, say, or a TV production company). The trust wouldn't pay any tax on these payments, because Jersey isn't really into making such things pay tax (or asking difficult questions about what the trust was doing in Jersey or who might be connected with it).

This trust would then lend those payments back to Jimmy. And, just in case you've forgotten this bit from earlier, loans do not make you any richer. Sure, you have some cash, but you also owe that cash to the trust. It's just that Jimmy would never actually be asked to repay the loan, so in effect he got the cash tax-free.

Well, not entirely tax-free. The promoters of these schemes would bend over backwards to make sure that these schemes were legal, which also meant abiding by minimum-wage legislation – so Jimmy would have to be paid a little bit of a real wage to make sure the trust wasn't prosecuted for breaching employment law.

So far, so good. Or do I mean bad? Either way, Jimmy was reported to be sheltering £3.3 million per year from the taxman via his Jersey account. But then the pile-on started.

Prime Minister David Cameron took a break from an official

government trip to the G20 chinwag in Mexico to denounce Jimmy Carr for using a scheme that was "morally wrong" and "very dodgy".

Chief Secretary to the Treasury Danny Alexander said that Carr and other users of tax loopholes are "the moral equivalent of the people who cheat the benefit system".

Fellow comedians went further, tweeting that Jimmy was responsible for how crap some towns in Britain were and for the fact that babies die in underfunded hospitals.[†]

At first Jimmy Carr was a bit on the back foot, and is said to have feared that the revelation of his tax dodging would be career-ending (though we would barely have any celebrities if it was). But then he apologised, paid the taxes he should have paid in the first place and made this statement on the BBC TV show *Room 101*:

> This is tax avoidance, so it's following the letter of the law not the spirit of the law, and leaving it up to us to decide how much you pay, and I don't think that's a good idea . . . it seems like it's one rule for rich people and one for everyone else and it doesn't seem fair because it seems to me they should make the law much clearer and much simpler to follow and it would be better for everyone.

[†] While I understand this rage, it seems a bit harsh, as you could use the same logic to say that someone who chooses to become a poet rather than an investment banker is choosing a life of not paying taxes, so will lead to babies dying in hospitals. Or, indeed, someone who puts more money into their pension (which saves them tax) is somehow responsible for how shit Blackpool is. Or, for that matter, anyone who doesn't give all their wealth away to help sick kids in impoverished countries is morally reprehensible. I think I'm saying it's not as straightforward as *paying less tax kills babies*. I mean, the government spends more of our taxes to buy missiles than incubators. Jimmy Carr put this a little better: "I didn't kill anyone – because there's a very clear law on that."

He did add, with a smile on his face, that "I should probably mention that I'm a recent convert to this view."

You may have gathered that this is pretty much my take on the subject. I have asked Jimmy Carr for an endorsement of this book, so if his name isn't on the cover then he clearly told me to fuck off.

As it happened, a couple of years later it was revealed that David Cameron's father had for years operated an investment trust incorporated in Panama and based in the Bahamas, and that (though it took him a few days to admit it), David Cameron had himself profited from investments in this taxless entity.

Jimmy Carr said it would be "morally wrong" to comment on Cameron's affairs.

Meanwhile Danny Alexander's Liberal Democrat colleague Vince Cable received a penalty for failing to pay VAT that he owed. In Vince's case it was an "innocent mistake".

It really was an innocent mistake in Vince's case. But he still had to pay the fine. Cameron didn't – he hadn't made any mistakes on his tax returns, he had just taken advantage of how the law is written.

Maybe Jimmy Carr was right. Perhaps the law does need to be simpler and clearer?

Interestingly, Kwasi Kwarteng, one of Vince Cable's successors as Business Secretary, had almost the exact opposite point of view when it was revealed that his colleague Rishi Sunak's wife, Akshata Murty, had been claiming non-domiciled status, and thus avoiding British taxes on her vast worldwide wealth.

If this news story passed you by, the facts were these: on the same day that Chancellor of the Exchequer Rishi Sunak (as he was then) raised taxes for "ordinary" Britons, it was reported by *The Independent* that rather than pay UK taxes on her more than £11 million per year of dividends, Akshata Murty paid a £30,000 fee instead.

This, of course, absolutely legal – though not for the reason Ms Murty's spokeswoman claimed, that this was somehow all unavoidable:

> Murty is a citizen of India, the country of her birth and parents' home. India does not allow its citizens to hold citizenship of another country simultaneously. So, according to British law, Ms Murty is treated as non-domiciled for UK tax purposes.

Domicile is not the same as citizenship, and neither British law nor Indian law forced her to claim non-domicile status. Rather, this was something she actively chose to do.

Many commentators also overlooked the fact that, under the UK–India tax treaty, by claiming non-domiciled status in the UK, Ms Murty would only pay inheritance taxes in India. Conveniently for her, there are no inheritance taxes in India, so her estimated £700 million fortune will escape death duties, too.

Just to put some figures on this, her decision to claim non-domiciled status will have allowed her to avoid more than £4 million per year of tax on her offshore dividends (no one seems to have suggested that the dividends are taxable in India either, incidentally). And neither the British nor Indian government will get any inheritance taxes on her estate, whereas if *I* died with a £700 million estate, my kids would expect to pay £280 million.

And she's married to the man who decided the tax rules!

Kwasi Kwarteng said, "Her tax affairs are a matter for her. There's been a lot of malicious attacks on someone who's a private citizen."

Energy minister Greg Hands said the commentary around the former Chancellor of the Exchequer's wife was "a little bit unpleasant, to be frank". I assume he means the kind of commentary like "Maybe there's a conflict of interest here?" Actually, now I write that, I do feel like something unpleasant is going on.

Odd that it's a "malicious attack" on a "private citizen" that's "a little bit unpleasant" when that citizen is married to the Chancellor of the Exchequer – the very person who decides the tax breaks available to his wife – but it was fair game to target a comedian. This despite the fact that Jimmy has never (I think) bedded a government minister.

—

K2 wasn't the only loan-based scheme out there. Katerina and Houghton's client Pierre had got himself involved in another one and, unlike Jimmy Carr, he hadn't settled his case. Now a new law was coming to bite him.

The controversial piece of legislation that Pierre was afraid of was a new Loan Charge, introduced in 2017. Over 50,000 people had joined these schemes, though unusually for a tax-avoidance scheme, most of the people who joined were not, by conventional measures, *wealthy*.

While Jimmy had paid an accountant to sign him up to the scheme, many of these 50,000 people had joined the schemes because their employer – people like Pierre – had insisted on it.

Because these schemes involved lending money to an employee, rather than paying them a salary, in *theory* the employees weren't any richer (as they had to pay the loan back). So the employees paid no tax on receipt of the cash from the loan, and then never paid the loan back either. So the employee got the cash, but not the tax bill. Their employer – the Pierres of this world – saved on payroll taxes, which is why they pushed these schemes on their employees.

In other words, yes, these schemes saved the employees tax, but more often than not the employees hadn't paid to join the scheme – rather they hadn't hired an accountant to get them out of it.

But, argued the government, *if no one paid back the loan, then that loan was really income.*

It's not hard to follow the government's logic. On paper the loans were wholly legitimate – companies often lend cash to their employees, to buy season tickets, for instance, or to get them through a rough patch. But in practice, some of the loans in these schemes hadn't been paid back for over 20 years, and it was pretty obvious that they never would be.

So the government came up with a plan. Anyone who had a loan outstanding from a former employer had either to pay it back, or to treat all the outstanding loans as income in one particular year.

This was designed to hit people hard. It's difficult to reconcile the softly-softly approach HMRC has taken with Big Business with the sledgehammer of the Loan Charge being swung at the poorer end of the dubious-tax spectrum.[†]

Of the people who used these schemes, 40 per cent earned less than £30,000 per year.

Imagine you were an IT consultant and, rather than being paid £30,000 a year for five years, you'd taken a £30,000 loan each year instead. You would have avoided income tax of maybe £4,000 a year, so £20,000 in total, and in theory you would "owe" £150,000 to your employer. Whether you view this tax avoidance as a moral outrage

---

[†] Only a few years before the Loan Charge, HMRC had allowed Vodafone to avoid interest on underpaid (or rather, not paid) taxes. Vodafone had set aside £900 million to pay the interest, but HMRC simply ignored their own rules to let them off. That's just the interest. Investigative journalist and former tax inspector Richard Brooks estimated that *conservatively* Vodafone had been allowed to avoid £6 billion in taxes, or roughly double what the Loan Charge was aiming to bring in.

or something you would have done (or indeed did do), this form of remuneration was widely marketed, well known to HMRC, and legal.

But flash forward to 2019 (when the Loan Charge began to hit hard) and you had a choice. Repay your employer £150,000, or declare £150,000 of income all in one go. And remember, that the more income you have in one year, the higher the rate of tax you'll pay on most of it. Also, although I just said that you have a *choice*, your employer was almost certainly an offshore intermediary that has since disappeared (as it was only set up to run the loan scheme), so really you have *no* choice but to declare all that income, and pay a massive tax bill.

This, as you can probably imagine, was going to ruin a lot of people. The government was saying, "You avoided paying £20,000 of tax a decade ago, so pay £60,000 of tax now".

It was a little as if someone in authority had realised that a country lane had been misdesignated as a 60mph zone, had set up a camera and caught a lot of people driving at 60mph, and *then* redesignated the road as 50mph and sent out a batch of speeding tickets to people who had been going 60mph when the speed limit had been 60mph.

Don't get me wrong – I don't believe people should drive like maniacs on country roads – but retrospectively changing a speed limit would be a gross injustice. Wouldn't you be cross if you received a speeding ticket for driving below the speed limit?

Many of the people caught out by this Loan Charge claimed that they were just doing what their employers told them to do. And most of them didn't have their own accountant, and didn't think much about tax. They were just told, "You'll pay less tax if you take this job", in much the same way as you might be told you'll pay less tax if you get a job in Dubai. Would you pay an accountant to double-check these claims? It seems more likely that the employers were at fault, rather than the employees.

"Don't worry," reassured Houghton, offering Pierre a brandy. "We can get you out of this."

For the most part, it wasn't the employers, like Pierre, who had to cough up. It was the much poorer employees.

Not only were the schemes legal but, unlike many dodgy tax schemes, they had actually been examined thoroughly in the courts – and *ruled* to be legal. So it's like the government had said, "This road should have a 50mph speed limit" and a judge had said, "No, 60mph is fine."

But HMRC saw an easy win, and sent out thousands of demands for tax payments that were going to literally bankrupt people. An independent report found that HMRC staff were "displaying aggressive and unreasonable behaviour towards taxpayers" and HMRC was accused of "misleading" the MPs investigating the situation, withholding "embarrassing" information, and prioritising their reputation "ahead of telling the truth".

HMRC denied these claims, though they did admit that they were themselves one of the employers who hired freelance contractors who were using these schemes. But they said that didn't mean that HMRC would have been aware of the contractors' tax status. Y'know, because knowing about such things isn't HMRC's entire point of existence.

But still HMRC pressed on. Going after billionaires is difficult. Pursuing poor people is much easier. HMRC has form when it comes to this.

An investigation by the think tank and charity TaxWatch found that between 2009 and 2019, HMRC prosecuted 23 times as many benefits cheats as tax cheats, despite tax fraud costing the economy nine times as much as benefits fraud. Eight and a half times more prison sentences have been handed out for benefits fraud than tax fraud.

Now it's possible that there are just more benefits cheats than tax cheats. It's also possible that benefits cheats don't tend to have good lawyers.

What's weird about the Loan Charge rules is that the government already has rules on fining people who don't pay their taxes. Normally the maximum fine is 100 per cent of the tax you avoided or, rather, evaded. If the government was confident that people had cheated the system unfairly, it could have just used its own normal rules and fined people based on taxes they hadn't paid, but should have.

But it didn't. Indeed, it couldn't, because no taxes had been *evaded*. So it used draconian retrospective legislation instead.

The All-Party Parliamentary Group of MPs investigating the Loan Charge said that seven people pursued by HMRC over the Loan Charge rules had taken their own lives.

—

The government has passed a whole host of laws to tackle *disguised remuneration*. Though right down at the bottom of the legislation (clause 554E(12) to be precise) is a little line that says that these rules "do not apply . . . to a member of the House of Commons".

Not that the government has exempted itself from everything. One of the last acts of the last Labour government was to ban non-domiciled people from sitting in the House of Lords. Five peers resigned as a result. Being a non-dom, with all its associated tax breaks, was more important to them than being a lord.

—

Of course, none of this is to say that governments don't know what they're doing, at least some of the time. There are two particular tricks up politicians' sleeves if they want to increase taxes without the electorate getting upset: *hypothecation*, and *fiscal drag*.

Hypothecation is the concept that some tax receipts are ring-fenced, meaning they can only be spent on certain things, like Australia's first tax being to build a prison, or the UK's Labour Party advocating a mansion tax to pay for the NHS.

A moment's reflection will reveal what a daft idea hypothecation is, especially as it implies that the NHS will get less money if house prices drop.

Indeed, more recently Boris Johnson's government introduced a "sugar tax" that was levied on the makers of soft drinks. Worried that the tax would be unpopular, Boris sweetened the pill by saying the tax would be spent on improving the health of children at school. Who could now oppose such a tax? Wouldn't they be jeopardising the health of our children?

Leave aside for a moment that if our children's health was in jeopardy then the government probably should have been helping them already, but what happens if the sugar tax doesn't raise as much money as was hoped? Because that is what happened. Originally forecast to raise £340 million a year, it actually raised just £250 million. That meant a lot of gym equipment and healthy meals for young kids went unpurchased.

Well, actually, almost *all* the gym equipment and healthy meals went unpurchased, because once the sugar tax passed through Parliament, the commitment to help the kids – the "hypothecation" – was quietly dropped.

Fiscal drag is even more pernicious, and much more widespread. One of the easiest means governments have to raise taxes is simply to not raise the thresholds at which people have to start paying taxes. This happens so ridiculously frequently that it's amazing they get away with it. Or maybe they get away with it because it happens so frequently.

Take income tax. In Britain, when income tax was first introduced, only the richest 1 per cent of people paid it, because you had to earn more than £60 a year (which was a huge amount of money, *then*) to be caught by it. But every year inflation dragged more and more people into its net. And lo and behold, now almost all of us pay income tax. Similarly there's *bracket creep* – when the thresholds where you start paying higher rates of tax don't increase at the same rate as inflation. When the "higher" rate of income tax was introduced in the UK, originally only one in ten people were paying it, now (by some counts) one in seven are, with between 1.3 million and 2 million more people set to be dragged into it over the next few years.[†]

It's the same story with pensions, and gift exemptions, and stamp-duty thresholds, and inheritance tax, and in fact with just about every single tax there is, in just about every country there is. You introduce a tax at a rate where few people will be affected, and then let inflation drag other people into it, so slowly that they don't notice, but over time you swallow everyone up.

If the justification for taxes is that they are *fair,* then shouldn't all thresholds rise at the same rate as inflation? But they don't.

—

I've not yet mentioned the most unjust thing in our tax system.

Surely, *surely,* the poorest people in society shouldn't have to pay the highest tax rates? And yet this is exactly what happens under the British system, by design, but in a way that never once mentions the word "tax".

In the UK, one of the recent Conservative government's big ideas

[†] In Australia, Parliament has estimated that people earning around $45,000 will be most affected by this *creep* over the next few years.

was to merge six different types of benefit (i.e. a handout to people who need financial help) into a single *Universal Credit*. Launched in 2012, it was supposed to simplify the benefits system, but to say it's had its detractors is putting it mildly.

For a start, calling it *universal* was a bit misleading, as there are plenty of benefits that aren't included in the Universal Credit. And it's calculated by seeing how much of the six old types of credits you were entitled to, so in theory nothing has changed, except now it's just a bit less clear how your benefit payments are broken down.

Actually, not just "a bit" less clear – the government doesn't even provide its own online calculator to check whether what you're getting is correct. Instead it suggests you use calculators set up by charities or you speak to your "work coach" – but neither of these are available if you're old, young, born abroad or in prison: in these cases, you're on your own.

I hope you can see the double standard here. If you owe the government money, you have to state precisely what you owe them, and are fined if you get it wrong. If the government owes you money, you have to weave in and out of different government agencies, deal with often conflicting or confusing advice, work it out for yourself and still get fined if you get it wrong.

Indeed, the one time I was eligible to claim some money off the government (for a benefit I was owed), I noticed that the amount I'd received was incorrect. The government was supposed to have backdated the claim I'd made, but hadn't. I thought about letting it go, but I gave them a call as it was clearly an oversight. That, and the backdated claim was worth about £300.

I was on hold for half an hour with the Department of Work and Pensions, which seems a bit odd, as you'd think they were the one government department that would have no trouble recruiting more people to man their phones, since "work" is literally in their name. Eventually I got through to a bored-sounding young man.

"Oh, yes, I can see what went wrong," he said.

"Great, can you fix it?"

"Oh, no, I can't, you'll have to send us a letter."

"Can't I email?"

"We don't use email."

"It's 2021."

"Not here, it isn't."

I sent the letter. They still haven't coughed up what they owe.[†]

Anyway – what has this got to do with taxation? Well, the Conservative government decided that to keep the system "fair", the Universal Credit you are eligible for in the UK is reduced if you go to work. I can see the logic of this. Benefits are meant to be a safety net – if you can't find a job and have no means to support yourself, the state will step in and provide, but if you don't need a handout from the state you shouldn't take one. That seems, well, *fair*.

But obviously you can't take all the benefits away as soon as someone gets a job, otherwise there would be no incentive to actually get a job.[‡]

So instead there is a taper, by which, and this is a direct quote from the government, "Your Universal Credit payment will reduce gradually as you earn more".

Ah yes, *gradually*. That doesn't sound so bad.

[†] He even suggested that the only way to get a response would be to make a complaint, as then the department had a statutory duty to reply. I made the complaint; they haven't replied.

[‡] The American version of this is a bit more brutal. You can get a handout from the government if you lose your job, but usually for a maximum of six months. After that, you get nothing.

The effect of the taper is that a recipient of Universal Credit who gets a job will have to give some of their wages to the government. This isn't officially called a *tax,* but a worker giving some of their wages to the government is pretty much a description of how taxes work, right? If I get paid £100, I don't expect to be £100 richer, because of tax. Likewise if a recipient of Universal Credit gets paid £100 from a new job, they can't expect to be £100 richer, because of the taper.

So effectively, the taper is a tax. Technically it's not – it's a reduction of benefits – but the mathematical, economic reality is that it's a tax. Indeed the Chief Secretary to the Treasury, Simon Clarke MP, referred to a reduction in the taper as a "tax cut", which implies that he sees the taper as a tax, too.

About 10 per cent of British society claims Universal Credit. Let's do a thought experiment. What would be a *fair* rate of tax for this poorest echelon to pay?

What rate do you think the government meant when they said your Universal Credit payment would reduce "gradually"?

The answer is 55 per cent, i.e. if a recipient of universal credit gets paid £100 from a job, they'll pay £55 of it to the government. That's an effective tax rate on income that's higher than a partner at a top accountancy firm will pay. In fact when I started writing this chapter it was 63 per cent, but, when he was Chancellor, Rishi Sunak oh-so-generously cut it in the same budget in which he cut air passenger taxes for short-haul flights (because, you know, fuck the environment).

Just to hammer this point home, let's see it with some more numbers.

If an unemployed young person on benefits manages to get a job, then for every £100 they earned they would get just £45 richer (and until recently they'd only get £37).

A millionaire accountancy partner would get to keep more than £51 out of every £100.

In other words, the millionaire keeps £6 more out of every £100 than the poorest people in society.

But this is just the tip of the iceberg of *fairness*. If you're a single mother the system is even harsher.

The UK's Conservative government decided that Universal Credit should be paid monthly, to mirror how wages are paid and encourage fiscal responsibility (no one seems to have mentioned to them that most lower paid jobs are paid weekly, but never mind). But unlike wages, the Universal Credit is paid and tapered differently depending on whether you have a kid to look after, or you're in a couple.

And amazingly, *shockingly*, if you're in a couple you'll get your Universal Credit *cut*. In other words, mothers are incentivised *not* to live with the father of their kids.[†]

And not just a little bit disincentivised, they face a 27 per cent pay cut if they couple up.

But even worse than that, if you live with someone else who earns some decent money, but then split up with them, *their* wealth will reduce the amount of Universal Credit you can claim even *after* you've kicked them out.

The government's thinking is that if your boyfriend or girlfriend receives a normal income from a job, then *you* don't need Universal Credit, because surely they'll be supporting you, even if they ditch you.

So not only are you disincentivised to couple up, you're penalised for breaking up too.

If this was how normal jobs worked, my boss could say, "I see you've

---

[†]   Actually there's nothing gendered in these rules: a single father would be similarly disincentivised to move in with a partner too.

moved in with that nice lady you met in the park, so I'm cutting your pay by 27 per cent."

If this new girlfriend then got a promotion, but afterwards dumped me for another man, my boss could say, "It must be tough now you're on your own, but I've decided not to pay you anything at all for a few months because I assume you've got some cash left over from park lady."

The government has at least acknowledged that this might trap vulnerable women who are victims of domestic abuse, as they won't be able to afford to leave their partners. The government helpfully advises women in this situation to "speak to their work coach".

—

The French poet Baudelaire reckoned that the best trick the devil pulled off was convincing the world he didn't exist, but the tax system seems to have gone one step further. The real art is in making a heinous subject so complicated, so turgid, so *boring* that no one spends too long trying to understand what just happened to them. I doubt Lucifer wears a red cape. I think he's in pinstripes.[†]

Underneath the veneer of dull respectability is a Byzantine tax system that entrenches inequality, stifles economic growth, does very little to promote environmental health and requires an army of accountants to operate it. In the UK there are about 66,000 government employees connected with the tax office, plus at least a further 30,000 people in the tax-consultancy industry; in the US there are a staggering 1.2 million people working as "tax preparers" to help the rest of the country file their taxes. That's more tax preparers than police officers and firefighters

---

[†] Since I wrote this passage it's been reported that Lucifer is now a more common name for new babies than Nigel, so we may well soon *literally* have some little Lucifers in pinstripes.

combined, suggesting that, at a certain time of year at least, tackling tax is a bigger priority than tackling both crime and fire. [†]

Worse, perhaps, than all of this, is that taxation is just about the most significant thing that governments do, so it should be something that electorates really understand, but despite almost half our lives being spent working to pay taxes, no one really understands how much tax they pay – or how much other people are paying or should be paying.[‡]

This removes democratic accountability. If we, as the electorate, don't understand something, how can we vote in a way that will make it change?

I've heard people argue that the solution is that "tax should be taught in schools", but frankly that's one of the worst ideas I can imagine. Double maths was bad enough. The problem isn't a lack of education, it's a tax system which is far, far too complicated.

It doesn't need to be this way. In fact, we only need three simple taxes to fix all the problems with our tax code: its incomprehensibility, its inherent bias against the poor, its stifling of businesses, its manipulability, its waste of resources, the fact that the Department of Work and Pensions still owes me a few hundred pounds, and all the rest.

I don't mean that we need three *extra* taxes. I mean we could scrap the entire system and start again, and have a tax system so simple a child could understand it.

Just three simple taxes, and one radical step. What follows is my attempt to make my career redundant.

—

[†]   This figure of 66,000 employees is from HMRC's own website, though when I phoned them to check it seemed that no one had the job of answering the phone.
[‡]   Except in Scandinavia. In Norway, everyone's tax return is public knowledge. In Sweden, everyone's salary is. Not surprisingly, both countries score well on equality indices, and gender-equality assessments especially.

(By the way, if you do want to cut your own tax bill, I've put the most likely way you can do it in the notes at the end of this book.)

13

TAXTOPIA

Houghton didn't quite understand what I meant about not enjoying my job any more.

"But I've just given you a pay rise," he said, as if I must have failed to realise the relationship between work and pay.

Worse, my children had started to ask me difficult-to-answer questions like, "What do you do for a living, Daddy?"

Perhaps it was a midlife crisis, perhaps it was spending too long eating hospital food, but I couldn't think of *any* jobs in tax I wanted to do. It seemed either my role would be helping rich people (or companies) reduce their tax bills, or failing those clients by *not* reducing their tax bills (even though the law said we could), or blindly inputting numbers into a computer to let the machine calculate the tax or, if I went to the other side, threatening otherwise innocent people with jail if they didn't correctly navigate an impossible-to-navigate system – HMRC recently lost a court case after they fined a man for not paying a *Child Benefit Tax Charge* that was due because his ex-girlfriend was claiming child benefits for someone else's kids.

(This might sound like a weird one-off, but they've also fined 160,000 other parents for not repaying (often someone else's) child benefits. The Child Benefit Tax Charge is payable if you earn both more than £50,000 *and* more than your partner, but you or your partner (or in some cases your ex-partner) are claiming child benefits. I feel a little confused just writing that sentence.)[†]

The Child Benefit Tax Charge is just one of so many really messed-up rules, and I didn't fancy working for the organisation that enforced them.

The conclusion I came to was that almost all jobs in tax shouldn't really exist. There's no need for the complexity, for the endless forms and years of exams. Taxation shouldn't be something that it's possible to be an *expert* in. It shouldn't be something that requires *analysis*, or *planning*. It should all be, well, simple. Here's how we could fix it.

—

You may have felt a sense of outrage reading this book at the huge number of rich people and successful companies that exploit loopholes and offshore rules to reduce their tax bills. I suspect that what gets to you is the unfairness of it. If two people or two companies earn the same, and spend the same, then they should pay the same tax. Because it's *fair*.

Politicians love this word, *fair*.

"Companies should pay their fair share!"

[†] But it gets weirder: because some people don't know how much their partners earn, HMRC allows you to write to your local tax office and ask whether someone *else* is earning more than you are and, if so, whether it's more than £50,000. It's probably illegal to use this resource to find out how rich your next hot date is, incidentally.

It's one of those statements that's hard to disagree with.

But what does it mean?

Presumably, in the case of companies, it's about the fact that companies benefit from the apparatus and infrastructure of the state – the roads, the legal system, the educated workforce – so should pay for it.

But there's a really big problem with that.

They don't.

Just to be clear, what I'm saying is that companies do *not* benefit from roads and laws and schools. Not one teeny, little, minute bit. This is such an obvious point that I feel slightly embarrassed to write about it. But think about it: have you ever seen a company driving down a road or hopping on a bus? How about a company taking the witness stand in a court room? Or a company graduating from school, or having its tonsils taken out?

Those are all things that real-life, living and breathing people do. And people already pay tax.

If Facebook's fancy London office burns to the ground, Facebook simply won't care. It can't care – it doesn't have feelings. The employees might care, indeed one of them might phone the fire brigade – a brigade which the employees are paying for, via their taxes. Mark Zuckerberg might care – it's his office (well, his and the other shareholders'), but Mark and the other shareholders pay tax too (I assume).

It's possible that some of the other shareholders aren't people – perhaps they're pension funds or investment trusts. But those funds and trusts are making money for their retirees or investors – who are living, breathing people too, who already pay tax.

Sometimes it seems that the whole corporate world – from its owners to its detractors – forget what a company actually is.

A company is nothing more than a legal mechanism that allows strangers to pool their resources. That's it. It no more exists in the real world than the joint account I share with my wife does.

Is it any wonder that nothing governments try and do to tax corporate profits seems to work? I'd say it's like hammering jelly against a wall, but the jelly is make-believe.

Yes, it is deeply unfair that one large multinational avoids tax when another small local company doesn't. Yes, that hugely distorts fair competition. But governments and pundits may just have reached the wrong conclusion about what the problem is.

I've discussed this with my peers a lot, and the reaction is normally, "No, that's not right, because . . ." And then the reason never comes. There are entire books about tax avoidance that just blithely say, "It's obvious that companies should pay tax" but never explain why. The best they usually manage is "Because that's where capital is accumulated." Well, my wife and I accumulate our capital in our joint account. Hell, a pile of bricks is an accumulation of capital – but it's the person who owns the bricks that you'll have to ask for any money.

You might think I'm descending into libertarian lunacy here, but I'm not advocating that we abolish taxes. Far from it – I'm trying hard *not* to argue whether taxes should go up or down, I just want a *good* tax system. One that both encourages economic growth and prevents the amoral wealthy from avoiding paying their dues.

Companies really do drive economic growth – simply by doing what they were invented to do: allowing strangers to pool resources.

What would happen if companies paid *no* tax?

That's surprisingly easy to answer (especially because, as we've seen, some companies don't pay any already).

There are two possible things that can happen to a company's leftover money:

1. **The money can be paid as dividends to the company's shareholders**.
   If the shareholders are people, then these people pay income tax.

   If the shareholders are other companies, then the money has just moved to another company, and the process starts again. Eventually a person needs to get their hands on the money. That person is probably *you*, incidentally, via your pension fund.

2. **The money can be used to improve the business.**
   This means either paying existing staff more, or employing more staff, or improving products, or designing new products, or improving working conditions, or investing in new machinery . . . all of which are good things. And all of which result in *someone* – an actual person – eventually getting some money, upon which they'll pay tax.

Many of the distortions and loopholes in our tax system are due to this weird abstraction that an entity that exists only in the imagination should itself pay tax (or be allowed to own a house). Accountants can spend hours calculating how profits should be extracted from a company to be "tax efficient". What an absurd use of resources. Billions – or even trillions – of pounds and dollars and euros and the rest get shifted around through different offshore accounts by international companies, via shady tax havens and dodgy dealers, all in an effort to avoid a tax which is itself a bit, well, *off*.

The justification that dividends should be taxed at lower rates is usually that they are paid from company profits that have already been taxed – but as we've seen, all too often the company has dodged the tax on those corporate profits, so all we're left with is lower tax rates on dividends – and wealthy people who own shares reap the benefit. I've also come across the argument that there should be *no* tax on dividends in order to "encourage investment". How convenient for rich people . . . perhaps instead we should have no income tax on salaries "to encourage work"? I'll leave that one with you.

There's a danger here that you may think I'm making an argument akin to "Hey, I know how we could stop needing to put murderers in prison – we could legalise murder!", but I'm really not saying that. It is troubling how deep into our psyche the concept of a company being akin to a real "person" has got that I even need to make such a clarification.

There should be no corporation tax. Instead, whenever – and however – the cash in a company bank account finds its way into a person's bank account, that person should pay tax.

That's so simple – and would have some wonderful effects.

It would do away with the incentive that companies have to load up on debt for the sake of tax relief (which would make them less prone to economy-destabilising shocks).

It would create a level playing field between *all* businesses – whether they're a sole trader, a partnership, a small company or a giant multinational.

It would remove the distortions of dividends being taxed at lower rates.

It would remove the dead weight loss of tens of thousands of people being employed to fill in company tax returns (which costs the UK around £10 billion per year).[†]

It would help businesses grow – boosting the economy and providing jobs.

It would encourage foreign businesses to set up shop in whichever countries introduce this rule, bringing in more investment.

And finally – and this is a pretty big rebuttal to anyone who thinks this is some dodgy right-wing idea – abolishing taxes on companies doesn't mean cutting taxes for the rich. If anything, it will mean richer people pay *more* tax, because they can't now hide behind false excuses for paying lower tax rates.

I'm fighting against the tide here though. There is a slowly emerging consensus among the rich nations of the world that there should be a global unified minimum corporation tax rate. The theory goes that forcing all companies to pay a certain percentage of their profits as tax no matter where they shift their money to will raise billions in extra tax revenues.

But this is wrong. If a company grows by 6 per cent per year, then in 30 years it will be five and half times bigger than it is today. If it grows at only 4 per cent (because of taxes) it will be only three and a half times bigger. That's a smaller pension pot for you. It's your kids or grandkids

---

[†] HMRC account for about half of this, yet infuriatingly *brag* on their website about it, as if it's something to be proud of. Their line is that it only costs 1p to collect £200. At first this may sound impressive, but they then let slip that they deal with 12 million tax returns per year, which works out at £333 *per return*. In fairness, they also deal with a few other things, but they shouldn't. That's kind of the point I'm making here – taxes should be so simple that we don't need a 100,000-strong army to work it all out. And ironically, HMRC's own stats show that it actually costs them 1p to collect £157 (not £200). I might try that sort of rounding on my next tax return.

not getting a job. It's your favourite restaurant closing down. It's the world being a poorer place. And indeed, critics of the global minimum tax have pointed out that it's the *richest* countries that stand to benefit the most.

Corporate taxes hit the most profitable companies hardest, so by design limit the growth of companies that (with a few exceptions) are selling things people want.

We should let companies grow – creating jobs and paying dividends to shareholders (including our pensions) – and then tax the employees and the shareholders when they take cash out of the company.

Encouraging growth really is the best way to increase the total tax take. By all means raise taxes on people, if that's what you believe in, but a company is only a joint account. Don't tax the account, tax the people who withdraw the cash.

Once we've scrapped taxes on companies, here are the three taxes we do need:

1. Something Witty

Let's start with some ground rules.

Two people who earn the same and live similar lives should pay the same amount of tax.

Hmm, that's just one ground rule, but it's all we need. Let's just check that we agree with it, because it seems like a very simple and obvious thing but virtually no tax system in the entire world enforces it – for instance, in the UK a landlord will often pay just half the tax rate that their tenant does; in New Zealand someone selling a company will pay no tax, but an employee of the company will pay lots; in the USA a billionaire presidential candidate will pay lower rates than the journalists covering their story. That doesn't seem right.

Though what do we mean by *earn*? I reckon that earning £100 makes you the same amount richer whether you were paid a salary or sold some shares that had risen in value or inherited some cash or were paid cash to put up a shelf. But most governments don't agree, which is weird, because what wages and share sales and inheritances have in common is that someone else transferred their wealth to you. *Your wealth has increased.*

So what we need is a *Wealth Increase Tax* – a simple, easy-to-understand, universal tax on *any* situation where someone else has transferred their wealth to you, for whatever reason.

This doesn't have to be a flat tax – i.e. a single rate of tax that everyone pays – though it could be. We could keep "progressive" rates that increase as you get richer, if you want. But it would be simple, and with simplicity comes a whole host of benefits.

If dividends and capital gains and salaries and benefits-in-kind were all taxed under the same regime – the Wealth Increase Tax (or WIT) – then there would be no need to pay an accountant to work out how best to *extract your profits*, there would be no convoluted ruses to convert income to capital. It would just be "Did you get any richer?" and if you did, you pay the tax. We'd all be in it together, as it were.

Compare that to what we have at the moment. The London School of Economics did some fantastic research in 2020 based on anonymised personal tax returns and found that one in ten people in Britain earning more than £1 million pounds per year paid an effective tax rate of 11 per cent. Another quarter paid less than 30 per cent. That's almost certainly less than what you're paying.

HMRC did their own analysis based on the same tax year and discovered that the average inheritance-tax rate on estates over

£10 million was just 10 per cent, which is the same *rate* you'd expect to pay if you inherited your auntie's £430,000 cottage, and is a quarter of the 40 per cent tax rate those big estates would have paid without any input from a tax advisor.

And in both these cases the analyses only looked at *reportable* wealth. A non-dom with an offshore trust doesn't even have to let HMRC know what they're *not* paying. (So while we're at it, let's scrap the non-dom rules and secret trusts, too.)

Effectively, I'm saying we should not have different tax rates for different types of earnings, but rather should merge together income tax, capital gains tax, inheritance tax and all the various different add-on payroll taxes and extra levies.

There should be just one tax that's based on how much your wealth has increased (wherever that wealth is) because someone else has transferred their wealth to you. I rather like the idea of calling it a *Wealth Increase Tax*, if only because then you could brag about your level of WIT.

If we did this, a whole host of opportunities would open up to us. For a start, it would be much more difficult to avoid tax. Did you get richer? Then pay the tax.

You'd no longer have private equity managers arguing that their fees were capital and not income, because it would make no difference, nor footballers negotiating higher payments for their image rights, nor billionaires squirrelling millions away a week to avoid inheritance taxes.

It would stop the wealthy avoiding taxes by claiming they had a different type of wealth – dividends and capital gains and salaries and inheritances would all be assessed the same way.

It would be much simpler to understand. You would know how much tax you paid, and how much other people were paying. The government wouldn't be able to hide tax increases in NICs or obscure levies.

It would make all the politicised adjustments transparent.

And it would leave the Wilhelms and Hals and Bazzos and Katerinas and Houghtons of this world looking for something more productive to do with their time.

—

Still not convinced? Well, how about this: If you're an employee, those taxes that your employer has to pay just to keep you on their payroll could be paid to *you* instead. That would mean a pay rise for you of somewhere between a few per cent (in certain US and Australian states), and 15 per cent (in the UK). Do you really want to argue with a pay rise? Plus, if we raised taxes on capital gains and dividends, we could then lower income taxes and keep the total tax take the same. How about that – a pay rise *and* a tax cut?

Also, something really special could happen if we merged inheritance tax with income tax, capital gains tax and National Insurance.

You might remember me banging on about the two big reliefs that the mega-rich get from inheritance tax: agricultural property relief (which removes most land from taxable estates) and business property relief (which does the same with businesses). Between them, they're responsible for a significant proportion of the entrenchment of wealth in the hands of a small minority of people.

The justification for them is that they allow businesses to continue beyond the deaths of the business's owner. That's not wholly unreasonable. On the eventual demise of a Richard Branson or a James Dyson or even a Donald Trump it would often be counterproductive to demand their heirs pay 40 per cent of the value of their inherited businesses, as doing so would usually lead to a break-up and fire sale of their businesses. Except . . . what if tax bills weren't always settled in immediate cash?

What if the Branson and Dyson and Trump offspring (assuming the kids inherit the businesses) could settle their tax bill in shares – or a proportion of their land?

The inheritors could agree that 40 per cent of any future income arising from their business or land that wasn't reinvested into their business or land would be paid to the taxman. The control of the business or the land could still be in the hands of the family – the business would continue unimpeded from the perspective of the outside world, but the rich would now be sharing their spoils, just like the rest of us do. The company or the land would still make the same cash, but when that cash was taken out of the company a good chunk of it would go the government.

After all, we already use this model at the other end of the wealth spectrum, with *shared ownership* of houses. In London it's almost impossible to get onto the housing ladder without agreeing to share ownership of your new house with the government. If it works for the poor, why not the rich?

Over time this could lead to what in effect would be a *sovereign wealth fund* – the government owning a share of the nation's businesses and land – and receiving an annual income (which might, just, take some burden off the rest of us).

Perhaps the idea of the government owning the right to income from land and businesses sounds a bit communist, but isn't that what all tax is? I'm just asking the rich not to be exempted.

Or was my suggestion earlier of a pay rise and a tax cut more convincing?

—

2. No Value Added

I have a real thing about toothbrushes. I'm not knocking the importance of clean teeth, but a toothbrush seems designed to make people sick: you get it wet and just a little bit warm, stick it in one of the top three most germy parts of your body, then leave it alongside the rest of your family's little germ-incubating sticks a couple of feet away from where you defecate.

And yet, whoever thinks about toothbrushes? It even took a child to point out to me that they should be called *teeth*brushes. They're so everyday and routine that few of us stop to give them a thought.

Well, here's something else that's routine and everyday and yet is making the economy, and possibly the planet, just a little a bit sick: indirect taxes. VAT, GST, duties, stamp taxes, sales taxes. There's something very wrong going on.

Take VAT. It's insane. The clue's in the name. It's literally a tax on *adding value*. It's the same with any tax on "goods". We shouldn't be taxing *goods*, we should be taxing, well, *bads*. It's as if someone sat down and said, "How could we destroy the economy?" and the best idea anyone put forward was "How about every time someone adds value or makes something good, we tax it?"

It's the kind of thing a bad guy in an Ayn Rand novel would say.[†]

How about – and I'll try not to sound too radical here – we tax things that *don't* add value instead?

[†] Apparently Ayn Rand's *Atlas Shrugged* still sells close to half a million copies in a good year. The heroes are the brave millionaire entrepreneurs and captains of industry and the villains are the people who try and drag them down (like employees, politicians or wives). It remains very popular with libertarians and billionaires. It's both bat-shit crazy and contains some pretty convincing ideas, often at the exact same time.

At the time of writing, almost all food bought at a British supermarket is effectively VAT-free, even if it's battery-farmed, picked by child labourers, flown in from far away and wrapped in plastic. Whereas (apart from a brief respite during the coronavirus) all food from restaurants has a 20 per cent tax, no matter how ethically sourced it is or how beneficial the restaurant is to the local community. It's pretty much the same story elsewhere in the world. Sales taxes get added to almost everything, but with some incredibly broad exceptions.

VAT and other sales taxes punish businesses that create wealth. And as they are levied on revenues and not profits, they harm low-margin businesses, like restaurants, disproportionately.

A 20 per cent sales tax is equivalent to a sixth of a business's turnover. So for example, if a restaurant buys a steak for £11 and sells it for £12 they will *lose* money on that steak, as they have to hand a sixth of all their turnover to the taxman (i.e. £2 of the £12 sales price of the steak, so businesses can go bust even if they can sell things for more than they cost.

The reason this is so problematic for "low margin" businesses like restaurants is that on a *turnover* of £1.2 million they might make *profits* (their "margin") of just £50,000, but be paying £200,000 in VAT.

This means that those restaurants could be five times more profitable if they didn't have to add a tax onto all their prices. That would mean more restaurants, more employment, more wealth.[†]

Surely we should be taxing products that destroy wealth? Surely the

---

[†] The rate of sales taxes and other duties and indirect taxes varies enormously around the world, and even within countries. The UK's rate is particularly high, at 20 per cent, though this is lower than in a lot of Europe. Australian and American rates vary from 0 per cent (in Delaware) to combined state, local and city rates around 13 per cent, but with a huge number of special rules and caveats, and before considering import duties or product-specific taxes. In short, this is an extremely messy area of tax law almost no matter where you live.

products that should cost the most are the ones that can't be recycled, that catch fire easily, that emit carbon dioxide, that blight local neighbourhoods, that encourage addictions and a dozen other ethical wrongs. How can it be that in the UK we have the same VAT rate on electricity generated from renewable sources as from coal? Or the same VAT rate on a delivery made by bicycle as by a diesel van? Why the flaming fucksicles is there VAT on Covid-testing kits? Why was there ever a tax on sanitary products?

What we need is an NVAT – a "No Value Added Tax".

We don't even need to persuade our governments of the merits of this, because they already have taxes on things that don't add value. In the UK there are already (at least) 16 different taxes on things due to, in theory, the harms they cause. These harms are what economists call "negative externalities".[†]

NVAT could merge all existing indirect taxes. It could be a percentage or a fixed amount. It would be clearly labelled. Imagine choosing between two packets of salad, when one costs more because its packaging is not recyclable, and the NVAT percentage clearly shows it to be worse for the environment.

Cars would cost more as their CO_2 emissions rose, and bicycles would become cheaper.

Locally produced grass-fed beef would have a lower tariff than the intensively reared kind, but both would be a little pricier. Almonds grown where water is scarce would cost more than peanuts grown sustainably.

[†] Brits have separate duties and sales taxes on alcohol, cigarettes, petrol, air travel, landfill, electricity, insurance, car ownership, betting, sugary drinks, plastic packaging, houses, shares, imports and aggregates as well as VAT.

Clothing companies that could prove their cotton wasn't picked by forced labour would have lower prices.

Private schools would charge different rates depending on how much they shared their resources or offered bursaries.

Professional advice on tax mitigation would have a higher NVAT rate than legal advice on pursuing the Department of Work and Pensions for not coughing up the £300 they owe me.

This may all sound complicated, but there's actually nothing new in distinguishing between products in this way and assigning a mandated tax. Businesses already do it when they import something – the UK has over 5,000 "product codes" to identify which import duty is payable. And do you not remember about the quadruply excepted Yemeni goat-fur kid's hat?

Both the NVAT and the WIT could be tweaked in different parts of the country, or in different industries, to encourage jobs and businesses in deprived neighbourhoods. Products made in some places could have a lower rate of NVAT, or workers a lower WIT, to reflect the benefit to society of those products being made in those places.

This would be a double win.

It would shift the burden of sales taxes onto products that are doing the least for society and the environment.

And it would give far greater understanding and transparency to us, the taxpayers, helping us make decisions that help the planet, help each other and help our own wallets. Isn't it weird that most of us don't know whether there's more tax on a pint of beer or a litre of petrol? Or on a flight to Scotland or the travel insurance you bought for the trip? Or a thousand other daily purchases? I think we should know.

We could easily alter our buying choices, led not just by price but by the NVAT rate – a rate which would indicate the societal and environmental harm caused by the product. Producers would have to alter their manufacturing and business practices to ensure they could charge a low rate.

"Oh look, this tuna fillet has a 62 per cent NVAT but that mackerel has only 4 per cent."

Suddenly restaurants could thrive, unless their food was unhealthy or unsustainable, or they didn't pay their staff enough, or they were noisy, or led to littering, or whatever else we wanted to encourage or discourage them to do.

If we want to save the high street we could lower the NVAT rate for goods sold *from* the high street. If we want to reduce traffic we could raise the NVAT rate on deliveries.

The government may be reluctant to make this change simply due to the amount of tax collected from the sale of goods and services: about £250 billion in the UK, about $125 billion in Australia, over $600 billion in the USA. I have two rejoinders to this:

1. The total amount of tax collected doesn't *have* to change. There could just be a baseline amount of NVAT and all the ethically better products could get a discount and all the stuff we want to discourage would be charged extra. And then if all businesses upped their game, like a rising tide the baseline could increase.[†]

---

†   There's an extension to this argument, but as it's slightly technical I'm hiding it in a footnote: cutting VAT by, say, £50 billion wouldn't lead to a loss of £50 billion in taxes, because that £50 billion would either end up as income for the owners of businesses (so be subject to income taxes or the WIT) or as savings for consumers, who could then spend it at other businesses.

2. The government could remember that VAT causes good, otherwise profitable businesses to go bankrupt, so is doing massive harm to the economy, especially to the hospitality trade. That is the very opposite of what a sensible government should be encouraging.

Actually I have a third rejoinder:

3. Window taxes raised a lot of money. So did hearth taxes and beard taxes and poll taxes and bachelor taxes and concealing your breasts taxes. Just because something raises a lot of money, it doesn't make it right. If it did, Britain may as well go back to plundering its old colonies.[†]

VAT is a 20th-century tax. Duties are even more ancient than that. Merging all our indirect taxes into one N VAT rate could help make business practices fairer, support businesses that are more environmentally friendly, encourage a fairer distribution of resources, help consumers make more ethical choices, reduce fraud, encourage economic activity in poorer parts of the country, and do all of this without changing the overall amount of tax collected by the government.

[†] Bachelors have been taxed in a number of jurisdictions, usually to encourage young men to get married and start a family. As exemptions were often given to men who had tried to get married but had been rejected, there are some instances of women earning a living as professional marriage-proposal rejectors. And in some parts of 19th-century India, "lower" caste women had to pay a tax to be allowed to conceal their breasts in public. The "lower" caste men had to pay a tax to grow a moustache (which doesn't seem quite as problematic).

3. Hold It Right There

Pretty much every report I've ever read into reforming our tax system (and I've read a lot of them) is written by the same sort of people. Indeed sometimes by the exact same people. It's always either partners from Big 4 accountancy practices ("make the system more complex") or inspectors from HMRC ("employ more tax inspectors") or professors in taxation ("we need a deontological manifest on the actuality of the Smith doctrine quid irrumabo the categorical imperative within the tax community").

I don't really mind if you agree with my tax ideas or not, but I do hope you recognise that a much simpler, much fairer, much more business friendly, much more environmentally friendly tax system is possible. The one big difference between my ideas here and the ideas for reform you'll usually read is that I'm not trying to create work for tax accountants. Quite the opposite. But there is one big problem with my ideas, so far: they wouldn't work.

If there was no tax on companies, then there would be nothing to stop any business transferring all their wealth offshore. I mean, a lot of companies *do* transfer all their wealth offshore, but we would have made it much easier for them.

To stop this constant offshoring of money – the dividends paid to Philip Green's wife in Monaco, the offshore trusts used by the Goldsmith family, the royalty payments paid by Starbucks, the payments to the Irish subsidiaries of tech giants, the Dutch sandwiches and so on, we need to revisit something we encountered earlier: a *Withholding Tax*.

We would need a Withholding Tax at the same level as the Wealth Increase Tax – so that anyone who made their money in one particular country had to pay tax in that country. You couldn't avoid it by shifting your wealth offshore.

For instance, imagine you pay your English phone bill to a big English company. What could that company then do? They could pay their staff, who'd pay the WIT, or pay their British shareholders, who'd pay the WIT, or pay another UK company for some service – in which case what does *that* company do?

If the money leaves the UK – whether to a foreign shareholder, or a foreign business – that payment will suffer a Withholding Tax. This rule doesn't have to affect *people* buying something from overseas, because we've already paid the WIT.

Put this all together and Big Tech companies will have to *onshore* their operations to avoid tax, Starbucks will suddenly decide that their royalty payments weren't necessary after all, and the Wilhelms of this world will have nowhere to hide. You make your money, you pay your taxes.

So just to recap, we need just three taxes:

- A universal tax you pay when you get a bit richer.
- A sales tax based on the harms caused by the products we buy.
- A withholding tax to stop offshoring wealth.

—

I'm a great believer in the theory that you don't really understand something unless you can explain it to a child. I think that's something Albert Einstein said, but then his name has been attached to a lot of sayings (including that the hardest thing to understand is income taxes).

Obviously having kids changes your perspective on things, but I hope that's a good thing. We all like to imagine what the world will be like as our kids grow up, and hope it will become more Utopian than it is now. The world I know best is the world of tax. I guess I'm hoping for a Taxtopia.

I also hope my kids follow their mother's career and not mine. And no, I haven't told you what my wife does for a living, but it's something wonderful.

I've read that Einstein didn't start talking until he was eight years old. This has been some comfort to me, as my own daughter has been a little late in this respect and prefers to use sign language (though I assume she's just been figuring out something about the universe).

All the same, I decided to try and explain the concept of taxation to her – how all the grown-ups pay for the roads and the parks and the schools and the nee-nors and I asked if she understood.

She put the side of one of her hands in the palm of her other hand and swayed it side to side.

This is the British Sign Language gesture for sharing.

I couldn't put it better myself.

NOTES

Although I'd like to think of myself as an expert in my field, most of the experts I know make mistakes *all* the time. Also, I'm not an economist or a historian (or an expert on ghosts). I won't be in the least offended if you want to fact-check anything I've said in this book – indeed, I'd positively recommend it.

To make your life easier I've compiled a list of sources for most of the claims I've made, as well as a few extra explanations of tax rules, just in case you *really* want more of that. That said, this is not a bibliography – I always assume academics are just showing off when they list the thousand books they supposedly read to form their thesis. Instead, I've mentioned a small handful of books I've enjoyed, and why. Let's just pretend I've read hundreds of others.

I've figured it's more useful to mention articles that are online (and not behind paywalls), so I've tried to stick to those – but be aware that most journalists are not tax experts, so some of these articles are a little light on the implications of the tax issues. (But hey, that's why we need more books on tax, right?)

Please don't take anything in these notes (or, indeed, this book) as personal advice.

Do say nice things in reviews or on twitter (@RebelAccountant) if you've enjoyed this book. And if you've worked out who I *really* am, please keep it to yourself.

Chapter 1

The Big 4 accounting firms are **PwC, KPMG, Deloitte and Ernst & Young**. Until it collapsed in the wake of its audits of Enron and World Com there was also Arthur Andersen, to make a Big 5. They really are big – PwC alone employs more than 295,000 people in 156 countries, according to their own 2021 Global Annual Review.

The bit about VAT on Mongolian goat-fur children's berets sounds made up, but really is in Britain's VAT Act. Have a look at Schedule 8 of the Act, if you're interested.

The VAT court cases are quite easy to look up, too. The **Pringles** case was in 2009: *Procter & Gamble UK* v. *HM Revenue & Customs*; the judge said it was worth £20 million per year to Procter & Gamble to zero-rate their Pringles.

The VAT tribunal for **Jaffa Cakes** was United Biscuits (UK) Ltd (no2) [1991], and see ***Domino's** Pizza Group* v. *Customs and Excise* for the wonderful argument that "the appellant contends that it is not its purpose in heating the products to enable them to be consumed hot".

Subway franchise owners Bookfinders Ltd took their case to the Supreme Court of Ireland in 2020, and you can read the Supreme Court of the United States' judgement on the X-men by searching for *Toy Biz Inc.* v. *United States*, 2003.

Spearmint Rhinos *Ventures (UK) Ltd* v. *Revenue & Customs Commissioners* [2007] is a less titillating read than you might think.

It was **Gordon Brown**'s March 2006 budget that lowered the VAT rate on contraception.

In my description of **carousel fraud** I glossed over the VAT rules on importing something. In the UK you usually have to pay a "normal" rate of VAT directly to HMRC when you import something, but historically there have been a number of exceptions to this, such as when dealing with other EU countries and importing items that cost less than £15 – something that was called Low Value Consignment Relief (which I believe is why if you ordered three things from Amazon you would get three separate deliveries, to ensure each was below the VAT exemption threshold).

A much simpler ruse, and far more illegal, was for the company that owed VAT to the government to just not pay it (which was also a lot easier to get away with for goods that cost less than £135 (because of another relief), like some cheaper mobile phones).

The numbers on how many **accountants** there are worldwide are ironically hard to pin down, especially as it depends on the definition of *accountant*. The professional body the Consultative Committee of Accountancy Bodies (CCAB) puts the figure at 275,000 in the UK and Ireland if you mean *accountants with an accounting qualification*, but well over half a million if you mean *people working in accounting*; equivalent US figures range from about 650,000 to 1.25 million, again depending on who gets included. The Institute of Chartered Accountants Australia and New Zealand represents 110,000 chartered accountants working down under, and another 10,000 or so globally.

Americans really do own a lot fewer yachts than Europeans. In a 19 April 2019 list, *Business Insider* put the figures at Americans owning 158 **superyachts** vs Europeans owning well over 500.

If any of the five-digit codes I mentioned are *actual* client codes, that's just a coincidence. Sorry.

Chapter 2

There are some fantastic books on the history of tax, and a wealth of information online, often written by accountants – it's almost as if accountants are really keen on compiling lists of facts and figures. Most of the books point out that it's probably accountants who invented writing, and counting systems, and generally were responsible for every major breakthrough or event in human history.

I particularly enjoyed Dominic Frisby's *Daylight Robbery* (especially for the title, which Frisby points out was a term originally coined due to the tactic of bricking up windows to avoid window tax). I hadn't heard of the Dog Tax War until I read *Rebellion, Rascals and Revenue* by Michael Keen and Joel Slemrod, and Richard Brooks's *The Great Tax Robbery* is written by someone whose tax knowledge I find a little bit intimidating.

A lot of the history of tax in this book was provided by a specialist in economic history whom I happen to know, but I appreciate that doesn't help *you* much, unless we know the same person. Maybe we do? But thank you, if you're that historian, for all your help.

The line about **the non-dom rules** being specifically to reward the backers of Britain's empire, I've taken from a Parliamentary debate held on 23 July 1914 in which the Finance Bill that contained this new rule was discussed. Financial Secretary to the Treasury Lord Montagu said:

> The citizen of the Empire who lives in one of our Colonies, and is not domiciled in this country, is exempt from this taxation. The official carrying on the Empire abroad, who pays an occasional visit to this country, but is not ordinarily resident here, is exempt from this taxation.

The rule as it stands today (May 2022) is that if you are non-domiciled you can be resident in the UK for up to seven years before you have to pay *any* special charge to exempt your offshore income and gains from UK tax. After seven years you have to pay £30,000 per year and after 12 years you have to pay £60,000 per year.

The **residency rules** in the UK are a bit more complicated than I have made out. In some situations you would only need to be in the UK for a very short period to be deemed a UK resident, principally if you have your only home or your main job in the UK. Luckily for the super-rich, if you have multiple homes and don't work for someone else you can visit the UK more frequently.

Zac Goldsmith gave the following statement in 2016:

> I have today published my tax return details, prepared and verified by PwC, who have represented me all my adult life.
>
> I gave a commitment to do so and today I deliver on that promise. I look forward to all mayoral candidates doing the same, so London voters can judge us equally.

As was well known to voters in my two elections as an MP, I became "non-dom" automatically because of my father's international status. It was not a choice, and I relinquished it seven years ago. I was born, grew up and have always lived in London – except for two years travelling abroad in my early twenties. Because of this I derived very little, if any, benefit from this status as my income came to the UK and was therefore taxed here.

I don't 100 per cent agree with his analysis of his situation. In particular I don't see how something can be "not a choice" but also relinquishable, by choice.

There was a Parliamentary Motion discussing the tax status of **Lord Ashcroft**, Deputy Chairman of the Conservative Party. You can read it here: https://edm.parliament.uk/early-day-motion/34315/tax-status-of-lord-ashcroft.

Charles Clore's case was: Clore (deceased)/ [1984] BTC 8101.

On 5 February 2010 the *Guardian* newspaper had an article about **Guy Hands** with the headline "I save tax by never visiting my family, says tycoon Guy Hands".

In 2019 it was widely reported that Hands was addicted to roast potatoes, which I appreciate isn't about tax but is very understandable.

In a 2007 interview with Michael Parkinson, **Lewis Hamilton** was asked whether the move to Switzerland was "basically because you've been advised to because of the tax laws". Lewis replies, "Also, that definitely adds to it." You can watch it on YouTube.

He confirmed his move to Monaco in a video titled *Monaco Is My*

Home and, according to the *Sun* newspaper, posted on social media: "Monte Carlo, a place I call home."

You can see some of the houses and apartments he's bought online, and hats off to him, he does seem to have good taste.

The situation surrounding the purchase of the Challenger jet was first revealed in the Paradise Papers leak in 2017, when confidential information from offshore law firm Appleby was handed to the German newspaper *Süddeutsche Zeitung*. On 7 November 2017 the paper published a thorough analysis of the jet, which was then widely reported by other papers. You can read the original source material at offshoreleaks.icij.org.

In a House of Commons debate on the same day as *Süddeutsche Zeitung* released their analysis, Dame Margaret Hodge said the following:

> I wish to focus on issues that have not yet received the public scrutiny and attention that they deserve. The Paradise Papers contain details of a tax scam that operated out of the Isle of Man, facilitated by the law firm Appleby, with advice from one of the big four accountancy firms, EY – Ernst and Young. It is a lethal cocktail of accountants, lawyers and the super-rich. This is how the scam works. The super-rich buy private jets, which can cost anything up to £70 million. Lewis Hamilton spent £16.5 million on his. To avoid paying VAT on the purchase, the rich buy their private jets through companies they set up in tax havens. Lewis Hamilton used the British Virgin Islands and avoided VAT. Owners want to fly their planes in Europe, however, for which they need a certificate issued by a European jurisdiction to show that they have accounted for VAT and any other taxes.

At this point, in steps the Isle of Man, a jurisdiction that boasts the Queen as Lord of Mann. The advisers, EY and Appleby, create a company in the Isle of Man, controlled by the private jet owner Lewis Hamilton, which leases the jet from the BVI company controlled by Lewis Hamilton. The Isle of Man government issue a VAT refund on the grounds that the jet is part of a leasing business, although the only customer is one Lewis Hamilton. The Isle of Man company then leases the jet to another offshore company in Guernsey, which is also controlled by Lewis Hamilton. This carousel of leasing companies, all controlled by Lewis Hamilton, exists simply to enable Lewis Hamilton to avoid a £3.3 million VAT bill, yet the plane has been leased only to Lewis Hamilton and he has never returned to the Isle of Man in his jet. Lewis Hamilton may wrap himself in the Union flag at Formula 1 races, but he should hold his head in shame at his contrived and deliberate refusal to pay the British taxes he should.

Check out Lewis Hamilton's vlogs on YouTube if you want to see the actual jet.

This is a bit of a long link, but you can read about the enquiry by HM Treasury into the **Isle of Man**'s treatment of private planes (and yachts) in 2019 here:

https://assets.publishing.service.gov.uk/government/uploads/system/uploads/attachment_data/file/839880/HMT_review_of_Isle_of_Man_s_VAT_procedures_web.pdf.

I mentioned that *The Guardian* is itself no stranger to avoiding tax. It acknowledged this itself in a blog post written on 22 February 2011.

In brief, the paper was transferred into a trust to avoid tax, and its ownership has largely remained there. It does some of the world's best investigative tax journalism, though, so maybe we should go easy on it?

Chapter 3

Most British chartered accountants have to pass about 10–15 **exams** (depending on the exact qualification), with pass rates of about 75–80 per cent per paper. So the odds of passing all their exams first time are pretty low. Obviously I passed all of mine first time, though I scraped through my first tax exam, ironically.

I mentioned how many of my firm's clients had **Russian names, registered offices in Ireland and profits of £300,000**. The Russian connection is, I think, just due to the industries we dealt with, and nothing more sinister. But the registered offices in Ireland is explained later in the book – often foreign companies would register in a particular tax-friendly jurisdiction, then fly their directors to that country once or twice a year to hold their key meetings, so that all the important decisions were made in that country, thus qualifying the company as, in these cases, Irish (despite being Russian-owned with Russian offices and Russian operations).

The profits of £300,000 are a lot more technical. This was due to an unbelievably daft bit of corporation tax legislation, whereby companies with profits under £300,000 paid a low rate of tax, companies above £1,500,000 paid a high rate of tax, and companies with profits between these two thresholds paid an *even higher* rate of tax on their profits between these thresholds. It was an unfathomably stupid rule. Rishi Sunak has said that he plans to reintroduce it.

You can read about the fines that **KPMG Australia** had to pay due to cheating on exams on the Public Company Accounting Oversight Board's press release (no. 105-2021-008) on 13 September 2021, and the fines that **KPMG US** had to pay on an SEC (the US Securities and Exchange Commission) press release of 17 June 2019. And you can read about **EY**'s monster fine in an SEC press release of 28 June 2022, which includes this zinger of a quote from the SEC's director of their Enforcement Division, "It's simply outrageous that the very professionals responsible for catching cheating by clients cheated on ethics exams of all things."

You probably don't want to just google "Big 4 fines", by the way, as there are *way* too many of them. **PwC** responded to the fines, due to their employees cheating on training courses, by saying that (as well as other things) they would introduce "additional ethics training". Hopefully no one cheated on the new ethics course. You can read all about it on the Public Company Accounting Oversight Board's press release No. 105-2022-002, dated 24 February 2022.

I made a reference to there being **32,000 pages of tax legislation in the UK**. No one seems to agree on this figure. In 2009 the website accountingweb.co.uk claimed there were 10,520 pages. In 2012, the government's Office of Tax Simplification (which is part of the Treasury Department) wrote a 14-page analysis of existing legislation suggesting that there were 17,000 pages of it, though acknowledging that the main publishers of legislation had reduced the margins in their books to keep the page count down.

The Office of Tax Simplification suggested that this growth wasn't especially relevant, as much of the new legislation was "repetitious . . . and can be ignored" and that elsewhere it was due to making the language clearer. I love the idea of the Office of Tax Simplification saying, "Just ignore the legislation, it will make it simpler" (though I accept that that's not *quite* what they meant).

I've found a few other references to there now being around 22,000 pages of legislation, but not from official sources – though 22,000 makes sense if the 2012 figure of 17,000 pages was right, as there have been more than ten Finance Acts since 2012, each of several hundred pages, plus a whole host of new rules.

So where does the figure of 32,000 pages come from? Easy. I own copies of the tax legislation. I counted the pages in each book and added them all together. It's possible I made a mistake (I'm not going back to check), though I think the most likely explanation for the difference between my count and the government's may be due to footnotes and explanations. But if the tax doesn't make sense without the footnotes and explanations, then it seems fair to include them.[†]

The United States has even more legislation than the UK does, allegedly adding over two million words to their tax code in the first decade of the 21st century alone. Hong Kong apparently got by with fewer than 300 pages.

The particular bit of legislation I've included as an example of how difficult some of this legislation is to read is section 59A from the Taxes Management Act.

When I wrote this chapter, the basic rate of income tax had been largely unchanged since the mid-Noughties and the additional rate hadn't been tweaked since 2010, so I felt pretty safe saying "I've used more recent rates" to explain how much tax we all pay. And then with only *days* to put my final edits through before this book went to print, the Tory party imploded, *two* new Prime Ministers and *three* new chancellors were appointed, the additional rate was first scrapped and

---

[†]   I frickin' love footnotes.

then unscrapped, the Queen died (passing on her estate tax-free), NICs went up and then down again and no one was quite sure what was going to happen next, or even whether nuclear Armageddon would make the whole thing moot. *Typical.*

The Sun analysed the cost of **NHS parking charges** on 2 November 2019, and even quoted their rival the *Mirror* as having spotted that almost a third of these charges were paid by the NHS's own staff. The House of Commons Library records the amount raised by the **BBC licence fee** as £3.75 billion in 2020/21. To put that figure in perspective, over the same period Netflix had global revenues of around $30 billion, according to their accounts.

I was quite a fan of the rock band **Mansun**. I think I may even have a cassette(!) copy somewhere of their album *Attack of the Grey Lantern* (which features the song "Taxloss"). It's all online now, of course. Give it a listen . . .

The Working Wheels case involving **Chris Moyles** was decided at a tribunal on 10 February 2014 (decision number TC 03314). Chris Moyles has tweeted on the issue, saying that he is "not a tax expert and acted on advice I was given. This was a mistake and I accept the ruling without reservation . . . I take full responsibility and have learnt a valuable lesson."

The New York Times reported on **Donald Trump**'s tax returns in an article published on 27 September 2020, headlined "Long-concealed records show Trump's chronic losses and years of tax avoidance".

Chapter 4

The famous test case about the **deductibility of your work clothes** is called *Mallalieu* v. *Drummond* (1983). The less famous, but perhaps more fun, case is *G Daniels* v. *HMRC* (2018). Ms Daniels was allowed a deduction not only for her lingerie and stockings, but also for her hair and make-up (she spent £250 per month on her hair alone). She was also allowed a deduction for her perfume, which she said she didn't wear outside of work as it would remind her of "getting naked in front of drunken men". The implication of this ruling is that if you wear a particular perfume only when at work, you can deduct the cost of it from your income for tax purposes (though maybe speak to your accountant about that first).

Pretty much all British accountants are taught about *Mallalieu* v. *Drummond*, but not so much about *Daniels* v. *HMRC*.

Private Finance Initiatives were introduced by John Major's Conservative government but their use greatly increased after Labour, under Tony Blair, came to power in 1997. The think tank the Institute for Public Policy Research published a report on 18 September 2019 that estimated that, for just £13 billion of actual investment, the NHS would pay a total of £80 billion to private companies.

The government's own Public Accounts Committee found that some investors in PFI schemes were making *annual* returns of 30 per cent (with the British taxpayer footing the bill). The committee also found that the Treasury Department was unable to provide any evidence that PFI schemes were value for money, even after using them for 25 years. The committee did hear, though, that offshore infrastructure funds owned around half of the equity in PFI projects, with the five largest of these offshore funds paying less than 1 per cent in tax on their PFI profits.

Under UK law, when a company makes a **Purchase of Own Shares**, the cash that the company pays a shareholder for the shares can be treated either as a dividend or as a capital receipt. Dividends can be taxed at rates of up to around 40 per cent, but the capital receipt will usually qualify for something now called *Business Asset Disposal Relief* or, more aptly, *BAD Relief.* This allows multi-millionaires to pay a 10 per cent tax rate, as a reward for being successful entrepreneurs. The independent think tank the Resolution Foundation reported on 29 August 2018 that BAD Relief (or, more accurately, BAD Relief's virtually identical predecessor *Entrepreneurs' Relief*) cost the Exchequer more than £2 billion per year in lost tax revenues. But the relief does nothing to encourage actual entrepreneurship because it gives no support to entrepreneurs starting their businesses. It is simply a reward for success. Wealthy businesspeople love it, for obvious reasons. The relief is specifically designed to give you no benefit if you are poor.

You can see pictures of **Chris Evans**'s car collection on a number of websites. Some of my favourite pictures are on the website motoringresearch.com. **Billie Piper** herself wrote about the gift of the silver Ferrari in her autobiography *Growing Pains*. She says the day began with a text from Chris Evans that said, "Why are you not up, you lazy cow?", though actually the description of their romance is rather lovely, in a way.

I will happily pay more taxes to support the **Office for National Statistics**. You can read more of their meticulous work on the distribution of wealth on their website – search for "Income and Wealth" on ons.gov.uk.

The Financial Times reported on 22 September 2021 that **average Deloitte partner income** was £1 million. The year before it was apparently only £731,000, poor guys.

You can read **President Biden**'s proposal for a tax on unrealised gains in a press release of 28 March 2022 at whitehouse.gov. The release begins: "For too long, our tax code has rewarded wealth, not work, and contributed to growing income and wealth inequality in America." Yes, indeed.

I got the information on **richest senators** from the American research group Open Secrets (opensecrets.org), who do great work tracking the money in US politics.

The **ProPublica** report about "true tax rates" was released on 8 June 2021, with the headline "The Secret IRS Files: Troves of Never-Before-Seen Records Reveal How the Wealthiest Avoid Income Tax".

Tesla's SEC filings state that since May 2019 **Elon Musk** has been awarded no salary. They also refer to him as "Technoking of Tesla". He gets pretty good share options, though.

The **Buy, Borrow, Die strategy** can perhaps best be understood by imagining the purchase of a house for, say, £100,000 (or $100,000). Imagine your house doubles in value, to £200,000. Rather than sell the house to get your hands on the extra cash, you borrow the extra £100,000, and spend it.

A downside is that you'll now be paying interest on the borrowed cash, though during the long era of low interest rates this wasn't such a problem (as the interest rates were *way* lower than the tax bills on "realising" the gain).

A bigger problem is that your house might then *fall* in value. Your bank won't mind too much, so long as the house is worth more than £100,000 – the amount you borrowed. But if your house looks like it will soon be worth less than £100,000, the bank would ask you to *post margin* – effectively pay over extra cash to the bank, in case you can't afford to pay the loan back. The bank will return your cash if your house goes back up in value, but otherwise they keep it.

There is a way around this problem – you can buy something called a *put option*, which for shares gives you the right to sell your shares for a particular price at a set future date (they don't really exist for houses, but let's pretend they do). So for our house example when you borrow £100,000 against your (now) £200,000 house, you also buy the right to sell your house for £100,000, should the need ever arise.

Of course, if the need does arise because of a house-price crash, you now have less cash than you started with – you sold the house for what you bought it for and paid the interest on your loan *and* paid for the put option.

Keep this in mind when reading the *Financial Times* article from 17 February 2022 headlined "Inside **Peloton**'s epic run of bungled calls and bad luck".

When **Warren Buffett** invested in the supermarket Tesco I thought, "If Warren thinks that's a good idea, then so do I", and I spent about a month's wages on Tesco shares. My investment soon lost almost half its value. Warren Buffett then wrote to shareholders of his investment company Berkshire Hathaway Inc. to explain that his investment in Tesco had been a "huge mistake". Apart from Tesco, his investment brain is practically second to none.

His philanthropy is also very well documented: you can, for instance, read about it in an article in *Forbes* magazine on 23 June 2021.

Besides my subscriptions to *Taxation Monthly* and *What Calculator?*, I rarely miss a copy of the *Bemidji Pioneer*, the newspaper of Minnesota's 72nd-largest city. It did some very fine coverage of **Minnesota's "theatrical loophole"** to get around the smoking ban back in 2007–2008.

The **Google masseuse** was called Bonnie Brown, and she was Google's 41st hire. She wrote an account of her experience in a book called *Giigle: How I Got Lucky Massaging Google*. She includes a nice line about how she "literally and figuratively felt the pulse of the company", though in truth I'd be a bit freaked out if my masseuse started feeling my pulse.

Chapter 5

I never saw the girl who loved **Take That** again, though a friend of mine once left a bunch of flowers on her doorstep, rang the bell, then *ran away*. He was even less cool than I was.

The **Take That song titles** hidden in this chapter are: "Get Ready For It", "Shine", "Greatest Day", "These Days", "Sure" (though I think that might be cheating), "Amazing", "Everything Changes", "Back for Good", "More Fun than Submitting EIS Forms", "Good Feeling" and "Relight My Fire". Though "Good Feeling" is officially called "Give Good Feeling," so I may have got that one wrong.

Gary Barlow's apology from 2 September 2014 is still on Twitter. If you want to read the long, legal version of what he was apologising for, search for the court case Acornwood-LLP-Others-v-HMRC-2014-UKFTT-416-TC.

The "Icebreaker" case was much-described in the usual legal and accountancy journals, but there's also a surprisingly well-written analysis of the tax-avoidance scheme on the website sproutology.co.uk, which, if I've understood it correctly, is a fan site for the 1980s pop band Prefab Sprout. I hope the guru(s) behind sproutology won't be offended if I say it's not where one might expect to find detailed evaluations of convoluted tax schemes. Look for an article called "Filthy Lucre and the Art of Tax Dodging".

You can read all about the **British Film Institute**'s points-based system on their website, BFI.org.uk. Search for "cultural tests". Weirdly, you can get points if your film's location, characters or subject matter are either British or *anywhere else in the European Economic Area*. Similarly, the dialogue can be English or *any other European language*. So your film could star Gérard Depardieu as Odin, Norse god of war and poets, speaking Spanish in Liechtenstein and *still* pass the "culturally British" test. I suspect this anomaly is due to EU state-aid rules (as they don't allow discriminatory state subsidies), so perhaps it will change post-Brexit.

TaxWatch's brilliant dissections of **Bond**'s finances and **GTA V**'s finances were published on their website taxwatchuk.org, in their reports section. Some of TaxWatch's reports are mind-blowing. You can read Rockstar North's response to the allegations on the video-game magazine *VG247*'s website vg247.com on 20 January 2020.

The United States Department of Justice formally charged a "regime-backed" North Korean citizen for hacking into **Sony** on 6 September 2018.

The **other celebrities** who got involved with Icebreaker were plastered over the news in May 2014 – search online for your favourite next to the word "tax" and you'll see what I mean. If you want a little more tax detail, accountancydaily.co had a good analysis on 12 May 2014, including the claim that Take That "are said to be considering undertaking a world tour late this year to raise the estimated £30m they owe in tax as a result of the scheme's failure". They did indeed announce a *European* tour in November 2014 – so if you saw them then it's possible you have the failure of Icebreaker to thank for your night out.

Enterprise Investment Schemes have two main advantages: when you invest in them the government reduces your tax bill by a percentage of your investment (usually 30 per cent or 50 per cent), and when you sell your shares you pay no capital gains tax (and, indeed, can offset any losses against your income, to save more tax). In some cases you even get to reduce or defer your capital gains tax on *other* investments if you use cash from those investments to finance your new acquisition in EIS shares. The rules are very fiddly, though, so as with *everything* in this book, get some proper advice before you make any rash decisions.

The database of clients of the **Liberty scheme** was leaked to *The Times* in July 2014, which led to a great number of reports of the various celebrities involved in the schemes. If you need your memory jogging about what they look like, Channel 4 News has a very good article from 9 July 2014.

Chapter 6

Of all the tax offices I've ever dealt with, the **Australian Taxation Office** (the ATO) has been by far the most straightforward. Between the ATO website and Wikipedia I think I managed to bluff my way successfully through an awful lot of Australian tax while I was out there (I did also go on some training courses). Many of the stats and historical observations in this chapter are from the ATO.

I don't believe **crocodiles** are seasonal, but nor do I believe that Hal really took me wake-boarding in a crocodile-infested estuary. Actually I can't parse those two points. I am terrified of saltwater crocodiles, which I'd never heard of before I went to Australia. Sometimes they eat people miles offshore.

Pick your own historical sources for the **Eureka Stockade** or **Bottom of the Harbour Schemes** if you don't trust mine, which you shouldn't. (Hal once laughed when I leaped out of the way of a washed-up jellyfish, saying, "It can't hurt you" and to prove it, he prodded it with his foot. His toes then *blistered* from the jellyfish's toxins and he was almost crying with pain for two hours.) There's some good history of tax on the Australian Treasury's own website: treasury.gov.au.

All the historical sources seem to agree on the facts of these events, but I guess the interpretation is the fun bit of history.

You can read the complete **Asprey Review** online, but be warned – it's 594-pages long. I actually quite enjoyed reading it (though I might have skimmed a few pages).

Chapter 7

If you want to read up on the **Papua New Guinean timber trade**, the Californian think tank the Oakland Institute has produced some detailed reports: go to oaklandinstitute.org

Starbucks's use of royalty fees and transfer pricing has been widely discussed, and you can view their accounts online (though as I mention that's a less illuminating task than you might think).

My wife owns a Starbucks coffee mug from the time when she visited America and was really excited by the concept of a coffee shop with *sofas* in it, so bought a souvenir.

If you want to read more about what they get up to, tax wise, try TaxWatch (again, of course), or check out the 27 June 2019 issue of *The Guardian* (or many other issues); for Starbucks in Australia, see the *Australian Financial Review* of 7 January 2013, titled "Starbucks avoids paying tax in Australia for 12 years".

One of the interesting *personal* things about moving to Australia was that I didn't have any prejudices about particular newspapers, as in I didn't know which were left or right wing, or supported particular political parties, or were owned by Murdoch.

Not every media outlet covers stories about **News Corp**'s tax situation, funnily enough . . . among those that do are the *Australian Financial Review*, msn.com, the *Sydney Morning Herald* and crikey.com.au (and, as I mentioned, *The Economist*). Are they left wing? Right wing? Is crikey.com.au a major media outlet? I'll leave that for Australian readers – pick your favourite and a News Corp tax story is never far away.

The Guardian Australia's analysis of **Qantas** and other major Australian companies was on 10 December 2021.

Harley-Davidson really did try to trademark their sound, but it was back in the 1990s, and they were unsuccessful.

According to a report by Reuters on 3 June 2021, the **Ford Motor Company** could face penalties of up to $1.3 billion in relation to the import duty dispute on their Transit vans.

Chapter 8

No, **swans** do not sweat. They pant like dogs to cool down, apparently.

Historytoday.com has a good analysis of **Churchill**'s tax dodging. Funny how that's rarely mentioned.

And no, **Scottish people** are not exempt from tax. In 2016, tax-raising powers were semi-devolved to the Scottish Parliament, which introduced new (mostly higher) tax rates in 2018.

As soon as you start reading about **Delaware** you can go down a real rabbit warren of tax-havenesque analysis. It may just be more fun to look at a map of America and see if you can identify where Delaware is. On my first go at finding it I was 600 miles out. Can you do better? Bonus marks if you can name the state capital.

The BBC report into **Amazon** that I mentioned was on 8 September 2021. You can read about **Facebook** receiving more from HMRC than they paid in corporation tax in a number of places, such as *The*

Independent on 4 March 2016. If you don't have to read tax cases as part of your job so you haven't come across them before, it's similarly easy to find tax stories online about **Macquarie**, **Thames Water**, **Apple** and the rest.

The state capital of Delaware is Dover.

The **Diverted Profits Tax** was designed to tax profits that are shifted offshore at a rate of 25 per cent, rather than the "normal" 19 per cent (which has since changed). The idea being that companies will be better off recognising their profits in the UK and paying the lower "normal" rate. I have my suspicions that it was all political theatre – a nice headline that had no real impact.

The interaction of corporation tax and income tax is tediously fiddly – you have to balance a host of different thresholds and tax rates to find out how much tax you're saving, but a very approximate example of the impact of **IR35** in 2021 to a truck driver earning £30,000 per year is as follows.

Before IR35, the trucker's "personal" company would pay the trucker about £9,000 as a salary (to be below the NIC thresholds), leaving the company (which the trucker owned) with profits of £21,000. The company would then pay £4,000 in corporation tax, leaving £17,000 to be paid as a dividend. The trucker receiving this dividend would pay another £1,000 in income tax, leaving them with about £25,000 out of the £30,000 they started with.

After IR35, the trucker's personal company would be deemed to be paying the trucker a salary of £27,000. The company would then pay £3,000 of employer's National Insurance contributions, and the trucker would pay £3,000 income tax and £2,000 employee National Insurance, leaving them with £22,000.

Which is a long-winded way of saying an extra 10 per cent of the trucker's income disappeared as tax.

Chapter 9

My goodness, the way female celebrities are described in the broadsheets has changed since I was a teenager – I'm not saying it's perfect now, and I fully appreciate that I am myself bound to have used some clumsy language that will have upset somebody (sorry), but in digging out the references to **Coleen Rooney** and **Victoria Beckham** getting caught out by customs duties I found this line in *The Independent* from 12 February 1998: "The dark-haired singer who has fuelled thousands of adolescent (and adult) fantasies has none the less had a run in with HM Customs and Excise." What is "none the less" doing in that sentence? Are we meant to think that *normally* the fuellers of adolescent fantasies are let off? Exactly what image of the event does the author have in their mind? And why are we being told the colour of her *hair?!* It's not even a distinguishing feature in her band – three of the Spice Girls had dark hair! I could just about understand it if they referred to Geri Halliwell as the "ginger-haired singer", because she was at least nicknamed *Ginger.* But actually what the fuck was that about? They nicknamed one of them *Ginger!* They might as well have called her *Freckles.* As for the other names . . .

And yes, neither Coleen nor Victoria was married at the time, so I should have used their original surnames, except . . . go on then, what *were* their surnames?

And I'm sorry for the bad pun about Old Spice. I spent far too long deciding whether to edit it out, so I flipped a coin and now it's in there.

Beckham's Law is known as *Ley Beckham* in Spain. Although my language skills aren't great, I think I can just about work out what *Ley* translates to.

Davos is in Switzerland, though a chukka is not a goal in polo; it's a time period. I stand by my comments about shoes.

The news about **Tony Blair**'s tax avoidance was the one time I was absolutely delighted to read about an outrageous tax dodge – I actually leaped up and raced to tell my wife and kids. I can even tell you the date of the story breaking without looking it up – it was Sunday 3 October 2021.

Bidding for the rights to this book began on Monday 4 October 2021. Thank you, Tony!

I got the quote in which Blair described the tax system as "a haven of scams, perks, City deals and profits" from the BBC news.

The **Nicholas Shaxson** article about the real owners of **One Hyde Park** was published by *Vanity Fair* on 13 March 2013. Shaxson is also the author of *Treasure Islands: Tax Havens and the Men Who Stole the World*, another brilliant book about tax avoidance and evasion.

Global Witness, which provided the statistic about the number of anonymously owned homes in the UK, is another deeply impressive organisation. Its co-founder Patrick Alley has written a book called *Very Bad People*, about the fight against the world's network of corruption. It's really, really worth reading. It features yachts, private jets, classic cars, money-laundering, deforestation – wait a minute, it's almost like we have the exact same publishing team.

I can't find any evidence that **Mikhail Gorbachev** ever lived in Hampstead, but it's what I was told . . . though I wouldn't say my witness was super reliable. Gorbachev did celebrate his eightieth birthday party in London, though.

I appreciate that the details of **Private Residence Relief** are only of interest to a narrow band of home-owning Brits, but it really is the number one thing I get asked about by friends and family (and old acquaintances who start emails with "Hey, long time, not seen you since 2004 – but could I ask you a quick question about my house sale?"). I've started billing them.

The issue for *you* is that the legislation is *constantly* being tweaked and case law is full of contradictions and inconsistencies. So if you do think you need to know more about this relief, speak to an accountant *before* you sell your property – indeed, before you list it on a property portal, either. One person got caught out because their supposed "main home" appeared on Zoopla, but the photos didn't show any dog paraphernalia, despite the homeowner having pet Labradors. Obviously your main home is a question of *fact* – it's just that you need to be able to prove that fact.

Photoshopping photos would be very illegal, in case it wasn't obvious.

In much of the world the main relief when you sell your house is a form of "rollover relief", whereby you pay no tax on your gain *now*, provided you move to a new house. This can have the unintended consequence of preventing people from downsizing, as doing so triggers a big tax bill. It's also relatively common worldwide (and used to be the case in the UK) to allow a tax deduction for your mortgage interest payments, which arguably leads to reckless over-borrowing . . . but that's a debate for another day.

Chapter 10

I mentioned there being tax effects for marriage, buying a flat and having babies.

In the UK, **married couples** can claim a *Marriage Allowance* if one of them earns less than roughly £50,000 per year and the other one earns less than about £12,500. The idea behind this is to encourage people to get married. But as the allowance is worth about £250 and the average wedding costs £17,000 (according to hitched.co.uk) it should take the average couple 68 years to break even.

And yes, I know you can have cheaper weddings and yes, this is the sort of fact that my wife asked me not to mention in my groom's speech.

The wedding presents you receive from your guests are also exempt from taxes, including inheritance taxes, normally up to £1,000 per gift. I wanted to put that on our gift list as a little *nudge* but, again, I was overruled.

Historically, in the UK married couples were treated as a single unit – which meant that if the wife of a high-earning husband went to work, she would be taxed at her husband's highest marginal tax rate. Inevitably this discouraged women from joining the workplace. Margaret Thatcher abolished this rule in 1990 – meaning it made economic sense for the wife to say, "You look after the kids, I'll go out and work." Despite this, I believe Thatcher is not particularly remembered as an icon of feminism.

In America you have a choice between "joint" or "single" filing; in the UK you can transfer wealth back and forth between married couples without tax consequences (normally), which facilitates a lot of tax-planning opportunities (of the non-controversial kind).

We had to pay about the same amount of tax on the flat we bought as the amount of cash I earned each year. One of the deeply unfair aspects of the UK's **Stamp Duty Land Tax** is that it's payable on the whole amount of a property, rather than the *step up* from one property to another. This is a bit technical, but the effect is that people who move frequently are penalised, as you get *poorer* if you move from one £400,000 flat to another (because of paying the tax). As a consequence people move home less frequently (especially between more expensive homes), which means fewer properties are brought onto the market, which means everyone suffers. It's a tax that isn't based on ability to pay, that makes homes more expensive (and yet decreases house prices), reduces choice, penalises movers and was avoided by Tony Blair. It's one of the first taxes I would abolish if I was in charge, but then I'm also in the process of moving home at the moment, so it's on my mind.

And while there are a few benefits and tax breaks for having **children** in the UK, we're hardly at the top of the international league of generosity. Whereas the government gave me £11 per week to put towards the £14,000 per year cost of putting *one* child through nursery, in Hungary women who have four kids are exempt from income tax for *life*. Though "life" in most tax laws actually means "until the next party wins an election and changes the rule".

The World Bank economist Branko Milanovic put the **income required to get into the global 1 per cent** as US$34,000 per year in 2012, which was about £21,500 then (and about what my salary was when I started as an accountant in the mid-Noughties). So when I said *any* job would put you into the global top 1 per cent I guess I was being a bit of a snob – the National Living Wage (which is the rebranded minimum wage) today is £19,000 per year for a 2,000-hour-per-year job, which is not far off £21,500, though the $34,000 figure may have gone up since 2012, and the Sterling equivalent has certainly gone up, as the pound has tanked.

You can read more about using boxes of **snails** to avoid business rates on the BBC news, 13 February 2020. I believe there's also a rule somewhere about how many chickens you need to own before you can call yourself a chicken farmer. My wife has asked me not to look it up, lest I get ideas.

I've tried to get the number of *greats* in the **Buccleuch** lineage correct, but it really is an ancient family – the first feudal Baron of Buccleuch died in 1492. A lot of them were called Walter Scott, but as far as I can tell they're unrelated to the Walter Scott of *Ivanhoe* and *Rob Roy* (and the expression "Great Scott!") fame, which is a shame.

Richard Murphy, the author of *The Joy of Tax*, is almost certainly the most prolific writer about tax (and tax avoidance/evasion) in the UK, if not the world. You can read his many – and detailed – blog posts at taxresearch.org.uk. For instance, a recent post is titled "HM Revenue & Customs really do not want to collect tax from the wealthy" (and it's hard to argue with his conclusions).

The Tax Justice Network asked me to include a link to their rankings, and I'm more than happy to oblige: https://cthi.taxjustice.net/en/

Chapter 11

Yes, obviously that was a joke about ***Phantom Menace*** being the best *Star Wars* film. We all know it goes *Empire, Jedi, New Hope, Rogue One, Ewoks Christmas Special, Force Awakens*, others. But only *Phantom* has any tax in it, so it deserves a special mention.

In the UK there is VAT only on *private* parking charges, not public parking charges, so you're probably only committing tax evasion in private car parks by not paying to park. Either way it's theft, though, so a decent public prosecutor could probably get you on a **money-laundering** charge, too, for concealing the proceeds of a crime. Oddly, if ever you fail to prevent money-laundering at your place of work, you can get off by saying that you didn't know how to spot the laundering – in which case your *boss* becomes criminally liable for failing to train you sufficiently (which is probably why your boss has made you do an online course on money-laundering, if you handle any invoices at all).

The **NatWest** fine was announced by the Financial Conduct Authority on 13 December 2021.

The Court of Justice of the European Union's ruling against Italy and the **Vatican** over unpaid taxes followed a complaint by a school and a bed and breakfast in Rome. They argued that it was unfair that *they* had to pay taxes when rival schools and accommodation run by the Vatican didn't. As early as 2012 the non-collection of taxes was found to be unlawful, but Italy was let off the hook because its property register was incomplete, so collection would be too complicated. I might try that line if ever I'm prosecuted for non-payment of tax: "My records are incomplete, so collection is too complicated."

The case dragged on through the courts for years, with further rulings in 2016 and 2018. Eventually the school and B&B won.

The **Cup Trust** scheme involved the charity buying government bonds, then immediately selling them at incredibly low prices to clients of the scheme's promoters. The clients would then sell the bonds for their real values and donate the proceeds to the charity. In other words, cash moved in a great big circle. But the law on donations allows both the charity and the client to make enormous tax savings.

The Guardian reported on 25 November 2021 that **HMRC had plans to move to a new office complex in Newcastle**, which was owned by a company that is itself owned by another company, based in the British Virgin Islands, that is itself owned by the billionaire Tory donors Simon and David Reuben, allegedly the second richest family in Britain.

This doesn't mean that something dodgy is afoot, and I'm not suggesting anything illegal is happening but, as *The Guardian* pointed out, it now means that the HMRC officials in charge of tackling tax avoidance will be doing so from a building owned via a tax haven. Most tax offices around the world have special teams that look at ultra-high net worth individuals, but it must be weird if one of them is your landlord.

The most generous type of **Research and Development Tax Credits** in the UK subsidises almost a third of a company's research expenditure. Claiming the credits requires a report explaining the research, which takes a half-decent accountant an hour or two to write. Accountants will typically charge somewhere between 5 and 10 per cent of the tax credits claimed . . . meaning that if a company spends half a million on R&D the government will pay for up to a third of it and some accountant will pocket £15,000 or so for a couple of hours' work. I think it's an absolute racket. *Always* haggle on your R&D report fee.

According to tasteofcountry.com, **Willie Nelson**'s album *The IRS Tapes* is "not generally remembered as his finest project".

I enjoyed my experience on **morphine** a little too much, which is a bit terrifying. I've been knocked off my bicycle more times than I can remember, and once came off a motorbike while on holiday in Thailand when I was a teenager. I was all alone on that occasion, and tore a hideous amount of skin off my arms and legs. I returned to the beachside hostel where I was staying and knocked on the door of the neighbouring cabin – I knew some English girls were staying there and I thought that at best they might be able to help; at worse my injury might be a good way of introducing myself. When one of them opened the door I tried to look as cool as possible, despite the blood all over me, and casually said, "I don't suppose any of you have any Savlon?" They looked at each other, said, "No" and shut the door on me. In many ways, that rejection hurt more than the crash did.

Chapter 12

As well as 12 pilots and 11 accountants serving in **Congress**, there are 17 doctors, 76 former soldiers, 175 lawyers and 4 members with computer science degrees.

Chancellor of the Exchequer Philip Hammond's comment that **Class 2 NICs** were "regressive and outdated" wasn't some casual throwaway remark – it was in his 2017 Budget speech to the House of Commons. He changed his mind by September 2018.

According to a *Guardian* report of 18 November 2021, **Richard Desmond** donated £12,000 to the Conservative Party 12 days after **Robert Jenrick** signed off Desmond's planning application to build 1,500 new homes in Tower Hamlets. Jenrick later conceded that the sign-off was "unlawful" due to "apparent bias".

I'm still not entirely sure why **Jimmy Carr** received so much more flak than just about anyone else for his tax dodging. Perhaps it was a slow news day. I'm not excusing it, I'm just saying it was no worse than what a lot of other people did. I'm also not entirely sure why **Ken Dodd** got off all his charges of tax evasion, but he did. Obviously you can read up on the K2 scheme and **Barclays Bank**'s foray into tax avoidance in various places, but it's far more fun to watch clips of Carr and Dodd (and less so of Barclays) on YouTube (though a few of Carr's jokes might not be to everyone's taste).

It's a little astonishing that the revelation about **Akshata Murty** – Rishi Sunak's wife – not paying tax on her £11 million income did not get more press coverage. This was such a flagrant conflict of interest that you would have thought the Chancellor would have resigned, but no, his allies defended him, his wife's spokesperson misspoke about the reason for the non-domicile claim, everyone carried on as normal and then he got promoted to Prime Minister.

But here's a bit of maths to bring this conflict of interest home: there are about 450,000 employees in Birmingham, the UK's second largest city. If they all received a £2,000 bonus, the tax rises brought in by Rishi

Sunak would cost them and their employers collectively an extra £20 million, which is roughly the same as what Akshata Murty is alleged to have avoided paying by electing to be treated as a non-domicile (though the real figure may be a lot higher). Or if that's too convoluted, she avoided enough tax to pay the annual wages of over 500 nurses – and that's just on her income . . . her heirs could save ten times that amount in inheritance tax.

Remember that she's only taking advantage of the law as it's written . . . but it's her husband who could have changed that law.

Worryingly, of the other 20 current Cabinet Ministers (in May 2022), ten have either been accused of earning income via tax havens, claimed to be non-doms, refused to pay taxes they owe, acknowledged breaking the law or been accused of over-claiming their expenses or lying about their income . . . that's *half* the senior members of government! So I doubt *any* of them will be changing the law any time soon.

The All-Party Parliamentary Loan Charge and Taxpayer Fairness Group is an official Parliamentary Group comprising Parliamentarians of all parties from both Houses of Parliament. You can read about their work at loanchargeappg.co.uk.

Members of the APPG "have concerns about the nature and impact of the '2019 Loan Charge' and they also have concerns about the wider context of fairness of tax legislation and about HMRC's conduct in enforcing it".

In 2019 the British government asked the former Auditor General Sir Amyas Morse to review the Loan Charge. He made a number of recommendations to make the charge less onerous.

I would recommend Richard Brooks's book *The Great Tax Robbery* again for its detailed analysis of **Vodafone**'s negotiations with HMRC. You might remember it was big news at the time, but now seems largely forgotten.

Try TaxWatch again for the analysis of **prosecutions of tax cheats versus benefits cheats.**

And the legislation with the delightfully worded exception for MPs from the **disguised remuneration** rules is the Income Tax (Earnings and Pensions) Act.

The **five peers who resigned from the House of Lords** following the ban on non-doms sitting were Lord Foster (the architect), Lord Bagri, Lady Dunn, Lord McAlpine and Lord Laidlaw. They all got to keep their titles.

The most likely way you can **save tax yourself** is to check your payslip. (I'm afraid this only works for British employees, sorry.)

Payslips are designed to be incomprehensible, but somewhere on that payslip will be a PAYE code. If you earn less than £100,000 and you only have one job and don't receive anything other than a salary and a pension (i.e. no car or gym membership, or such things), then this code should probably be something close to 1257L. If it's a tiny bit different I wouldn't be too worried – it changes every year and there are some decent reasons why it might not be exactly 1257L.

But if it says something else, then you may need to get it fixed. The most common error is to be on a "BR" code. This stands for Basic Rate and means that every penny you earn will be taxed at 20 per cent (plus NICs). That might sound correct, but it actually means you won't be getting your Personal Allowance – that is, the twelve and a half grand or so of tax-free income. The net effect of this is that you could be over-paying your income tax by over £2,500.

Seriously, check your PAYE code. Yes, it's boring, and yes, your work have probably made it difficult for you to access your payslips, but my experience of this is that about one in five people are on the wrong code. That means, on average, every British person reading this book might be overpaying their taxes by £500.

In theory HMRC will eventually realise their error and repay your overpaid tax, but in practise this can take years. One of my colleagues was once on a BR code for six years before HMRC realised. In her case, she was earning enough to be a higher rate taxpayer, so was actually underpaying her taxes for six years. She returned home one day to find a demand for payment from the tax office for over £12,000. Ouch, right?

Chapter 13

I've got a big rant in me about the **Child Benefit Tax Charge**, but maybe I'll save it for Twitter (or another book – I'm wondering about calling a sequel *Richard Osman's Guide to Tax*, but I suspect there might be some legal issues with that idea).

I hope you liked my proposal for a **simple tax system**. If you find any holes in it, or think you can do better, tweet me @RebelAccountant.

I am open to invitations from Big Business to give after-dinner speeches about abolishing corporation tax. My rates are very reasonable (less so if you want me to gloss over the *tax the rich* bit).

Thank you for reading.